D0856524

"[A] **blistering yet tender** story of a woman transforming Midwestern cooking, in a fresh voice all her own."
— *Publishers Weekly*

"A chef-savant unlike any other in the U.S." —*Eater*

"With this **deeply personal work,** Iliana reminds us that there is great strength in vulnerability. Her story is one of resilience, determination, and vision."
— **René Redzepi, chef and co-owner of noma**

"It turns out that Iliana Regan writes the way she cooks: with **a voice that's bold and soulful, tender and tough, impossible to ignore, and utterly her own.** *Burn the Place* is much more than an account of hustling in the kitchen. It's a story about identity and addiction. It's about getting creative and becoming a boss. And it's full of scenes of gothic drama that still give me goosebumps when I think of them."
— **Jeff Gordinier, author of *Hungry***

"Renowned chef Iliana Regan . . . is **self-taught, charismatic, delightfully foul-mouthed, and utterly devoid of pretension** as she parallels her ascent in the culinary world with a past strewn with AA chips, jail cell stints, and brutal family losses. This groundbreaking memoir reinvents the well-worn trope of the "bad boy" superstar chef, presenting us instead with a **palpably vulnerable, complicatedly feminist, and sexy-queer-girl genius** who takes no prisoners, including herself."
— **Gina Frangello, author of *A Life in Men* and *Every Kind of Wanting***

"Iliana Regan is Alice. The fields and farms where she forages for ingredients comprise her Wonderland. We are along for the ride, and it behooves us not to be late." —*Chicago Tribune*

FIELDWORK

FIELDWORK

*A Forager's
Memoir*

ILIANA REGAN

A MIDWAY BOOK

AGATE

CHICAGO

First printed in January 2023

Printed in the United States of America

10 9 8 7 6 5 4 3 2 1   23 24 25 26 27

Cover design by Morgan Krehbiel

Author photo by Sara Stathas

Library of Congress Cataloging-in-Publication Data
Names: Regan, Iliana, author.
Title: Fieldwork / by Iliana Regan.
Description: Chicago : Agate, 2023. | "A Midway book".
Identifiers: LCCN 2022019146 (print) | LCCN 2022019147 (ebook) | ISBN
    9781572843189 (hardcover) | ISBN 9781572848696 (ebook)
Subjects: LCSH: Regan, Iliana, 1979- | Cooks--United States--Biography. |
    Restaurateurs--United States--Biography.
Classification: LCC TX649.R44 A3 2023 (print) | LCC TX649.R44 (ebook) |
    DDC 641.5092 [B]--dc23/eng/20220705
LC record available at https://lccn.loc.gov/2022019146
LC ebook record available at https://lccn.loc.gov/2022019147

Midway is an imprint of Agate Publishing. Agate books are available in bulk at discount prices. For more information, visit agatepublishing.com.

This book is dedicated
to my ancestral family,
my immediate family,
and to the forests I love.

"You don't want to ever be frightened in the woods, Nick. There is nothing that can hurt you."

"Not even lightning?" Nick asked.

"No, not even lightning. If there is a thunderstorm get out into the open. Or get under a beech tree. They're never struck."

"Never?" Nick asked.

"I never heard of one," said his father.

"Gee, I'm glad to know that about beech trees," Nick said.

–Ernest Hemingway, "Three Shots"

PROLOGUE

THE MEN CAME IN THEIR PICKUP TRUCKS. I KNOW because I saw them. Big silver and white pickups: Super Dutys, Platinums, King Ranches. Trucks with a four-ton payload—3500s. Some trucks had double wheels under the beds that might have held even more. I learned those were called "dualies." Some trucks were so big they had diesel engines, rumbling while coming in over the washboard pathway. The men had mustaches. The mustaches were a logging thing, I've heard, and it seemed true. I read that about loggers and mustaches in Suzanne Simard's book, *Finding the Mother Tree*. Simard came from a family of loggers and worked in the industry. She wrote that the mustaches came along with the job. In addition to the mustaches, the loggers I've seen often wore aviator sunglasses.

The first of them to arrive were the *surveyors*. They came to *test* the soil and *design a reforestation plan*. But you know, the forest didn't *need* a plan to accomplish what it has done for the last hundreds of millions of years. The timber companies turned it to monocrops—it's mostly pine out here. If you look around, you'll realize it's everywhere, this sort of fixation on product. And it wasn't the loggers' fault. I wouldn't say they were the enemy because they weren't. It's far deeper than that.

The surveyors tied neon orange and blue plastic ribbons around the boles. After they left another guy arrived. He didn't wear sunglasses but squinted against the sun instead. He got out of the truck's cab, a smaller truck this time. He shook a spray paint canister that went *rattle-clank*. All the oldest, biggest trees got an X. The ones with the ribbons didn't. The thin ones were left alone.

From where I stood watching, feeling helpless, it seemed to me it didn't make a difference which tree was tagged or ribboned. The map was clear. Go for the heart.

After the pickup trucks left, the John Deeres and Caterpillars crawled in. They rolled over everything with their large mechanical mandibles that tore the forest to shreds. They cleared the way, slicing the birch, pine, beech, maple, elm, and aspen, taking almost everything. A few skinny oaks remained, which soon would die due to the wounds left along their young bodies. Those machines were operated by a guy too, but behind the turbid windows of the cockpit I couldn't see if he had on sunglasses or a mustache.

It didn't take long for the trees to be stacked in pyramids twenty feet high and a hundred feet wide. The trees were stacked and the semis crept in, further wearing out the path. All thirty-six wheels of the logging semis carved large ruts, making it harder for us to get in and out from the cabin. I knew how many wheels they had because I'd counted them.

The cabs of the semis had wood placards above the windshields with blue or white paint that spelled out, *Whiskey Bent, Bob, Willy, One-eye, King Tom,* and *Log Man.* Recently I saw one that read, *I'm Best In The Bush,* and that made me feel strange. I didn't often see the guys who drove the semis. Like the guys in the machines, they were ghosts. But sometimes you can see ghosts, and once I saw one in the middle of the path. He revved his chainsaw, holding it up above his head. He reached up and severed the last bits of branches and twigs that were hanging outside the width of his semi's trailer. He was good with the machine; his ancestors might have been swordsmen. He flung it side to side, pirouetting all the while, releasing the overhang. He wore thick canvas dungarees and had a gray, frizzy beard that grew down over his rotund belly. I waited patiently for him to finish. I didn't honk my horn or make a spectacle of it. He politely moved the rig, though it took a full ten minutes to back it up. We waved to one another, and I drove past.

After a while the path was demolished by the machines. From where they crawled into the forest, roots were left exposed like bony fingers from one side of the path to the other. The brambles and roots of wild raspberries, blueberries, blackberries, chokecherries, goldenrod, violets, clovers, elderberries, Solomon's seal, dead nettle, dandelion, and aster flowers, to name a few and there are thousands more, got pushed back, torn up, and trampled. Last year, chestnut and birch boletus grew under those destroyed trees. I would walk a mile, hunting the mushrooms, and find so many aside from those: boletus, rishi, oysters, chanterelles, cauliflower, coral, sheep's head, lobster, and wood ear. But not now. The embankment was crushed. The path was changed and so was everything around it.

Chapter 1.
WHEN I FALL ASLEEP

A BIG STORM WAS COMING. I STOOD AT THE BEDROOM window while getting settled for bed and beyond the window I saw the shadows of trees, the ones left behind, cast by the moonlight on the forest floor. I felt tired and scared. I got into bed as quickly as I could, pulling the covers up to my chin. I was afraid because I knew the big storm was coming. The lightning and thunder began. I imagined trees splitting and fires sparking. The approaching storm reminded me of all the things Dad had said about big storms. I tried hard not to think of those things.

For many years, most of my life in fact and still to this day, in the dark or daylight, I looked out windows, up to the sky, under the water, or into the forest; I looked somewhere beyond where I was, waiting for the mothership to come and take me back home, but she never came. I turned to other things instead.

When you thought enough about all the things you could eat in the wild, and you remembered all their uses and ways to prepare them, things weren't so empty. Sometimes at night, lying in bed, if you thought of all of them, it could help you fall asleep.

That night I lay in my bed, staring into the dark. Fear had come over me. I was rigid with it. I had the flat sheet and quilt pulled to my chin. I lay there stiff, almost as if I were dead. There were burglars in the basement, I was sure of it. I thought they had gotten in because I forgot to latch the door and you could hear them talking but not what they said. I was convinced it was something about how they would kill us or mess things up. I heard their footsteps coming up the stairs.

I wasn't sleeping yet, though it was early in the morning. Sleep had become troublesome. I had a somewhat unrealistic fear I would die. For a long time, I had been living with the fear I would die at thirty-nine. While I lay there, at forty-two years old give or take, according to my calculations it meant death was going to happen any day now. My sister Bunny died when she was thirty-nine, with none of us there. She died in jail. It was awful, the thought of dying alone. I thought all the time about what she was thinking the moment she knew she was leaving this earth. How she was probably thinking of us (her sisters), our mom and dad, her daughters, her partner. She was thinking about how she couldn't say goodbye. When I talk to others about this, they say that's what trauma is. That I felt the way I did about dying because of something bad that happened in the past. I don't know, because for a long time, I was also certain I was going to die before I was thirty, but now I don't remember what stopped that fear. It may have been that I got sober and stopped behaving as dangerously as I used to behave.

Sometimes at night, I fell enough asleep that my arms and legs tingled. Somehow, I knew when they tingled it meant I had fallen asleep or was on the way. In the dark, once the tingling began, I worried I'd never wake up. That I would die in my sleep. Occasionally I'd wake up enough to take a few deep breaths to make sure my lungs were working, that my heart was pounding. Taking those deep breaths often caused my eyes to jolt open. I'd take mental note of my body; if everything seemed to be functioning, I might begin to tingle again.

I was afraid of the dark and I was afraid of dying. It was a selfish, human sort of thought. One less human would be one less parasite on this planet, which it certainly needed. I know that sounds dark, but it isn't untrue.

Crying was a good antidote to insomnia. When I was little, I had the same problem with sleep. At times I would go into Mom's room (I slept with her a lot on account of being afraid of the dark) and I'd cry because I couldn't fall asleep. She'd move over in bed, and I'd get in next to her. I slept better next to her. Once I was next to her, I would fall asleep, worn out from the crying.

When I did sleep, I had vivid dreams as if I wasn't sleeping at all. Often I didn't feel rested because I exerted a large amount of energy on whatever it was I did in the dreams. Lots of times I was an animal running on four legs and climbing up something steep, or running through the forest, or searching for mushrooms or berries or things I couldn't find. I was the birds in the trees or the mushrooms themselves and someone was aiming to cut me down. It might sound nice to be an animal or mushroom in your dream, but those dreams were often stressful. There was the sense that wherever I was, I was not safe.

And on that night before the storm came, while I lay awake, staring into the dark, keeping my mind busy, it was early morning, around 2 AM and I couldn't see anything. It was black in our room, as well as outside. Outside it was so black the sky was also purple and blue. It was the sort of black that allowed your eyes to see the colors of the stars. In places other than here, looking up at the sky, if you were asked, you would probably say the stars were white. But out here, you might say some were blue, some yellow, and some were pink, because that's how well you could see them. There weren't any real cities, not for hundreds of miles. There were a couple towns that the people in them might have thought were small cities, but the largest was only about twenty thousand people, and that one was two hours away. The lights there weren't like real city lights. The industry and population simply weren't there. Even there you could see the color of the stars.

But our room wasn't so dark when the moon was above the trees. I knew my cardinal directions very well. The moon was often in the southeast but sometimes it was in the southwest and even sometimes in the northeast though it was never directly north, at least at the times I was looking at it. If the moon was in the southwest or southeast, then our room went from pitch black to gunmetal. We often kept the curtains open because it was hard to get up if we didn't. When the moon was out you could still see the stars but maybe not so much of their color. And that night, staring into the dark, I heard all four of our dogs breathing. They sensed the storm coming, a bad one, which was why they were all in the bed. We have a little one that can bite faces while sleeping and we learned that the hard way, but when he was afraid like I was, he was awful sweet.

I heard the men talking. My entire body tensed like my white knuckles over the quilt. There was another sound but this time it was outside. I determined there were footsteps in the leaves, not far from where the forest began, just beyond our bedroom window. There were lots of squirrels, chipmunks, field mice, porcupine, fox, coyotes, deer, and other small creatures that made a surprising amount of noise, considering how small they were, walking around at night. It was probably just that.

When I heard noises like that, I held my breath and listened with intent. George, our 140-pound Newfoundland, blew breath from his mouth, ruffling his jowls. I exhaled, realizing that was the sound I had been hearing. It wasn't the men in the basement or walking up the stairs. It was George. He was lying perpendicular to me and Anna at the foot of the bed. He was dreaming, and when he moved his legs, the bed creaked. It was all coming from inside our room. Then adding Bunny, the Old English Sheepdog, plus Bear and Clementine, the Shih Tzus, and us, our combined weight was five hundred pounds in the bed, give or take a few. Our queen-sized bed was a little small for the six of us. I knew it'd be fine, but Anna worried while we were all on it that it would collapse onto the guns we stored beneath it. I told her not to worry because none of them were loaded. The pearl-handled .38

Smith & Wesson, Dad's cowboy gun that he gave to me when we moved out here, was loaded, but that one wasn't beneath the bed. That one I didn't place beneath the bed, but on the dresser behind a few photos. I kept that one loaded in a spot I could get to fast if I needed, because if there were two men in the basement or footsteps in the forest that didn't belong to the small or furry creatures but the ones with hardened flesh around the face, then I'd need to get it. Out here there was no one to help. We couldn't call an ambulance. We couldn't call the police. We sort of couldn't call anyone for anything. Just recently, the cell phone service got a tad better when AT&T put up a new tower. For a long time, we didn't have service for the thirty-plus miles between here and the next place, so if anything happened while driving between that place and our cabin, we'd have to walk to whichever place was closest and that could be a long way through the forest, especially at night. There were bears and wolves, but they weren't the scariest ones even though Dad thought so.

Dad gave me his .38 special. He said I should always have it on me in case I broke down or got stuck in the mud. He thought I'd get stuck or something unfortunate would happen, that I'd get lost on my way back to the cabin and starve to death or worse. He said out here the wolves would make a snack of me. Like I said, I wasn't worried about the wolves, and with all the fears I sometimes had, I wasn't worried about the bears either. Anna worried about those things more than I did. Dad worried about them most of all. He was certain they'd kill me. If not them, he was certain something would. But I, like the animals, thought people were scarier.

After I realized the sounds came from George I tried to

calm down. I took a few deep breaths, remembering meditation groups I've been in; I paid particular attention to my limbs, telling them to relax. I flipped on my side, becoming more comfortable with one ear on the pillow. Things became quieter and the muffling of noises made me less afraid.

But when the storm rolled in. It clobbered all other noises and it was not muffled. It started with a bolt of lightning that lit up the room along with some of its items: the dresser where the .38 was, the guitar on the wall, my bookbag on the shelf, the mackinaw jacket on the hook with my Thermos and ballcap over it. This lightning made the room brighter than when the sun came through the windows. I had never seen the room without shadows until that moment. I sat upright. And then, after the lightning, there was the loudest crack I'd ever heard in my whole life. Anna stirred. I knew it had woken her. I could tell by the way she had shifted after the thunder and lightning that her eyes were open too.

The dogs, with the storm now here, tucked in closer to us. I scooted from where they had me pinned, finagling myself out of bed. I was already up so I went to the window. I watched the storm. I don't know how long I was at the window; I might have fallen asleep while standing there. Though at that moment I knew I was awake more than asleep. I felt like how I slept on airplanes, like when you knew everything that was happening, yet your neck was bent in a way that seemed broken and there was drool from your lips to your chest. On airplanes I worried about crashes so I didn't sleep well on those either, but I was so afraid, there was nothing I could do but close my eyes and squeeze the arm rests as hard as possible. On the other hand, I thought if the plane ever crashed, I would do well helping myself and those around me to get to safety. As fearful as I'd become lately, I was more fight than flight.

I don't know how long I watched the storm, but Anna came up behind me and, putting her hands on my shoulders, steered me back to the bed. I sat on the bed for a long while, looking to the window before lying down again. She asked me what I was looking at. I wasn't looking at anything, I don't think. More than looking I was waiting. I was waiting for something to happen, something deep in my gut that Dad had planted there for harvesting in moments like these. I waited for the orange glow, following the electric blue bolts that zapped as they came down. The forest was going to catch fire, I was certain. If not this night, then someday. I loved this forest and would fall apart if it went away. And in many ways, it was falling apart, regardless of the storm. And though I was afraid of storms out here, I wished for the rain. I just didn't want the lightning to happen. We were surrounded by thousands of acres of forest, deep in the Hiawatha, and a lot of it had been logged. Where lots of the trees had been felled, their branches, dried leaves, and needles all remained and had been curing to kindling one summer after the next. In many ways, we lived within a tinderbox.

One time Dad told me I'd need a boat for the river. He said if there were a forest fire, I'd need to get Anna and the dogs on a boat and take the river out. At first, I thought he was just being how he was, anxious, thinking of the worst as he often did, but then I became afraid too and began to prepare.

The first time I came out here he was with me. As he left, he begged me not to stay alone. He said the overnight temp was going to drop to forty-five degrees Fahrenheit. He swore if I stayed the night and it wasn't any warmer than sixty, I'd get hypothermia. I told him I had plenty of blankets with me. I had the gun. I had the wood-burning fireplace I'd keep stoked throughout the night. He said if the fireplace had creosote built up in the chimney, there'd be a back draft. "A back draft shoots out fire like a jet engine," he said, telling me I'd burn "like that," snapping his fingers. I told him in that case hypothermia was out of the question. I remember having a cocky smile on my face because I wasn't as afraid then and I continued eating the granola bar I had from the breakfast bar at the Travelodge we'd stayed in the night before. I took a sip of coffee, smiling at him behind the cup. I was very cocky I think because at the time I was still thirty-nine, and sober.

"God damn it. I'm serious," he scolded.

"Oh Larry, stop it, she's an adult," Chris, his wife who was along for the ride, said to him. "Let her sleep in her cabin, she's excited." Chris was right. I was excited. More excited than I'd been about anything, probably ever. I never really thought my dream to have a cabin deep in the forest and off the grid would come true. But it had because I kept dreaming about it and doing everything I could to make it happen. Maybe somewhere deep down it was all about escaping. All I knew was I wanted out of the city and the grind of restaurant life. I didn't want to be a boss lady anymore. I didn't want the awards. I didn't want any of it. So much so that my idea was to give the restaurant away, which I did, and this cabin, this Inn I'd call Milkweed that I'd create would be the answer. Little did I know at the time, that in a sense, I'd be betting my life on it.

It was all dependent on if I lived or died. Over two years into the pandemic, we still found ourselves with several years of reservations to fulfill, then there was road maintenance, cabin work, a lot more things too and not much in the bank to show for it. Even with success, as good as it looks on the outside, we still must live day to day on tight budgets, especially in the hospitality industry. I was never good with money anyways.

But Dad was a ridiculous man with crazy ideas, derived from his constant obsession with worst-possible outcomes. Things most people wouldn't ever think of, he thought of, and he worried about all of them. In one way or another he revealed to me his fears. Every single time I talked to him, he told me to take the gun with me wherever I go. He has said that every single day since we first arrived out here. Never mind I don't have a license for it. Also, he wants me to keep it loaded in my glove compartment. Never mind a lot of people end up accidentally shooting themselves that way. For some reason the fear that I could hurt myself with it, he didn't have. But he'd told me all these fears of his, many times, and now they were beginning to become mine too.

"You're making the dogs anxious," Anna said. She pulled the back of the oversized men's undershirt I slept in, making me lie back down.

I fell back against the pillow and threw my right arm behind it, propping my head a bit, listening to the rain ping against our corrugated metal roof. I worried about where it sometimes leaked to our bathroom counter during heavy storms. I turned back to the window, seeing where the rain fell in a wide stream from the roof. We didn't have gutters out here. The snow in the winter would tear them off. I imagined the stream fell below, where I had planted the dragon tongue beans and nasturtium flowers, worrying their roots would be broken by the fall, uprooted from where I'd found the skeleton of a hummingbird I had buried a year before. I told myself I shouldn't worry about the storm too much. It had been dry lately, this was good for the seeds.

In the past, I hadn't done a good job at planting things out here. I should have gotten a rototiller so I could have dug up more of the earth before I mixed in the soil and planted everything. I should have applied more manure and soils with nutrients. Plus, I might have found something cool, like when I was little and found arrowheads after Dad tilled our garden. I had a whole collection back then. At the farmhouse where I grew up, all we had to do was till the earth and mix in the manure and the compost that Dad had prepared in the barn, and everything grew beautifully. We did have to weed frequently, but it wasn't like what I had going on out here. I had dug a couple gardens by hoeing the ground, pulling out weeds and grass, then adding new soil over the top. The existing soil was sand. There weren't many natural nutrients, and I didn't put enough new soil down and didn't have manure or compost like Dad had back at the farmhouse. I did buy some, but by the time I did, it was already too late, and I hadn't dug down far enough so along with my cucumbers, zucchinis, watermelons, gem and butter lettuces, radishes, and beets there grew lots of grass and weeds between them. The buckwheat grew wild, twisting its vines around everything, strangling it to death. I was learning, and eventually I'd fix it, but at the time, the wild buckwheat, which eventually had gone to seed, was killing the vegetables. After the buckwheat turned to seed I figured I'd at least pick them and make my own buckwheat flour. It'd probably take an entire day to harvest enough to make a cup's worth, but things like that were worth it. Along with the buckwheat grew wild mustard and not long ago, last year or maybe the year before, I got about a tablespoon full of seeds, which was enough to pickle and stretch out on some special dishes for our guests at the Inn. There was also a weed called lamb's quarter that's like spinach. There was burdock root right down the hill. Out here there were thousands, if not hundreds of thousands of wild carrots also known as Queen Anne's lace; there's parsnip, dock, and wild asparagus. But sometimes if not picked at the right time these things could be very fibrous.

When I finally closed my eyes, I thought about the wild things and what I'd do with them. I thought of nettles. I thought how I'd wilt them with homemade vinegar and sizzling lamb fat. I thought of nettle tea. I thought of blueberries with fresh-juiced sorrel. I thought of the ramps and how I liked grilling them over the open fire. There were the trout lily flowers I fermented that tasted of cucumber. I thought of the raspberries lining the big yard. The Joe Pye weed and chokecherries. The gooseberries with prickly skin that looked like medieval weapons. Clusters of elderberries hanging low when ripe, the finches that bent the branches, picking them off one by one. The spruce shoots and cattail pollen. I thought of the hawks that flew across the path with garter snakes in their talons while all these things grew beneath. I thought of how the strawberries were the first berry to grow. I thought about the wood turtles that crossed the road and how I stopped, getting out of my vehicle to remove them. I believed they liked the fallen berries that lined the paths. When I moved the wood turtles from the road, I found black currants and groundnuts. I thought of chanterelles, oyster mushrooms; the thick lobster mushrooms that stained your hands like iodine. The boletus with their porous undersides that arrived after the fairy tale mushrooms, the fairy tale mushrooms—fly agaric—the kind that would make you hallucinate if you ate them, or give you dysentery. The blackberries that ripen right after them. I thought of how brilliant and beautiful these things were. I thought how, out here, when one thing got messed up a chain of events followed and how the logging really messed things up. I thought about the healing quality of turkey tail mushrooms, chaga, and rishi. I thought how, out here, we had everything we could ever need. How there was no need to escape and even though my mind and body pitched toward it, the truth was, in a way, I already had. I felt a little better after I thought of all those things and keeping my eyes shut, listening to the storm, I fell asleep.

CHAPTER 2.
OUT HERE

FISHERMEN AND HUNTERS WELCOME.
MICHIGAN CHERRIES. SUGAR BEETS AND
CORN. The banner at the truck stop rotated with these simple phrases. It hung above the front door and there was another one matching it stretched between two posts, next to
the single-lane highway. The truck stop was set far back from
the highway. The seasons out here were determined by what
there was to fish, hunt, forage, pick, and so on, you understand. Most people were hunters and fishermen and animals
were their prey, which left the flora to people like me.

The truck stop was a long rectangular building, nothing
spectacular—brown brick—and at the northern end of the
parking lot, which doubled as a Michigan Department of
Transportation carpool, at the furthest end from the highway, grew pines, red and white, hemlocks, maple, and birch.
To the east of the squared-off asphalt were several rows of

elderberries. Queen Anne's lace with its collars of white flowers around the stems. In the middle of summer, when you knew the fishermen were welcome, wild milkweed grew in the front ditch. When you pulled in and your truck's windows were down you could smell the sweet floral blooms. Sometimes I had to park at the northern end for different reasons and the trees were of an age that if the timing was right, beautiful young pine flowers grew. They'd get powdery not long after they blossomed, and all you had to do was give them a little flick to release a fair amount of pollen, which I used as a seasoning in bread, crackers, and so on. After the pollen stage, small young pinecones formed, and sometimes I did stuff with those too. I made vinegars, pickles, and turned them into syrups. I mean, don't get me wrong, we had plenty to forage in the forest, but that didn't mean I wouldn't collect pollen at the truck stop in between doing this or that.

I liked truck stops. Sometimes I had cravings for that sort of meat and potatoes type of Americana cuisine you could find at a truck stop. Because I'm a fine-dining chef, people think I eat fancy most of the time. That is very far from the truth. And out here the truth is if you are in the right place at the right time, you can get an exceptional meal from a truck stop. If you don't already know this about me, I love cooking, but I don't love being a "chef." It isn't as glamorous as the television could make it seem. A lot of chefs express an extreme amount of bravado. I'm not that type of chef. But I'm serious when I say that anyone who sets their mind to it can make a great meal. Many, many people can be chefs if they want to be.

Inside the truck stop the lady behind the deli counter had on a net over her white hair. She'd spent time under the dome-shaped hair dryers, the ones that when you were little, waiting for your mom at the salon, doubled as an astronaut's helmet. I hadn't been to a salon in so long I didn't even know if those hair dryers existed anymore, but wherever she went to get her hair done, they did.

"I'll have two chicken thighs and a side of mojos," I said to her. Her mask was on over her mouth but not over her nose. That's how a lot of people did it. Her hands were in gloves; she wore an apron, and of course the hair net. I had on my mask over my mouth and nose. I wasn't too worried, though this was around a time when many of us were still worried for good reason. She picked up the chicken thighs and mojos with tongs from under the heat lamp and placed them into a rectangular box. Those truck stop chicken thighs were some of the best fried chicken thighs I'd ever had. The breasts could be good too but only if they were fresh from the broaster. If they sat under the heat lamp for too long, then they got a bit dry. But the thighs, they didn't seem to get dry even when they were shrunken from the heat. Occasionally, I'd get one that might have been sitting for a short forever, but it was still delicious as heck. The wings I wouldn't go for unless you wanted to smother them with hot sauce. The thighs were easy, fist to mouth, no fussing or picking around anything, two bones and that's it.

The mojos were a whole other godly thing. Mojos were potato wedges, lightly breaded and seasoned and then broasted as well. Honestly, I didn't truly know what broasted chicken or mojos were, but I believed a broaster was a sort of deep fryer with a lid. I couldn't begin to imagine how that worked. Or how terrible it must be to clean.

The woman's nametag read, *Lucy*. She was there every Monday. I was there on Mondays because that was my day to run errands. From our cabin Anna or I went to town two days a week, and it's a long way to any of the towns. Mondays were when I drove the fifty miles to take the trash and recycling to the dump. I also went to the UPS store if we had any packages or mail delivered. I went to the hardware store, the grocery store for basic goods and home supplies, then I did whatever else we needed to get done in town. I left early because during the school year I had classes through Zoom on Monday afternoons. From 2020 to 2022, I was enrolled in the School of the Art Institute of Chicago's Writing Program, studying for my MFAW. I'm restless and I have backup plans for backup plans.

I had to give myself an hour and a half each way. It was fifty miles one way but going the first ten miles on the logging road and then the next five miles along the gravel road, I couldn't drive so fast without some sort of danger, whether animals, or fallen trees, mud, ruts, washouts, or what not. We had a Jeep Wrangler, a Dodge Ram, and a Toyota 4Runner, and each needed to get worked on several times a year just from the effects of driving those roads at a decent fifteen miles per hour. It was a hell of a thing.

Lucy set up the chicken and mojos on the deli counter in the red, white, and blue rectangle box with a block print of a chicken on it. There was a basic tagline, something like, "best broasted chicken," and they weren't wrong. I thought it was darn good and I got the broasted chicken every Monday, almost religiously.

Lucy asked me if there was anything else I needed and I

said no. I grabbed two napkins and headed over to the counter where I used a squirt of hand sanitizer. I paid the four dollars and fifty-two cents in cash. In line there were several people behind me. It was busy that Monday. I was excited to get to the truck and eat the chicken and mojos as I drove, using my knee against the wheel, the rest of the way to the dump.

The truck stop was often busy. Lots of people stopped there traversing the long Upper Peninsula. Often the customers were men—truckers obviously but also hunters, fishermen, loggers, and construction workers. I'd say 80 percent of the people roaming around were men, purchasing Monster energy drinks, Red Bull, coffee, and snacks for the road. Chicken too. Several were ahead and behind me in line. I kept my head down, my face shaded by my Realtree camo baseball cap. My hair was in a low ponytail beneath it. I had on Carhartt work pants, steel-toed work boots, and a hooded sweatshirt.

Two men talked with one another behind me. They were talking about the fishing season, and the forest work to be done. One said to the other, "This is god's land," which caught my attention. He was right, though I didn't feel like he meant it in a spiritual way but more of a strange way. It sounded like he meant it in a way that *god's land* wasn't for people who might not look like him or didn't like the things he liked.

I was being judgmental. I knew that when I judged others it made me fearful: fearful that others were judging me. Though I looked like a lot of the other people—women—out here, with long hair and white skin, that didn't stop me from feeling different on the inside. And it felt like he meant this wasn't land for people like me—queer people, or people who weren't white, which were many of the people I loved. I kept my head down and wanted to disappear under my ballcap. Even though I knew I blended in I was afraid to turn around. I wanted to see what he looked like; his voice was familiar.

The landscape out here was like what the land would be if it were *god's land*. It was beautiful. Though it came along with a lot of people who thought it was only for them. Or that they owned it. Anna and I often used a small path, smaller than the main one we drove in and out of the forest on. The path was like many other paths in that it ran through some people's property but in essence was an old logging service road, and therefore some of it was also on public land. One day someone put up metal posts in the middle of the narrow path so we couldn't use it anymore. I don't know what was so important that they didn't want people passing through. I don't know if they did it because it was *us* using it, but for some reason, they didn't want it accessed anymore. I was sad that they felt they had to block off a path to get from one place to the next. I couldn't help thinking it was because Anna and I were the ones often driving down it, looking for foraging spots, and that they didn't like us. We didn't know them, and they didn't know us, though we knew a lot of people out here had heard about us coming to the area. Everyone we had met was extremely kind, the midwestern sort of kind.

This truck stop with the broasted chicken and mojos was where we picked up the guests who visited our Inn. It wasn't easy getting to our cabin unless you had a 4x4, and we weren't on Google Maps, so Anna and I picked up our guests at the truck stop on Fridays. Some of them rode with us, but some of them, if they had a 4x4, followed behind.

The Milkweed Inn was also our home. Before we had it,

our cabin had been built by two men who loved to hunt. Most of the people with camps out here were hunters. By the way, cabins out here were called camps. Though others who didn't hunt just liked the scenery or riding their quads or things like that. The men before us also must have rented the cabin to snowmobilers, because there were a lot of magazines and other materials on such activities that had been left behind when we moved in. One of the men, we were told, had MS. We heard he used a motorized wheelchair with big traction tires to get through the fields and forest to hunt. He had a license that allowed him to hunt from his truck with another person driving and a window rolled down, his arm with the rifle propped in its frame. Because he was in a wheelchair, the cabin had a ramp leading up to it and a wide washroom on the first floor. Our kitchen counter was quite low where the stove was built into its surface, for easier access. I got used to it. Sometimes it caused a pain in my lower back, but I held myself with my core while bending over it. I'd never had a fancy kitchen or equipment, even at my restaurant, so I was familiar with cooking in any sort of kitchen, fancy or not. Honestly, I never learned how to use some of the fancy kitchen equipment that other chefs had, like combi ovens or Pacojets or steam injections or other things like that.

If you looked at the cabin from above, you'd see a large rectangle of corrugated green metal—that'd be the roof. Beyond that you'd see the thin wooden fence of the small yard we'd set up allowing the dogs their bathroom time at night and in the morning without worrying about them running off after the wolves or barking at chipmunks running up the trees or the occasional flying squirrels. Around the cabin there was about one acre of grass. I didn't cut the grass in the early summer and that made the mosquitoes worse, but I didn't cut the grass because in between all those blades were hundreds of wild strawberries, dead nettle, clover, plantain, and violet. There were garter snakes, toadlets, toads, crickets, grasshoppers, and ant colonies. Lots of other things I couldn't see, I'm sure. It was much better, leaving it be. The birds liked the berries. The bees and other pollinators liked the flowers.

Past the yard was forest, for miles and miles each direction, though occasionally large chunks were empty and somewhat brown from where logging had occurred. Down the hill from our back porch was a serpentine river that you could easily see, especially from above. I wished Anna and I were able to spend the holidays here with our families but it was near impossible to get here during the winter, through the snow, unless we got a Sno-Cat. A Sno-Cat was the sort of machine explorers used in Alaska, the northernmost ends of Canada, Greenland, and Antarctica. A Sno-Cat is like an enclosed tractor cabin with large tank-like treads. With something like that you might never get stuck. And I thought if we had a family ourselves, with children of our own, it would be exceptionally nice to have holidays here. But we didn't have that now. It would be nice to have children and our own family. I thought about it a lot. I wanted to pass on my cravings for the land, the enchantment of it, the feelings and memories I had, like the ones the farmhouse I grew up in had welded into me. In a sense, I did it for my guests instead.

Our cabin out here, *our camp*, is called The Milkweed Inn. We are deep in the Hiawatha National Forest. The cabin was constructed of large cedar and pine logs cut from the surrounding forest. I'd found the cedars and cedar swamps along the riverbed that people before us had left untouched. You could tell a few of the leftover cedars at the river were ones too big for them to get up the hill and because of that they were now older growth. Because the cedars at the river were so tall, they got struck by lightning sometimes, or the earth around them eroded into the river. Their roots became loose and they fell over too.

I loved the cedars. I loved how they smelled. For our guests, I often made a frozen custard from them. I clipped the cedar branches and greens, slightly warming them to bring out the oils, then I soaked them in milk and cream from the local Debacker Family Dairy. I let them steep with the milk and cream in the refrigerator for forty-eight hours or so, strained them, then cooked the scented dairy gently with egg yolks and sugar until it thickened, without curdling the eggs—that's a very important thing—then I spun the mixture in a small ice cream–making contraption. I served a single large spoonful with a syrup I made of pine flowers and crunchy bits of toasted, locally grown oats.

The rusted log splitter used for building this place was in our basement for a long time until I gave it to a man I knew, a logger I met out here. The hunting partners who built this cabin finished it in 1999. When they eventually left, they left everything in it: beautiful enamel pots, plates, silverware, bed sheets (which we didn't use); even some dry foodstuffs like microwave popcorn and Maruchan ramen were still in the cabinets (which I may have eaten). There were KitKat bars in bowls on the counters with lots of holes in the wrappers and mice dung sprinkled throughout.

This was the newest building I had ever lived in. The floors didn't creak and there were outlets everywhere. The men built it well. Our neighbors have told us they were surprised when the men hired an architect to help for the construction. It showed. Inside it felt like a normal home that could be anywhere, despite there being no power or water or sewer from urban types of sources. The house relied on the sun, propane, septic, and well water. In small ways I knew how to be out here from what I had learned watching Mom and Dad as they homesteaded on our small farm. For example, I learned growing up, it was important to ensure the septic was well maintained.

When you entered the cabin, you smelled the sharp scent of the cedar and pine walls. If the wood-burning stove was going you could smell that too, usually before you walked in. It was a nice thing to drive up and see and smell the smoke coming from the chimney. Pure comfort. Unless it was mid-July we often had a fire going in the wood-burning stove, which was our only heat source. In July it was usually warm enough and all, but even in July we sometimes needed a fire at night. The weather was never certain. I loved that stove. It was made of soapstone and the glass door shined with a warm glow when the lights were off. At night I pulled a beanbag chair up to it, opened a book, and with the soles of my feet stretched out towards it, read until I fell asleep. Sometimes that was the only way I could fall asleep. I'd sleep there until Anna woke me and ushered me to our bed. Once in bed, I didn't sleep, but at those moments, with the heels of my feet and my toes cooking to a nice medium rare, it was a really good thing.

From May to October we host ten guests each weekend. We pick them up at the truck stop on Fridays and bring them back Sunday mornings. I always suggest they get the broasted chicken and mojos for their drive home or to the airport. Anna is usually the only one who drives them out of the forest because over the weekend the guests become friends, and they all don't mind getting in each other's vehicles to carpool back into town. That way we don't need both of us to go and I stay back to clean the rooms.

Guests come from all over the country and even from other countries. We've had guests from Canada, Australia, the UK, and Europe. Once a couple brought us warm chorizo, eggs, and beans with homemade tortillas from their favorite restaurant in San Diego. How they did it I can't say, but it was one of the best gifts anyone ever brought us. It's a great effort to get to Milkweed, but in the end I hope people feel that the weekend with us is worth it. That in some way they get that magic of the farmhouse I grew up in.

After the guests arrive Friday, I cook a family-style meal over the open fire. It might be smoked trout or lamb, pierogi, and salad made from wild things, flowers, and our garden. There might be other vegetables from the farmers markets. On Saturday mornings I prepare pastries that are ready for the early risers. These pastries might be babka, cinnamon rolls, or monkey bread, things like that. Sometimes I make a glaze out of sour cherry vinegar I've made from Dad's garden or the truck stop cherries to finish over the top of the pastries. The rest of Saturday, we feed our guests like hobbits:

two breakfasts—the pastries and then a second breakfast at eleven (elevensies) usually of eggs, potatoes, and wild greens like nettle, ramps, or marsh marigolds cooked inside homemade tortillas made with locally milled flour from Freedom Mills—then in the early afternoon we have lunch, usually something foraged and from our garden, after that and before dinner we serve cheese, charcuterie, and homemade pickles, and on Saturday evening there's a multi-course tasting menu with anywhere from ten to fifteen courses, and beverages. On Sundays, I feed the guests brunch and my doughnuts, which I have to say, have been memorably described as "going down on a cloud."

We have five accommodations, so guests usually come in groups of two, either partners or friends. We offer three cabin rooms, one sixteen-foot silver bullet Airstream Bambi Sport, and a wall tent with a wood-burning stove on a wooden platform. In a sense, it's like glamping. In another sense, it's like a summer camp for adults; aside from the food, guests can forage, hike, mountain bike, fish, swim, kayak, or play bocce, croquet, cornhole, read on the porch. Best of all, if you're a night owl, is the stargazing. It's a chance to see the constellations, meteor showers, the aurora borealis, the Milky Way, and the International Space Station, which rolls through every forty-five minutes or so, give or take.

The Milkweed Inn is something I dreamed of for a long time. I always wanted something that felt more sustainable and holistic rather than the grind of the city. Here I have gardens, and I can forage and use the local ingredients. I can make small batches of ferments that last several years in a row. The meals I serve are a story of the land. You get to taste what the Upper Peninsula—the Midwest—tastes like. Cooking for just ten guests at a time allows me to do these things with very little staff and it gets to come from deep down.

I don't mean to say that what I did at my restaurants didn't come from deep within me. But as the years went by, things got harder. I didn't like managing the size of staff I needed for those places. And I couldn't get past the anxiety of the turn and burn, the waste, and the worrying about how much water or gas or electric we were using to make it happen. I was frightened to think of all the power and resources needed to create a fancy meal for people. Of course, eating artistic and thought-provoking food is a fun thing to do and I'm not trying to take away anyone's joy in that but it's also a privileged thing to do. Doing it out here doesn't make it any less so, but I figure if I'm able to be more conscious of our resources, I can do it with a less heavy heart. I reconciled with myself that this is what I do, so right now this is how I must do it.

I do love cooking food and cooking for others. Here, I get to tell people stories about the land and my life that I might not be able to otherwise. It's an exceptional feeling to be able to cook a whole Lake Superior trout over the fire that my neighbor has caught. Grilling fresh wild greens with homemade wild berry vinegar and oil allows me to give people something they'd never thought of eating before. The berries I serve are from our yard or the forest, the leafy greens I serve are from our garden or nearby paths or even deeper in the woods, the fish I serve is from the nearby rivers and lakes, and the red meat proteins I serve are usually from our friends and neighbors that have shot and butchered the animals themselves or from the Upper Peninsula farmers.

When Dad was younger, he was skilled at hunting and fishing and we always had something smoked in the fridge or hanging from the rafters of the barn or garage. It's true that what I'm doing here is trying to give people something like the feeling of what I experienced as a child. Being in an untamed place yet feeling safe and nourished. I'm showing them the magic I experienced, welcoming them to how I once felt. If I don't give it to them, I don't know who else I can give it to. And not yet having children, like I said, the need to share is strong. I'm determined to give people good experiences of what it's like to be in the wilderness and what better way to experience or create a memory than through a meal? The Upper Peninsula of Michigan is abundant. I want to share that with others. Milkweed is an enchanting place, as astonishing as the farmhouse I was raised in.

At the same time, it's as dangerous as it is beautiful. Once we got here, we learned that a lot of the forest was getting torn apart. I think there were many things about this part of the country I didn't realize. I'd been naïve. National forests are not protected like National Parks; instead, they are tree farms. I can't say that's fact but it's what it seems like.

꠸

When I got back in the Dodge Ram with my box of chicken and mojos, I used hand sanitizer again. I took down my mask, and before I pulled away from the gas pump, I dug into the red, white, and blue paper box. I sat for a moment before I put the truck in drive. I watched the man who came out behind me, the one I'd heard say this was *god's land*. I watched him get into his Chevy 3500; his eyes were shielded with reflective aviator sunglasses. He must have sensed me looking at him because he raised his hand over his steering wheel and gave me a short wave as he pulled away. I shaped my hand like a gun, extending my index finger and pulling in my other fingers, and snapped my thumb as if shooting it at him. He smiled, perhaps thinking I was admiring him. His front license plate had a frame that read, TREES ARE OUR RENEWABLE RESOURCE. When I saw the plate, I realized I knew this guy for certain. It was just, at the time, I didn't recognize him right away with his new cowboy-style mustache. Thing was, I liked this guy. Really liked him. We got along. He was the one I gave our log splitter to. And I knew he wasn't a bad guy, and when he said *god's land* it wasn't about what I thought. We just had different ideas of what that meant. Even though he was a logger—in fact, owned the company that did a lot of logging here—he was a good guy. He wanted the earth to be okay, I think, probably just as much as I did. You know, sometimes people just need to do a job. He and I weren't so different.

I'd see him out here each spring, parked somewhere in a new plot of land. A plot of land I thought wasn't possibly going to be logged. I'd see his truck backed into a small clearing with his license plate facing out at the edge of the path. It wasn't long after I first saw his truck that the machines came and then the trees were cut, the stacks piling up, the semis hauling them out, and all that was left was a clearing and a large mess with a lot of flora and fauna all messed up.

I thought there wasn't much I could do. Not unless I bought it all, but I didn't have those kinds of resources.

We get out here in the spring, just after the snow begins to melt. There's no real way to get through until the snow melts. And at first there is nothing. But after the earth shifts, and the sun gets higher, suddenly there is everything. The Hiawatha Forest is our home. The trees, the paths, the animals; it's our own rare neighborhood. We are, in every sense of the phrase, off the grid. After we get up here, within a short time, we become different. The water from our well, the oxygen, the trees, the soil, it all changes us. We look different, smell different, taste different. My skin clears up. I believe when I'm here, it's something like how it was when I was little at the farmhouse growing up. I'm more a part of everything around me and I'm like that again—more a part of the place, in a way.

All the berries are out here, all of them, nearly all I could dream of using in the meals I cook for others or for snacking as I'm out foraging. Turns out wild blueberries are the best blueberries you'll ever have. But before the blueberries come, the strawberries ripen. The strawberries dangle under trifoliate leaves and before the strawberries grow, the ferns curl like G clefs, eventually unfurling into long spindly leaves. Each fern is a fractal. One leaf looks like the entire thing and one fragment of the entire leaf looks like the entire leaf. It's a phenomenon that is all over in our universe: our bodies, our fingerprints, the trees, the mycorrhizal networks underground, the constellations. But before the ferns open, the trout lilies sprout, shiny, they are, exposing their green tips through the dormant forest that's mostly brown and tan at the time. Beside the trout lilies are the icy-blue reindeer lichen. The reindeer lichen is very nice; it's the thing most alive in early spring. As it gets a few degrees warmer, the trout lilies grow taller and slide open. They are called trout lilies because the spots on the rubbery leaves are a bruised color that fades into the green of them, somewhat like the skin and scales of the trout from the rivers. In the Sturgeon River (the river running through our property) there's brook trout (brookies), perch, and chubs, which are a small minnow-type fish. Because of climate change (yes, being a key witness, I believe in it) and overfishing, there aren't very many sturgeon, if any, in the Sturgeon River.

From the trout lily stems, running up the center are flowers with yellow silky petals that bloom like miniature sunflowers. They bend their heads the same way sunflowers do when they go to seed. Flowers, animals, and humans are alike in that way. I see the trout lily flowers and think how now, Mom and Dad are like them, both with their backs bent and heads hanging. I pick the young stems with the yellow petals and ferment them in salt amounting to 1 percent of their weight and compress it together inside a vacuum-sealed bag. I keep them at room temperature for seven to ten days and the result is like sour cucumbers.

The trout lily's petals fall off quickly. The forest floor becomes more yellow. That's when the ferns wake up, in a way, stretching. Sometimes when they are small and tightly curled, I gather a few and pickle them, but I mostly leave them because they are a special part of the forest. The ferns provide good nourishment to the animals that eat them. Along with the ferns emerge two different kinds of sorrel—wood and sheep. Wood and sheep sorrel are also called sour grasses or oxalis. Then there's club moss, which looks like miniature saguaro cactus, white and purple clovers, dandelions, even white and yellow violets. But that's not all, there's plantain, nettle, gooseberry, elderflower, and Joe Pye weed, and that's not even a fraction. You wouldn't believe how many things out here are nutritious. And they aren't just out here—a lot of these plants are everywhere in the Midwest and beyond.

The paper shells of maple and beech seeds stick in the ground where they've fallen. Tiny white arteries sprout from the cotyledons and dig themselves into the earth. New trees grow from there. At first, they come up with just a stem and two leaves. At that time, they are small saplings and not all of them turn into trees, but rather tiny versions of themselves. Sometimes I pick those and ferment them like I do with the trout lilies, or I dry them to use in a blended tea I call a forager's tea that I serve to the guests. In some areas the entire forest floor is full of maple and beech saplings. If we, *Homo sapiens*, had never arrived here, this entire part of the Midwest would be crowded with these trees. I walk through them, wishing for them to grow, careful not to step on the tender twigs that will someday become trunks.

Out here there are hundreds of thousands of critters. Truthfully, I don't know how many—it's probably more than hundreds of thousands. Let's say millions. Some you can see and some you can't. Many of them fly, such as ants, wasps, bees, gnats, mosquitoes, moths, butterflies. And above those flying ones soar thousands of feathered ones: blackbirds, finches, robins, woodpeckers, geese, cranes, ducks, turkeys, grouse, warblers, and woodcocks. When you least expect it, hummingbirds suspend before you, seeming motionless but with a sound like a mechanical drone.

Where the ferns give way, knee-high shrubs of berries emerge. As the ground warms, the reindeer lichen becomes stiff. When I enter the forest, the lichen crunches beneath my boots. Where the blueberry shrubs are low, before you know they're blueberries, you find pointy pink buds within the fold of the two green leaves. You know these ones. I know them too and studying them can make you or me blush. When you really look at it, the forest is an erotic place. Another week passes and those pink buds turn into white bells. Shortly thereafter the clusters of white bells fall away, forming tiny green globes. The cells continue to divide until a soft flesh fills up the skin, pushing it out and turning it from green to white. The sun warms the white globes. They turn pink, first the ones on the outside of the cluster and by the time the ones on the very inside get pink, the ones on the outside of the cluster have turned red or purple and so on until they're blue. Once the cell division stops and they are fully who they're meant to be, they grow fatter and become pale from the waxy film of the forest's yeast that has spread across their surface. This is when they are perfect. Wild blueberries are forest caviar.

～

One day I was out in the Polaris Ranger UTV, foraging as I promised myself I would. I liked foraging alone. This particular day was quiet and beautiful. I had been thinking of how rapidly the seasons change here. Some of those sleepless nights when I made my lists of what I would do with all the things I could forage, I would promise myself that the following day I'd go out and collect all of those things.

I was scanning the edge of the forest along the path, moving slowly, when I saw a baby crane run across a logged field. The young crane had many brown fluffy feathers, and a bit of red on her face. She was incredible and cute. Seeing her run through the logged field like that made me worry she was lost. It was a very human thought to think she didn't know where she was, but I thought it. She probably thought the same of me.

Later I drove to another spot. I parked on the path and got out with my mesh sacks, foraging bags, and the corrugated pint containers I saved from the farmers markets for collecting berries. I found the blueberries, more than last year but not nearly as many as the first year. By that time, we had been out here for three full summers. The logging changed things a lot one year to the next.

The grass grew tall in the middle of the path. *Amanita muscaria*, the fly agaric mushrooms stood proud, right between the wild grasses down the center where the tires of trucks and semis and logging machines hadn't messed things up too much. They seemed to appear overnight, taking a cue from the blueberries. These mushrooms were the sort that belonged to the book covers of fairy tales and in each direction I looked, they were there staring back at me. A forest floor full of mushrooms stopped me in my tracks. I inspected them closely, wishing I could eat one, but I knew if I did it would hurt my stomach. Possibly I'd hallucinate. Instead, I moved to the side of the path, where other wild things created a division between the path and the forest, closer to where I saw milkweed flowers growing in clusters. I inhaled. I gave the Inn the name of Milkweed because of the millions of milkweed plants around us. Ants and monarchs thrive on them. The milkweed plants are a sage color of green with purple, white, and pink flowers. Beneath the milkweed I found burdock root, which I loved to harvest for pickling, and I marked its location on my hand-drawn map.

Out here, the pine and birch are thick. Beneath the thin, sandy surface of the Upper Peninsula, beneath the path, the trees' roots reach out like hands linking and twirling. Water penetrates the soil and when it can't go down any further, the soil perspires, and the mushrooms emerge. At least that's how I imagine it. Their networks spread beneath the sandy soil, roots, and rocks, where the synapses of fungi teach each other about the earth. I plunged a spade into the earth and lifted out the burdock and, along with it, the membranes of roots, mycelium, critters seen and unseen. I gathered two roots of burdock.

The fly agaric mushrooms alert the boletus (the cousin to the porcini) when the time is right, and under the hemlock and birch and other trees they appear. First, only a thimble-sized cap, brown and sleek, peeps up. Their color makes them more conspicuous than the fly agaric. The fly agaric is red or yellow with white spots, but if you don't see the boletus, then you just don't see them. They are the color of the leaves. Mushrooms hide like that. But if you do see them, especially when they are young, trim them at the base with a pocketknife. The mesh sacks I carried were for the boletus and when I had collected a few and was satisfied, I packed everything neatly into the canvas bag I strapped next to me in the passenger seat of the Polaris.

The boletus and the blueberries come at the same time, like soul mates. I collected a pint's worth of blueberries that day too and was happy. The birds, bears, wolves, foxes, and tortoises could share the rest as far as I was concerned. I didn't need too many mushrooms, the forest and its inhabitants needed them more than I did.

There are several places in the forest that with no other noise for miles, it sounds the same as standing at the edge of the ocean. The echo through the trees is like a conch shell over your ear. At one of those places, where the forest was like the ocean, I walked the path, hunting for chanterelles. Depending on what I'm searching for, I change up where I go. Not all that I forage or hunt grows together, of course. This forest has many microclimates and I'm astounded by the continuous surprises.

Hedgehog mushrooms would be here any day now. The hedgehogs have little toothlike filaments beneath their small caps. Oyster mushrooms, which smell like oysters and often have a shiny gray cap, have been frequent. I scanned for mushrooms that looked like cauliflower and lion's mane, both appropriately named for their shape, and coral mushrooms, which look like coral and are often orange or pink, growing up as if they were in a body of water. As it was, perhaps millions of years ago, this place was covered in water so when you thought about it, it made sense.

I really wanted to find lobster mushrooms. I looked through the trees and leaves for their bright red-orange bodies, but they weren't ready yet. Ever since we first came here, I've been searching, foraging, and hunting for them. This was a priority for me.

A common mushroom in the hemlock groves, of which there are many, are lactarius mushrooms. These are a perfectly ivory-colored mushroom that shouldn't be eaten. I pulled the hand-drawn map from my pocket and marked the location where I saw them. I did this because lactarius mushrooms can turn to lobster mushrooms. I marked all the lactarius on my map.

When Anna first saw my map, she laughed. She said I should use the GPS coordinates or satellite from my phone to mark the spot instead. "No, no," I told her, that seemed like too much trouble.

"I'm an anachronist," I said. "I like my hand-drawn map."

Anyhow, there is no other mushroom that will look like a lobster mushroom. When you know what they look like you can see them from far away. Lobster mushrooms aren't really a mushroom but a parasitic fungus that grows over the lactarius mushrooms, giving them the deep red color of a boiled lobster, so much so that they stain your hands. There is something about the parasite which makes it so that the lactarius, once they are the color of lobster and smell of it, can be eaten. I'm not a mycologist but a few of these things I know. Some people even say they taste like lobster. I don't think so, but when you bite into it with your eyes closed the texture is a match.

After each rain, I searched for the lobsters. I took from my pocket the folded and somewhat tattered map, on which I'd outlined our topography to the best of my ability, even including the Dodge Ram pickup parked next to our cabin. The aphid-riddled pin-cherry tree was there, and then a little northeast to that—the red pine, the fallen birch, and the grove of hemlocks along the steep hill, the river, the ancient cedars, and the cedar swamps. On the other side of the pickup and the cabin, I had drawn the two lines that form the path, which then went on another ten twisting miles out into the Hiawatha National Forest. I was looking for all these mushrooms, though my intention was to at least collect blueberries or soon, blackberries. At times I wanted to keep it simple but always kept my eyes open.

If you looked at the map with me, I was that dotted line, moving not far from the cabin, between the wavering parallel lines of the path. The first year out here, I added a sketch for the trees. It was of little arrows without the stem, a small pen mark of an upside-down V. On the map, you could see where I was being very ambitious and marked several upside-down V's over one another according to the tree's size. I stacked them on top of one another, putting larger upside-down V's at the bottom and smaller at the top—a child's version of a forest. The map was drawn on two yellow sheets of legal pad paper that I'd extended with scotch tape. And that time, it was folded into sixteen rectangles, and fit in the back pocket of my Carhartt dungarees.

In some places, where the forest had been logged, it was no longer the cover of a fairy tale. The fly agaric was sparse. There were no boletus, the ferns were brown, and everything was broken. I stopped to inspect a blackberry branch lying in the path. The stalk had a clean cut where a machine had clobbered it. The bottom half of the stalk stuck up from the ground, sliced clean enough for a scientist's slide. Epidermis, pith, and xylem all circled around each other. Their insides were like the trees' lifelines. A few unripe blackberries hung onto the sad branch.

In all the places where the destruction happened, it

meant things weren't growing well anymore, at least for the moment, or perhaps the next decade. It takes a long time for a forest to recover from logging and when you think about everything the forest does for our planet, it's no wonder why. Again, I unfolded the sixteen rectangles of my hand-drawn map. I took a pen from where I had it tucked in the neckline of my T-shirt, and I put X's over all the upside-down V's where the trees had once been. I crossed out the blueberries from where more of them should've been undergoing cell division, growing larger. Those got an X. Where blackberries should be green, beginning to ripen in the sun—X. Looking around, there was so much brown. Where yellowjackets should be collecting nectar and ants carrying away ripe, fallen berries, another X. Turned out the guy I knew with the cowboy mustache and aviator glasses, the guy with the Silverado, the guy who had become my friend over many talks passing one another on the path—he and his crew had been taking whatever trees they could, and all the other things surrounding them. And I couldn't blame them, but when things got messed up it was always the most beautiful ones first.

CHAPTER 3.
BLACK WALNUTS

IT IS SAID THAT BLACK WALNUT TREES POISON THE ground and everything that grows beneath them. Black walnuts are a beautiful tree. I learned how to crack black walnuts before I was born.

The thing is sometimes you know things because they've been told to you and you can imagine how they happened. You can piece the stories together yourself. And sometimes you know things because the forest has whispered them. Or your ancestors are inside you, so you know things because it's in your blood to know them, deep in your bones. I knew about the black walnuts, and how they were the precursor to my conception. I knew they were there the day I had been formed.

Here, let me tell you. Though I must rewind.

Our dads—Mom's dad, and mine—poured a bushel full

of black walnuts onto the gravel driveway. Dad got in the Oldsmobile station wagon and peeled out of its spot. Gravel clipped the undercarriage of the long vehicle. He gunned it in reverse down the drive where the gravel gave way to grass, then in drive he rushed forward over the walnuts, spraying them like bullets all over the place. Wayne, Mom's dad, ducked when one came flying at his bald head. Dad laughed. He rolled down the window. "That'll do her, yeah?"

Down on his hams, Wayne squinted, looking through the fragments. "I guess. Lot of picking to do." Dad and Wayne looked to the farmhouse, where a nut had busted through the kitchen window. They looked at each other like, *uh-oh*.

It was late in October of 1978 when Wayne brought over the black walnuts to crack in the drive. Wayne was good at foraging black walnuts but not great at shelling them. Cracking walnuts was a hard thing to do. After he'd collect them into a large bushel, he'd bring them to the farmhouse. Dad tapped the toe of his boot against the bushel of nuts. Several of the green knobs spilled over the top, not quite the size of a tennis ball, but bigger than a golf ball. They discussed the situation for a moment and that's when they poured them from the bushel onto the driveway.

Mom watched from the kitchen window. She thought her dad was a real jughead, a lot like the black walnut trees, poisoning other things deep down. She knew about the black walnuts too. Dad's voice carried. He shuffled his boots over the gravel, doing a sort of slow dance, jabbering on about something. Mom rolled her eyes when he said, "My dad knew a guy who had saplings. If we'd gotten them from him, we'd have a whole damn thirty-acre grove. That'd be a lot of money." Wayne nodded in agreement.

The rest of their conversation was muffled by the sounds of my sisters upstairs with their friends from the *Tamburitzas*. They practiced with their tamburas and tambourines. They also did things they could get in trouble for if they were caught.

Upstairs, Bunny sat on Nina's bed and her long blonde hair, parted down the middle, formed a perfect encapsulation. She was high on a couple things and her hair felt safe. Because she was the oldest, she gave the other girls (six including herself) these instructions:

"There's a sequence for it to work." Bunny peeked from her hair, scanning their level of attention. Her eyes went to each one sitting around her in a circle. "Pay attention," she said. "I can't always be doing everything." The other girls nodded. She continued, "Okay, so you have to take this thing out of the metal compartment."

"What thing?" Kelley asked.

Bunny held up a thing that looked like a small tampon so that they could see. "This thing," she said.

"We have to hurry. Mom's going to check on us soon," Kelley said. Bunny handed the tampon thing to Nina. "You try," Bunny said to her.

"Okay, now, you wrap your fingers around it at the top." Nina wrapped her fingers around it where Bunny pointed. "And then you squeeze, running your fingers down this little cylinder thing. See?" Bunny mimed the motion.

"Okay," Nina said, making note. "What is it?"

"Or if you want, you can just soak it in the Coca-Cola

but it's more effective if you squeeze," Bunny said and after a beat added, "It's propylhexedrine. See here?"

They all looked. "Yeah," they said eagerly.

"Then you squeeze out everything that's in it, into the Coca-Cola." The white milky substance dripped down into the drink, which fizzled and popped in the glass full of ice. Bunny helped Nina by running her fingers over it several more times, trying to expel every bit of the substance into the cola.

"What's it going to do?" asked Tammy, one of my sisters' friends.

"It's going to be a little like cocaine but last much longer. It will keep us awake and energized." After Bunny was satisfied that all the drug was in the cola, she stuck her middle finger in the glass and swirled the contents. "Okay, let's drink this motherfucker. You first, but only a little, we've got to share. I've only got one more." Bunny narrowed her eyes at them. "We've got to share," she said again.

Nina did as instructed. Kelley was next and took the glass from her, gulping it as fast as she could. The taste was nasty, bitter, and astringent like crushed chalk. "*Ew*," she exclaimed, puckering her face.

"It's not that bad," Bunny said, punching her in the arm for being greedy. Kelley held her arm and after the other girls drank Bunny finished the rest. She didn't make a face. She wiped her mouth with the back of her hand and poured in more cola, then extracted another one of the tampon things from her purse.

From the driveway they heard the blast of a car horn. They jumped, looking out the window. It was just Dad in the driveway with Grandpa. "They're so annoying," she said.

Feeling buzzy, Bunny had Kelley do the next one for

them. She told Kelley she was going to be last on account of her drinking so much the first time.

Mom didn't check on them. She was watching the men act like boys in the driveway and was pissed about the window. Whatever Dad said, it didn't matter—she knew the rest of it. He'd say how the saplings were such a good deal and they could have made back three hundred times the amount of money they had put into it. *Where would he have gotten the money in the first place? Almost four kids. The basement knee-high with water after rain. Broken-down cars, my teeth need repairs, a restaurant.* The list could go on. Instead of fixing any of that, he shoveled out a swimming pool. He reversed the backhoe machine into it and almost killed himself. Regardless, there had never been any money to buy the walnut trees in the first place. But she couldn't deny she loved the smell of the husks though not enough to have a grove of them. He'd say he'd sell the walnut trees for their wood value, but she knew he'd never get around to doing it.

After plenty of debating, finagling, and attempting multiple methods at cracking the walnuts, they had decided like two boys who loved to throw rocks through the windows of vacant houses to drive over them with the Oldsmobile. They used the same Oldsmobile I'd later drive around the yard while sitting in Dad's lap. Mom would be the passenger, both hands pressed against the dash. My sisters would sit across the long bench seat in the back, without seatbelts. I'd fling them from side to side each time I cranked the wheel. Everyone was laughing because it was funny when a little kid drove a car around the yard.

From beneath the weight of the beat-up station wagon,

the black walnuts shot out with the whiz of a missile. There was the one that had busted through the kitchen window. Others punctured the siding of the house. Mom ducked. This began the count of how many times she'd have to duck in her own home as something flew through the window. With all the tape and glass they used to fix and replace the windows over time, Dad could have bought those saplings.

They separated the broken husks, cracking the shells. Black marks lined the driveway where the station wagon's tires crushed out the stain for which the walnut was named. The nuts were crushed enough that they could finish the job by prying them open. They used a small nail and pliers and a pick to get the meat out. The meat went in one bucket and the shells went in another. After they were through, Dad brought in both buckets, set them down, and went toward the bathroom, asking Mom about her tweezers. "You don't touch anything of mine," she called to him. "Don't you dare use my tweezers on those walnuts." That was when she buried her face as deep as she could into the bucket of shells, without letting her nose touch nature's incense and dye. When Dad came back in the kitchen, he mentioned something about an amaro. Mom hadn't heard of it. He swore the Sciara family, his childhood neighbors, made it by soaking things like walnut husks in moonshine, which he said he had plenty of in the barn.

"Okay," she said, "but get them off the kitchen counter and put them outside in the garage or the barn or somewhere else. I don't want them staining the counters."

That was Wayne's last forage for black walnuts, right before the last maples he would tap. He would die before I was born, and I'd end up with the same birthmark at the back of my head as he had. It didn't seem that long ago to Mom, because so much would happen between the walnuts and when she had her fourth kid—me. Bunny, my oldest sister, would have her first TKO with alcohol, including arguments, hiding, conniving, and other incidents braided therein. My sisters would enroll themselves in the public school and just pretend in the morning they were going off to their Catholic school, and then once they got there, they'd change into regular clothes and walk over to the public school. Mom would quit her job at Jennie's Café, the restaurant they owned. Eventually Mom would find out she was pregnant again, thirteen years since the last one. "Medium" was how she'd describe it when the doctor asked how she felt. She added a question mark at the end, "Medium?" And when the doctor left the room, she cried.

Wayne came into the farmhouse that day and his hands were black. Mom was sweeping up the broken glass. He went to the cupboard, found a nice glass and the bottle of whiskey and fixed it for himself over ice. Mom assessed him. He didn't seem quite ready to die. There was always going to be the time when (Mom waited for it not with anticipation but more with a shiver in her spine) he would no longer be able to function. Whether his organs would stop their advanced fighting and filtering techniques against the toxins he consumed, or the kneecap-busting debt collectors would come, something was going to take him out.

When she thought about it hard enough at his funeral, remembering that day, all she could think was, *He looked more worn than usual*, but not as if he was going to die. She thought the dust storm that had been chasing him for years finally caught up, covering him in its dander.

Dirt settled in the wide pores at the tip of his alcoholic nose. He didn't stay in the kitchen long. He was never quiescent, as though afraid to be looked at for too long. She couldn't catch his eyes because he rarely looked up. He thanked her for the whiskey, which he'd helped himself to twice in the few minutes he'd hung around. On the way out, conscious of his hobble from another drunken incident, he blamed it on a pain in his leg. He took the second glass of whiskey outside with him. The cubes cracked under the liquid, clinking against the glass as he walked down the few back stairs toward the pool and out to the drive. Before he got all the way back out there, he appeared below the broken kitchen window and called her name, "Sandra Lee?" he said.

"Yeah?" She slowly went over, careful not to step on or crack the glass on the floor any further and looked out at him.

"You're doing a real good job," he said.

She was happy to hear it, so happy that tears welled up in her eyes. She had no idea that affirmation was going to make her feel as good as it did, but it did. She swept up the glass, smiling a little as she put a plastic bag over the window and taped it closed. She watched as he drove away and dotted her eyes with a kitchen towel.

Far out in the distance it looked as if a storm was coming.

⌒➤

It wouldn't have been weird for Mom to dream of black walnuts that night so she did. She stood in a barrel of them, big as the ball pits kids liked to play in, which weren't very safe—*e. coli*, hypodermic needles, and once a severed thumb, withered as the casing of a pig intestine. She sank into the walnuts. The smell was mesmerizing. She loved this smell and I know that because she's told me. I loved it too. She began her descent to the bottom and watched the knick-knacks from her childhood bedroom float up like seals along an aquarium's walls.

That night in bed, Dad's arm was heavy over her abdomen. Her eyes opened to his other hand in front of her face. His hand looked like Frankenstein's, lit by the bit of moonlight coming through the window on the west wall. His dumb, dirty hand pissed her off. It wasn't like Dad to scrub his hands entirely clean of stains. His hand was dark around the nail bed, stained at the tips of his fingers, across each crease of his knuckle, and in the lifeline of his palm. His fingers spasmed, grasping at something. His teeth were a grist mill. She closed her eyes, playing possum. He thrashed around a few more times. She sensed his eyes pop open, hearing his eyelashes drag across the pillow. Her eyes were closed but she knew he was awake now, alert in that certain way against the curve of her lower back. He moved closer. She scooted away, pretending to shift in her sleep. She threw her arm over the side of the bed to create the affect of sleeping. He moved in again. His sharp whiskers were pointy against her ear where his face nuzzled against her. Then his breath was warm and wet against the back of her neck as he exhaled. There was nowhere for her to go that wasn't over the side of the bed and onto the floor. *Why is he in bed in the first place?* He usually slept on the floor, claiming pains in his hernia.

That was his schtick, for anything. "I can't sit in a booth, my hernia. . . . I can't sleep on the bed, my hernia. . . . I can't pick up that thing, my hernia." Some other nights, Nina slept in bed with her, being a real mama's girl. But tonight, she was with her sisters and friends upstairs.

And now, because I can't picture this sort of thing, I must change the nouns.

The lady went with it feeling she had no other choice, but with no more sexual energy than a fish, long out of water. She opened her eyes then closed them, picturing our one black walnut tree in the yard, while the man—eager but not a craftsman when it came to angling—did his thing. And this night his minnows, chubs, and tadpoles, with all the force of being shot through a torpedo, raced ahead. The lady didn't orgasm. She pretended like she was half asleep through it all. The guy did. His eyes were clenched and mentally, he might not have been there either. He was also thinking of the black walnuts.

The storm finally came in. Lightning cracked across the sky, so close that the entire room was illuminated by the cold, blue light. There were no shadows when the man's hair fell over his face. Partly clothed, he had on his yellow-sweat-stained, stretched-out undershirt, and gloomy boxer shorts. The top half of her was covered in a nightgown and her panties were at her knees. The room went black again and she closed her eyes when suddenly behind her eyelids she sensed an orange glow in the room. She opened her eyes to see, and he was looking out the window. The tree they had been thinking of was on fire.

Tucking himself back into his underwear, he raced outside. He unspooled the hose from the side of the house, running to the tree to douse the flames. Bunny, Kelley, Nina, Tammy, Toni, and Daniela appeared in the yard. Mom opened the window, yelling at them to get back to bed. Dad saved what he could of the tree, while fast as ever, inside Mom, his sperm banged against the egg.

As it happened, it was a mediocre day, hyphenated by stale lovemaking, a burdensome father who said a nice thing, black walnuts, and a lightning-struck tree, when I began to yolk.

And when I thought about it, it's no wonder I was afraid of the trees catching fire.

CHAPTER 4.
MEADOW MUSHROOMS

THE ANGEL OF DARKNESS ARRIVED. MY SISTERS SAID
to each other jokingly but also somewhat seriously, ". . . put
goat's blood around the doorway." Dad yelled at them, he
was the king of this castle and they must obey. They jumped
from windows, off the roof, and ran out into the darkness.

～

In the summer of 1984, I learned a lot.

Summers were everything because I didn't have school,
and I hated school. I wasn't good at it like some other kids.
And there were a lot of kids at school. I liked to keep to
myself, so things like school or anything that brought kids
together made things sort of difficult. It was a people thing.
In the summer, I kept track of time by what we foraged, like
mulberries, meadow mushrooms, boletus, chanterelles, hen

of the woods, blueberries, and by events like Mom's birthday, the Fourth of July, my birthday, the county fair.

But 1984 was important because it was the year I fell in love with the forest, though sometimes it was scary. Seemed like I also liked things that made me afraid. Fear was the proof we were living, or something like that. Somehow, I knew I'd come to live in the forest someday. Maybe I willed it? Maybe it was my trips to the forest with Dad? Or it could have been the way Mom cooked mushrooms or how we collected hazelnuts and mulberries together. Or maybe I ended up out here because sometimes things like that are in your blood. It's who you are. A lot of scientists do years of fieldwork to come to their conclusions. I started my fieldwork in 1984.

Standing in that farmhouse yard, in my boy shorts packed with a sock rolled up into a ball, shirtless and staring up into the sky, I saw my whole life. I might've even known how it would end. I was only five, but I think I knew things because I was possessed by my ancestors, or by something else altogether, like the trees, the air, the earth. Mother Nature.

That summer I learned so many things. Like, I was better at finding mushrooms than Dad and that mushrooms could also make you sick. Horses could hurt a person. Mom and Dad were the same species as me, though Mom was also the kitchen and Dad was the forest. I loved being beneath the trees. The farmhouse was a living, breathing organism. I learned how much I loved animals and how Dad wasn't great with them. I didn't like how he killed them, because that made me feel awful.

I learned we didn't own this place. That we didn't truly own anything, that no one did. I learned how to shoot a pearl-handled .38 Smith & Wesson revolver with Dad's guidance, him behind me with his finger over my finger on the trigger, which Dad—who was very fond of it—called his cowboy gun. I learned some men were dangerous, though I was already suspicious of that. And I learned that when you kissed the walls, you could travel through time.

That summer, before the county fair, Mom canned peaches. She set all the canning jars, still steaming from the boiling water bath, in several rows on the cutting board island. Everything she did was precise, scientific. She placed the jars all facing the same way. With my chin resting in my hands, curious, the cursive *Ball* label faced where I sat on the other side of the island, a narrow box on wheels with a drawer and cabinet underneath. The top was a thick slab of maple. Most of the kitchen work, and even some meals, happened here.

On this day, Mom wore a terrycloth jumpsuit that left bare her tanned, freckled shoulders, arms, and legs. I could tell she was still warm from the sun. I touched her arm gently as she was doing things, fascinated by the small skin tags she had on her neck and legs. This was common for a woman of middle age, I'd come to find out. Her curly brown hair was pulled back into a small ponytail like a bundle of sprouts and as usual, a bandana was tied at the crown of her head to catch the sweat from the humid kitchen. She dropped fresh peaches into the jars. The peaches were from the tree out front that Dad had planted, which he'd later lose to a battle with Japanese beetles. I'd get a terrible rash around my eyes from drinking the water from the hose he used to pump pesticide. It's hard to say for certain if it was the pesticide though, because that same day, I watched the cartoon version of *The Hobbit* and cried my eyes out using toilet paper to wipe them. Either way, the next day the rash swelled my eyes shut. The bonus was I'd get to skip summer school and tutoring for one full week.

Mom dropped a slice of peach into my mouth like the mama bird does with worms to her nestlings. I knew this because I'd seen it happen in the nests at corners between our gutters and roof, and in *National Geographic* magazines too, all of which were stacked in a wicker basket along with *Gourmet* magazine in front of our toilet. I liked to look through the pictures even when I wasn't on the toilet. I also had the *National Geographics* Dad collected lined on a bookshelf in my room, some of which dated back to the early forties.

Canning was never a perfect thing. Sometimes we heard glass shatter in the night, or at breakfast, causing Dad to jump, thinking someone had shot at the house. Mom blamed it on the yeast, and for a long time, I never knew what that meant. At the time, I understood it as shards of glass ending up all over the coffin-sized pantry floor and wet, sticky, sour-smelling things splattered on the walls, doors, and the perfect, color-coordinated jars. Mom liked the preserves color-coded. We cleaned it up and Dad took out the trash, holding the bag far away from him so the shards of glass wouldn't break through the thin plastic and cut his leg, because that had happened before too. He grumbled something about it, but grumbling was how he reacted to a lot of things.

Into the jars of sweet peaches, Mom added cloves, cinnamon sticks, and star anise. I drooled from the aroma. And
becoming restless I said to Mom we should go outside to
collect mushrooms.

"Okay, in a minute," she said. Sometimes she collected
mushrooms with me too, though it was usually a thing Dad
and I did. Mom was more of a nut person. She showed me
how to pick the hazelnuts in our front ditch, being careful
not to get too close to the road.

"Let's do one thing at a time," she said and wiped her
forearm across her forehead where the bandana couldn't hold
back any more sweat from her eyes. "I have to wipe the floors
first."

In the farmhouse kitchen you could lick the walls and
taste the air from several hundred years ago. I had accidentally licked them before while practicing kissing. The taste
was ancient. After it rained and Dad had tilled the garden, I
searched between the unearthed rows for arrowheads. Slick,
obscure rocks like flint and obsidian pounded into sharpened,
slate-colored points. When I found one protruding from the
dark, damp soil, I brushed it off and put it in my pocket. The
top of my dresser was layered with findings so well-crafted they
could spear the thick skin of a bison (though there weren't bison
anymore out here). One time Dad said that all the royalty from
England used to come to the Midwest on bison-hunting expe-
ditions, and they'd wiped them out. I don't know if that's true,
but at the time I listened to him tell the story.

After I came back inside on the days he tilled, my pockets sunk to my knees through the bottoms of my shorts, full
of arrowheads, snail shells, and anything else that looked

interesting, I placed them onto my dresser top in a way that made the most sense, lined in several uniform rows from big to small and dark to light. They were next to the set of nesting dolls. Also, there was a box that held a ballerina and when you opened it, music played and she spun in circles. I felt like the ballerina was too girly for me, so I pulled her off from where she was connected to a spring and put her in the bottom of the box and closed it. She was dead now, in her coffin.

Meanwhile, that canning day, Mom finished wiping up the floors. She was always cleaning the floors.

See, the thing was, Mom scrubbed the floors more than wiped them. On her hands and knees, with a bucket of soap and two rags, one for washing and one for drying, she went down the hallways, did the bathrooms, got every corner in the kitchen and back porch. Basically, anything that was tile instead of carpet, from one side to the other, she scrubbed and then dried. She told us to take our shoes off and we tried but sometimes forgot. We shouldn't have forgotten though. When we forgot it made her feel we weren't thinking of her. Taking our shoes off equated to a kind of love and thoughtfulness. It'd take me a long time to figure that out, but I get it now.

Because you don't forget why things were the way they were, one time, I sat at the top of the stairs awaiting the implosion between the upper and lower level as all six oracles—my sisters and their friends—sat with blue smoke curling above their heads, now paranoid. Their giggles subsided beneath their chests, which were feeling heavier. Their minds grew heavier too as the second hand on the clock suddenly could be heard ticking. Toni Petrovic, the second oldest of all, shushed them. The stairs creaked. They listened. The old farmhouse tended to settle and sigh on its own. *Was that what it was?* They looked at me, sitting ten feet from them at the top of the stairs, as if I had the answer. And I did, though I didn't know how to say it, so I just opened my eyes wide while I played with my pink spongy action figures.

The stairs were creaking. Dad in his work boots, he stepped on the bottom stair first. The boot was caked with mud, soil, and manure. The heels were worn to extinction, duct tape mending the sole to the arch, over and around it, where they always got wet and later caused an itchy rash. At night he'd take them off, not always where he was supposed to, then scratch his foot like a dog.

He slowly put his other boot up on the second stair.

It was confirmed, they did hear a creak on the stairs. They looked into each other's eyes, still with their fingers over their mouths to shush one another. It wasn't helping. Kelley wanted to laugh, and Bunny put her hand over Kelley's mouth, because she knew if Kelley let it out they would all buckle. Then another stair sounded off. I looked at Dad's face. I was a mostly innocent bystander, in the middle. He put his index finger over his lips. *Wait. I was now a double agent.* All six heads looked through the doorway, floating above the bed. I looked back at them and told them with my mind to stop whatever it was they were doing. I conjured every bit of Yoda I could. I shut my eyes tight and opened them again. They began to scuttle like bugs. Smoke hung from the ceiling. Kelley picked up the floor fan; she brushed her long brown hair from her face with her fingers, leaving rake marks across the top of her head, and held the fan to the ceiling. They all joined in, waving their hands, as if they could grab the smoke and throw it out into the night.

Dad was the angel of darkness. Someone joked, "Quick, put goat's blood around the doorway," then they laughed. Nina covered her sore mouth. It hurt to laugh, and a few tears came from her eyes. They thought if they could just get the smoke out, maybe it would be okay. *Wasn't he already sleeping or something?* But there was no goat's blood, no lamb's blood, cow's, pig's, duck's blood, or any for that matter to save them. They knew if they didn't get all the smoke out, they'd be putting their own blood there after it was done. Bunny thought about taking the cue from our calico cat, which bolted out the opened window. I still hadn't said anything. Dad was ascending. His steps reverberated.

Dad reached the landing like a deep-sea diver returning to his boat. He flipped off his helmet and his eyes beheld all twelve of theirs. With their arms and legs waving it was as if he'd brought some deranged octopus on board with him.

Madness erupted. Dad created a vacuum when he inhaled, puffing up his entire body and about to erupt, he yelled *not in my castle*, or something of the sort. The room became cosmic ripples, like looking up at the Milky Way, but instead of stardust, we were floating through hair. Meteor-like legs, arms became shooting stars, and torsos were satellites, belly buttons turned into wormholes, as one by one the girls vanished. One slipped past me down the stairs. One went out the window right at the top of the stairs, ducking under Dad's arm and somersaulting out onto the roof. Another went out the bathroom window. One crawled through Nina's bedroom window.

They knew these routes. They'd memorized the feel of the rough sandpapery roof against the soles of their feet. Sometimes when they sunned themselves up there, they rubbed their heels against it, exfoliating them. They knew which gutters were most secure to lower themselves from to prevent breaking legs, ankles, feet, or other delicate bones. They knew where the earth below was soft and grassy. Beyond that, they ran through the greasy blackness from the spilled-over septic Dad had once again put off getting emptied.

Nina was the only one left. She pulled the bedspread around her neck so that only her head was visible. Dad turned to her. He would hold her responsible; being his least favorite, she was the obvious choice to blame. But when he looked at her, her lips were curled in over her missing teeth, and there was a white scar where her lip had torn where the horse had kicked it a few months before. She looked frightened whether she meant to or not. He couldn't hurt her, not now, not after seeing her this way.

Instead, he was able to pivot, reach out the window and snatch Bunny by her mane before she could drop from the gutter. She had delayed, watching Nina and ultimately sacrificing herself. She knew that whatever Dad decided to do, it wouldn't be something he hadn't done before. She had met this angel before. And maybe because he also knew what she knew—that it wasn't worth it—he gave up, even as he had her neck cupped in his hand, as if he could break her rebellion with a quick twist. His fingers released. He removed his palm, and she slipped away, unharmed.

Now Dad, Bunny, Nina, and I were bobbing together like the room was a boat on the waves. I felt the bile in my stomach start to rise and my mouth water with the saliva that always preceded vomit. When the back of Bunny's neck had been cupped in Dad's hand like he could snap it if he wanted to, the bile had risen like sap through the trees, up through my chest and esophagus. I ran to the toilet, where I threw up for the first time I can remember. Mushrooms and ramen noodles. Dad ran to me and knelt beside the toilet, his hand gentle on the small of my tiny back.

He told Nina while carrying me downstairs, "This isn't over." She nodded in agreement with the covers pulled up over her face so all that was left were her eyes. He seemed unfazed until he saw two of the Petrovic girls through the front picture window of the living room, running through the front yard with Kelley right behind them. "God-damned son of a bitch and bastard," he hollered. Bunny was outside with them now and turned to the house, held up both middle fingers, and pumped her pelvis at him.

Dad handed me to Mom and tore through the front door, but not long after, he came to a stop when his own foot got stuck in an especially deep part of the septic swamp he'd created among his rows of cedars. He sank up to his knees. He used both of his arms to pull out first one leg, then the other. They came out with a squelching sound. He tried to wipe away the greasy shit but gave up. He tried to come back into the house, but Mom blocked the doorway. I watched, horizontally, from where she'd laid me on the wicker couch and I held my stuffed ewok, before she followed him outside. The streetlamp lit up Mom's frame and the dusty door like she was on stage. She held up her finger, pointing him away from the door. He sulked his way around the house to the hose, and I heard the water splatter. That was also where Mom made me wash after I'd played too hard. She was already pissed that she'd just finished cleaning up the mud he'd tracked into the house and all over the stairs. If she let him in, she'd have to do it again.

⌁

No matter how much Mom scrubbed, wiped, or polished things, the wild yeast was everywhere. The farmhouse was fermenting. Wild yeast and pollen were all over our shoes, lined at the back door. It was on our clothes and on every hair of our skinny arms. If you took a fiber of that hair and put it under a microscope, you would see hundreds of little particles form around it, and what looked like a thin wisp would transform into a wavering tentacle with hundreds of legs belonging to critters you had no idea were there. The farmhouse was alive. Wasps lived in replicas of honeycomb beneath the siding on the back porch. Bird nests formed in the armpit of every gutter where water ran off from the roof. Anywhere there was a crook or bend, the sparrows, finches, and what not brought in twigs, vines, leaves, dirt and built their fortresses while never once looking at us with both their eyes. That was a thing about birds. You never got two eyes at once. I supposed that was okay with me.

The leaf duff, bird dander, wings of wasps past their prime, mosquito proboscises, and wild yeasts were carried in at the tips of the thin blonde hairs on my head and stuck to the door jambs, sheets, walls, floor tiles, couches, and shower curtain, and then traveled down through the pipes into the basement, settling into the pool of water around the washing machine. If at any time you also took the water from beneath the house and put it on a slide beneath the microscope, you could transcend time. I did that once and there was a universe inside there. That was for a science project, but I didn't win anything—though one time I did a project on acid rain and went downstate because I had won locally, but I didn't win anything downstate. Bunny had helped me build a block out of sugar cubes to replicate a building that I used to show how they would melt from the acid rain, which in my project was lemon juice. I explained to the judges that this was what rain would be like in the future. They didn't care, but I might have been on to something.

The water from the farmhouse was what came from the sky, ran off the apple, peach, cherry, and mulberry trees, around the raspberries, slid from slippery corn leaves and dropped from the ends of scarlet runner beans, falling into beads on the silky skins of zucchinis and squashes, through the slices of grass, into the crumbled soil and sand, between the membranes and veins of the mycelium and down into the walls of the well. I was always afraid of what the past might be. It seemed like it was brutal based on the arrowheads I found. Then I kissed the walls, and I could tell it was a lot of things by tasting it. Turned out, as a family, we were the well water and the walls. We were all the things the farmhouse was and we were in the present and the past, all at once.

On another day in the not-so-distant future, I'd get near the threshold of my bedroom, wrap my arms against both sides of the wall, and kiss the wood panel that held the door in its frame. It was some sort of cedar or pine, and the splintery kiss would not be what it would eventually be like meeting two other lips in real life, like biting into a plum. Don't judge me, you know you did this too. If you say you didn't, I won't believe you.

I tasted the farmhouse walls in so many ways, so many times. My sisters had tasted them too, whether they wanted to or not. The year before Dad pushed Bunny up against the wall of the stairwell. Dad held her arms behind her like she was under arrest. He had caught her smoking. The side of her face was smashed against the wall, and when he made her open her mouth so he could shove her forbidden cigarettes in, she too, had kissed the wall. That's how it went down and that's how she became a time traveler like me. She and I had a lot in common.

~

But on this day, the day that Mom canned the peaches, things were more or less normal. No one was fighting yet, no walls were kissed, no rain, and boots had been taken off at the back door. So far. I waited, practicing patience, because Mom said we must do one thing at a time. I sat on the kitchen floor. Soon, she would scrub it again. The tiles were like a tessellation and many of these spear-like shapes had come undone. We kept all the loose tiles in a wicker basket beneath the bar counter in the kitchen. In a nook, between two stools where the wicker basket was, I picked out the tiles and, matching each shape, put them back in the spots where they fit best. Mom said if I was going to do that then I should Superglue them, because Dad would never get around to *really* fixing them with the grout and everything they'd need to stay secure. My dexterity, though decent, we knew wasn't good enough that I could handle Superglue without every limb being stuck together until I formed my own shell, so I knew she must have been being passive-aggressive and just wanted to complain about him. I didn't have those exact words for it at the time, but I knew what it meant when adults said stuff like that. I knew she wouldn't give me the Superglue though I looked at her excitedly when she said it.

At my side were the Russian nesting dolls, which I loved to handle. Mom always said, "Be careful with them," as I held the round wooden things, painted as ladies with aprons and woven dresses. *What could I do that was uncareful?* I undid them, then did them again. Fitting each woman perfectly inside the next. I imagined the small ones were the babies, myself, and my sisters. I told Mom who was who and she smiled. I matched each line of apron or hand or whatever it was that was sliced through the hourglass shape of painted lime tree and put them back together. What I didn't know was that I was also matching fingerprints: mine over Mom's over her sister's and her mother's and her mother's mother. The dolls were heirlooms. If you took iron particles and dusted them with a brush over the dolls, you'd see the rings of each tree, splintered at each generation, with new DNA, stories, ideas, passions, knowledge, trauma, pain, recessive and dominant traits. That's what those dolls were all about. I just didn't know it then.

Mom watched me fit them together. I felt her eyes anchor into me, analyzing how it made sense this strange child came out of her so many years later than all the others. She concluded without thinking about it too much that it was because she was tired, and hadn't had the energy to say no and then comfort Dad through the rejection. It was easier just to give in. She loved us, though. She does. Seriously, she does.

The back porch's screen door creaked open on unoiled hinges, then made a snapping sound. Dad shouted a cluster of bad words and ended it with, "fucking door." Mom pressed her hands to the edge of the sink, sighed, and—I didn't see, but I was sure—rolled her eyes. I watched her, holding the dolls in my lap.

"Maybe the hinges need to be fixed like I said back in May?" she said loud enough for him to hear in the next room. Without having to see him, I knew he wasn't listening and instead was fixating on the door. He wrestled the flimsy door off its frame and set it on the side of the house by the hose, beneath the bathroom window. Before he got to us, he must have shaken off his frustration because when he got to the kitchen he said, "Mmm, the peaches smell good." He added, "Apples are next."

"I know," Mom said unenthusiastically, but that wasn't how she truly felt. She loved when we pressed the apples for cider. How everyone came over that following Christmas and drank the cider after it had gotten full of fizz and alcohol, sour and sweet at once. "Country champagne," Dad called out, handing out glasses and bottles. But it wasn't country champagne. It was overly sweet and gave you excruciating headaches. I know because I drank some too.

"Came in to get this guy," he said, lifting me into the air by my armpits and setting me on my feet. While he held me midair, the steel toe of his boot struck the nesting dolls, scattering them beneath the stove. The worn heels of his boots, caked with soil and manure, crunched the tiles I had fitted back into where they were missing. He ruined the puzzle.

"Okay, go now," Mom said, her eyes resting on the disemboweled nesting dolls and the mud that had fallen out of what little tread was left on his boot. All the dung the outside held sat there in a V-shape where a kitchen tile should have been. If she didn't clean it, who knows what would have grown there? She knew she had to clean it. *She had to.*

He shoved my boots on.

"Meadow mushrooms are in the yard. Let's go hunting."

Our yeasty farmhouse was carbonated like a jar of sauerkraut that needed to be burped, always on the brink of explosion. That old place had its own central nervous system. It flushed out its systems below the ground with things we did that didn't serve it, and pushed up the things that did. The xylem in the mulberry tree pulled up the rainwater from near the top of the slope where its roots went down under the ditch out front, where the hazelnuts were, and the water coursed through all the limbs, exiting through the millions of mouths on the undersides of its leaves, because the roots were capillaries and the garden pulsed like kidneys and the trees breathed like lungs and the gland-like fruits on the cherry tree shone like ornaments under lights, heavy and low, and when they pulled the branches down I could pick most of them. The peaches were fuzzy like arm hair and the raspberries were tiny beating hearts because the farmhouse was alive.

Past the stubbly field and at the rear of the barn, the horses made noises by clicking their shod hooves in the dirt, *clip clop, clip clop.* The pigs grunted. In the yard, chickens clucked. A rooster aimed to peck my toes. When Mom took me outside with the damp sheets that she hung out to sun dry, she'd set me in the laundry basket so the rooster couldn't get me. She said, "He thinks those toes are corn kernels." I wasn't one for expressing myself, but I tried out, "He's an asshole." I wasn't wrong because once he drew blood. I didn't like being around him, he was too unpredictable. But I got reprimanded and Mom said she was going to wash my mouth out with soap. Later she took me upstairs to the same bathroom where my sister would sneak out that window and took the bar of soap from the counter and told me to put it in my mouth. I looked at her, catching myself in the long mirror behind the sink and the whites underneath the green of my eyes shone with tears. "Do it," she said, and I put the bar of soap in my mouth. It didn't taste too bad, so I kept it there, and then she had to wrestle me to get it back out. I was fine eating the fucking soap.

After a good summer rain, the meadow mushrooms sprouted out from the wild grasses in our yard. I didn't know it then, but those were sex organs. White dots on a green canvas, they came in all sizes. The undersides of the caps were lined with gills that looked the same as a fish's gills. We moved slow, being sure to collect every single one. We sliced them at their chunky stems with our pocketknives. I used the knife Dad gave me. He gave me the dull one since he thought I'd cut myself. Over the years he'd give me hundreds more pocketknives, each time telling me, "Be careful, that's sharp." When we brought the mushrooms inside, Dad had us check the spores by conducting a test, he said to make sure they were edible. First, we used a damp cloth to wipe off any grass or soil from them. Then we set them on a sheet of paper for several hours after which we checked the imprint for the color. In this case, they were good.

Mom got out the cast-iron skillet and warmed it over the propane burner she'd set on the cutting board island. She added a knob of butter. When the butter got frothy, she added the sliced mushrooms. Meadow mushrooms were close to perfect. Not as good as morels, boletus, chanterelles, or even hen of the woods, but good enough that farmers replicated them in manure beds and mediums of the like to sell to stores as white button mushrooms. These were better than the kind you got at the store; their bloodlines ran under our farm for who knows how far. Probably as far as forever.

They existed all year beneath the soil, grass, and seeds. They endured the harsh midwestern freezes and thawed into soggy sponges in the spring. The summer heat and rain drove them to fruit. In the fall, they emerged one or two or more times before going dormant for the winter. They thrived above our well and suffered over the septic. Their membranes spread in thin white strands, too thin for our eyes to see. Even when we made mud pies, we didn't notice them. After tasting the mud pie, though, we could detect that subtle, savory quality that kept us craving our land. Because of that, I'd always want that land, forever. I still do.

Close by were the rows of cedars whose root systems ran near the mulberries and hazelnuts to the north of the ditch, over and back around to the cherry and peach trees, where eventually Dad would set up the Japanese beetle traps and spray the trees with pesticides as if he were the one flying the

Agent Orange over the eastern jungles, spraying them within an inch of their lives, taking out so many things in the process. Still the mushrooms endured. Their intricate webbed systems cleared the farmhouse and met up again in the backyard near the apple and pear trees. They swung down under the clothesline, which I walked under, along the shadows pretending I was a tightrope walker in the circus. I held out my arms like a semaphore, trying to catch my balance, signaling messages to my future self that said, *remember this.*

Under the electric fence they burrowed deeper. Underneath the tilled soil of the garden they shifted toward the barn and around the foundation to the back, where in the last stall of the lean-to against the pole barn sat a large pile of manure where Dad grew shiitake mushrooms from spores he'd bought from a catalog. Sometimes they grew and sometimes they didn't. Sometimes even the meadow mushrooms showed up there. Dad said it was from their spores being carried in the wind.

Together in the barn, he showed me the fungus. I stood beside him with my hands in my pockets where I had a couple of arrowheads. I rubbed them with my thumb. He used a spade to pull up a fine layer of manure. At this point the mash of soil and manure and whatever else he'd put in there didn't smell so bad. But when he turned it over, a sinister aroma rose. A yellow and white film coated the lumpy mass. The fibers of the white against the brown were no more visible than dandelion or milkweed gone to seed, stuck in the moist soil. It was fuzzy.

Where shiitake had come up, he clipped the fruited bodies. They were ready when the caps darkened at the top and fanned out into hues of violet, purple, and light brown around their edges. He liked them to be at least the diameter of a half dollar and pulled a coin from his pocket to measure, along with various tissues, empty seed packets, pennies, nickels, quarters, and dander. He held the coin against the mushroom caps. "These ones are ready," he said. He harvested a pound's worth and I proudly carried some back to the kitchen in my cupped hands. After twenty minutes he had the mushrooms sliced thin with iceberg lettuce we grew in the garden. He fixed us two bowls of Maruchan ramen. To my bowl he added the fresh, sliced mushrooms, lettuce, and one egg yolk. I watched the egg whites drip through his thick fingers. Then he opened his hands to my bowl and let the yolk slide down to his fingertips before he released it in the center of my bowl. He added a spoonful of Kikkoman soy sauce and a drop of fermented chili paste he made from the tiny red chilies in the garden.

That first night I puked it happened again, several times. I heard the angry whispers from my parents in the kitchen. There was an interrogation by Mom.

"What did you feed her?"

"Same thing I always do."

"But there must have been something different."

"No. Same thing I always do."

"The mushroom sack wasn't in its spot."

"So?"

"So? Did you feed her the shit mushrooms?"

"Fuck you."

I also had a fever dream that night, but it was one I'd had before a bunch of times, a reoccurring one. We were out walking the field, Nina, her boyfriend Devin, and me. We were searching for mushrooms again, beyond the pole barn and lean-tos, further than where the horses ever went. Out here, beyond the fences, paddocks, and pens, was an overgrown midwestern prairie. I saw an Indigenous person on a horse. I'd seen him so many times I no longer knew if it was a dream or real. We had climbed the fence to get back there, and the pigs came up to us so that we could scratch their prickly heads. Nina joked, "Hopefully Dad fed them or they're gonna eat us." All of us knew that. He warned us, repeatedly, that if the pigs were hungry, we'd be their dinner. But this pink one with brown spots, after I scratched her head, jutted out her chin so I could rub the needly hair on the underside of her jaw. She flopped down onto her side and lifted her back leg, exposing her massive belly and nipples like little garden hoses. I scratched her belly. She was like a four-hundred-pound dog. In the dream I always cried a little as I pet her, knowing Dad was going to kill her. April, Nina's goliath horse, came over with her angel-white hair and mane, the sun behind her shooting out light in geometric designs. The sky was periwinkle, and the clouds were melted marshmallows. Grasshoppers flittered above the pointed grasses, crickets jumped, and some ants flew around, still with their wings—prior to mating—while the more mature ones formed colonies in sand dunes beneath our feet. Butterflies caught prisms on the edges of their wings and other flying insects buzzed next to our heads. Mosquitoes bit up my legs. Bats roosted in the top of the barn, waiting for night to fall.

When it did, they swayed their shoulders like kayakers on a river up into the sky.

And in this dream, Nina and I walked ahead of Devin. He straggled behind, taking in the view. He was gentle in that way. He was the sort of guy who stopped to look at the pretty flora and fauna. He pointed them out to me. First, the purple daisies and then the goldenrod, followed by the aster flowers and buttercups that blended into one purple and yellow show for the ultimate pollinating attraction. This made me like him more, enough to include him over and over in this dream. Devin wasn't weirded out by me. Sometimes at night, he and Nina cuddled in her bed and when I brought in my doll that was nearly big as me and we were all in our underwear, I said, "My girlfriend is going to cuddle too," and he was okay with that. Plus, he never frightened me even when I was almost naked. He was a kind person.

The prairie stretched out for five more acres. Near the horizon was a big hill that separated our yard from whatever empty land was behind it, then further beyond that we knew was the old highway, US 30. We never went past that hill, though. But out there was where I saw the man on his horse, on top of the hill. Before I could say anything, my legs buckled; Dad had cut me off at the knees because I'd turned into a mushroom. He collected me into his mesh sack. I bolted awake and reached for my kneecaps. My legs were still there.

Not long ago I asked Nina if this had happened for real. If we were once really out there with Devin. If we all saw the Indigenous man together. She said anything was possible but didn't remember. She didn't remember the man on the horse. But even if she couldn't confirm it, whether it was real or a dream, I remembered him perfect with his hair, long and shiny, so dark it was violet in the sun. He wore a colorful bandana around his neck. His chest was bare under a soft leather vest. He had on tan pants that also looked like they were made of animal hide. Long fringe ran down each side. His bare feet rested in the stirrups. He was more beautiful than any woman, with a wide jaw and sage-tinted skin. And each time, whether real or not, we saw each other and it was the same; we froze, and silence followed. A crack in time. A crack in the tree.

CHAPTER 5.
APPLES

MOM USED TO DRINK A CASE OF BEER A DAY. I DON'T remember her ever being drunk though. I don't really remember much about it, but I do remember her always having Miller Lite in the refrigerator. Our perfect oxidized avocado-colored refrigerator, where the beer was stacked neatly among the pig's feet, sauerkraut, beet and horseradish spread, and homemade pickles. She's admitted to me that she used to drink that much. She said she had to maintain a steady buzz all day—you know, to take the edge off. That she needed to numb all her feelings, ones like sadness, and the beer made her not think about being so sad. I don't know exactly when she quit or how she did or if it was hard. I've heard that once you're a pickle you can't go back to being a cucumber. But she'll still occasionally have a beer these days.

My sisters remember though. They've said Mom got up at 6 AM, stood next to the kitchen sink, lit one of her unfiltered Camels, and cracked a beer. They were much older than me when I was born. Sixteen, fifteen, and thirteen. I was born when Mom was thirty-six and Dad was forty. That's fucking old parents when you're born in 1979. Obviously, at one point Mom had been a young mother, with three daughters by the time she was twenty-two or twenty-three. She married Dad when she was eighteen. My oldest sister, Elizabeth (Bunny) was born not too long after they were married and if I have the math right Mom was pregnant on their wedding day. But she probably still snuck some drinks. In the early sixties women weren't taught to pay attention to their bodies like they are nowadays. So, she might not even have been sneaking. She might not have known she was pregnant. I don't know what the legal drinking age was back then, but I do know no one in our family would have cared because everyone drank. Some normally, some heavily, and some alcoholically. Mom's dad was an alcoholic. He died right before I was born. If reincarnation is a thing, which I sort of think it is, I'm certain I'm him. A large part of me is him, and if I ever transition into a man, then that will be my new name, Wayne. Right now I am both Wayne and Mom.

~~~

Like Wayne, I have a small birthmark at the base of my hairline on the back of my neck. Mom forgot about my birthmark once I started to grow hair, which took a long time. For the first six or so months, I was a bald baby. But I clearly remember the day she talked to me about the birthmark. It was in the important summer of 1984. We had her big fortieth birthday blowout. Banners that read, *Over the Hill*, also streamers and balloons. Everything was green, so someone had given thought to it. Green is her favorite color.

Dad roasted a whole lamb in the driveway. Friends and family were in the pool. There was a large plastic bin full of ice water that held a bobbing metal keg. My sisters took turns drinking from the spigot attached by a rubber tube to the pump. There was birthday cake. The kitchen went black just before the large wax numbers of a four and a zero were lit. The cake floated toward her, as if Dad willed it in her direction, and the small flame's glow wrapped around her face. Everyone's shadows grew large on the ceiling. Mom's eyes were big and glassy. She blew the candles out and her lips pressed together, resting in a smile. The lights turned on again and the shadows on everyone's faces went away. She tilted her head back when she laughed at what someone said, and you could see through her few missing teeth to the back of her tongue. Her teeth weren't as bad as they had been a few years before. They were in the middle of repairs since Dad now had a dental plan at work. But she'd have to postpone filling the last few gaps when Kelley's horse reared her hoof against Nina's mouth.

Mom always made sure I knew how much she hated the farmhouse's basement. She hated that it was always flooded, that she had to do laundry in Dad's waders, that he wouldn't make repairs to at least make things a little easier for her. And I knew when she said *she hated it* she was for real.

I did most of her chores with her. One day that summer I was fiddling with something nearby while she checked off tasks. She was wearing the waders, the same ones Dad used for netting smelts. I went down there in just my swim trunks and the water came up to my thighs. We weren't worried about me drowning because Mom took me to baby swimming classes, and I could doggy-paddle before I could walk. I tried to climb into the plastic laundry basket for fun. You know, to see if I could float in the murky basement water. I tried this every time we went down there together and each time I sunk or tipped over. Mom was pissed that somehow, I would have fun in the water she hated so much, but she wasn't pissed at me. It was more of an overall pissed-off emotion. I thought she maybe also hated the basement because it was scary. I was afraid of the hole in the wall that led to the crawl space under the house, but that always sucked me in.

Along the wall I climbed up milk crates that held logs just above the water line, getting a good look into the hole. Dad didn't want the logs to get wet and rot because we'd need them for the furnace come winter. Sometimes in the fall, he'd get the basement water pumped out, which was just a Band-Aid on a larger problem, so that in the winter it wouldn't explode the foundation of the house like a can of pop left in the freezer. "A half-assed fix," Mom said out loud to anyone listening, usually just me. "It was still high tide come spring," she'd say, pointing at her waist, gratuitously exaggerating the depth.

So, there we were, with my fingers clinging to the ledge of the crawl space and pulling myself up just enough so that I see into the maze beneath the farmhouse. It looked like archaeologists had recently excavated. Where the basement walls met the underbelly of the house, a patchwork of cracks let in pale sunlight, marking the dirt like a plaid shirt. I hung on tightly, the whites showing behind my fingernails. I stretched up on my tiptoes as far as I could reach.

I thought I saw a skeleton, maybe the skeleton of a man. I thought I saw lots of obscure things at the farmhouse. There was a crack in the skull, and I imagined the brains inside the skeleton were as dried as the peach pits we plucked before canning them.

There was a crack in the skull. Beyond that, the rest of the carcass faced away from me, and it was hard to make out what it was through the crumbled earth. An arm or leg was outstretched. I could see what looked like fingers but might just have been chalky nuts and bolts, and they held something brassy, but that could have also just been the sunlight. Or maybe it was a lamb's skull with bits of dried skin strung from it as though tethered. It's hard to understand how memory works, but later I'd look back at this moment and wonder if it was a real man. And if it was a man, if someone had really buried him beneath the house? I'd wonder if it was a dream or a dream of a dream. Or a memory of a memory—or even someone else's memory, which could also happen, especially when you're still in the womb. Once, when my mom was pregnant with me, my cousin got a tick in his belly button. I swear I saw him in the back seat between my sisters as they hollered about it and tried to get it out. Mom must've looked over the seat and that's when I saw what she saw, through her own eyes because pregnancy can be a strange phenomenon. She says I couldn't possibly remember this because I hadn't been born yet, but I even knew that the seats in the car we were in were brown vinyl when we didn't ever have that car after I was born. When I recalled the details, she looked at me with her head cocked.

I stayed there at the crawl space, looking in, while I wondered about a couple more things without thinking too much about them. A willow root that looked like a snake came at me. I knew it was a willow root because that was the closest tree to the house where the root was. The earth on the ledge of the crawl space felt like hardened flesh beneath my fingertips. I didn't have the words for any of those creepy, crawly feelings at the time. I was breathless after seeing all that I saw while hanging on tightly. The root wound in and out, between the ground and the floor where my bedroom was above. The root was split at the end like a snake's mouth with sharp fangs. I thought the root-snake might have also gobbled up all the gold and silver that Dad thought was buried there. When I closed my eyes I could see him out in the sun with the metal detector scanning the yard. He wore a headset, listening for the machine to tell him when to drop and dig.

Suddenly a force beyond what my fingers could hold onto pulled me away from the ledge. My arms and legs folded together until I was touching my toes. It was like I was being sucked through a tunnel, but I realized it was just Mom carrying me. I felt the warmth of her side and the water-repellant waders against my back. "It's dangerous over there," she said firmly. I was snug on her hip. She hunched forward, holding me in her left arm and using her right to press the plastic basket of wet laundry against her stomach.

At the clothesline just outside of the paddock, while she hung the sheets, I sat with my back against the post. I tossed corn kernels as far as I could to keep the chickens busy. If not, they'd come for my toes. "I want short hair," I said.

"Like how?" she asked. I saw her eyes stare out beyond

what she was doing. Then she looked at me and I turned my eyes to the grass.

She wanted me to say it, but she knew what I meant.

So, I said, I said to her, "Like a boy." By this time, I'd still only ever had a few haircuts, which left me the way I was now, with a bowl cut. Mom's nesting bowl went upside down over my head and she cut around it.

She didn't respond right away. She just kept pinning sheets and asked me to hand her several more clothespins. Her lips pressed together, twisted-like. She knew what I wanted. It wasn't just the haircut; she knew what I meant went beyond what I said. I was more than a tomboy. In a sense, she already knew I was her little boy. She thought this was going to make my life hard. She was a good mom and loved me very much so she'd prepared herself for whomever *I* was going to turn out to be. She had already begun looking up *gender dysphoria* and other such terms at the library not long after I'd screamed as she'd tried putting me into dresses, when I'd refused to wear anything pink, when all I'd wanted were boys' toys, when as early as I'd known the difference and I'd told her I was a boy. She knew from the beginning this was more than a phase or confusion. She believed what little kids said.

She knew she'd have to tell Dad and make him aware, because he wouldn't put it together by himself—even though he went along with it and introduced me to everyone as his boy because he knew that was what I wanted, and he thought it was funny. Plus, he wanted a son. They had been certain I was going to be a boy. But she had to tell him that it was okay, that they might have a homosexual kid or one who wanted to change their gender someday.

Mom let me get my hair cut how I wanted. First, she took me to the lady who cut her own hair. The lady refused. I can't remember that lady's name, but I remember her being a wide woman. Her hips stuck out from each side of the chair as she stood behind me. She had blonde curly hair and large boobs, like Dolly Parton, though she seemed more fragile. I sat in her chair before the mirror, her hips flanked at my sides. She pumped it up with her foot using a lever beneath my bottom. I watched the neon outlines of hairdos flash on and off in the windows. I got a tingling sensation at the back of my neck when she touched my head. She held my baby-fine hair and, like sprinkling sand, let it fall while little dunes formed along my arms.

"It's too fine, Sandra, her hair can't be cut short. Can't do it too short." She said it to Mom, but also to me. I knew she was talking to me even though she said Mom's name, because she was looking at me in the mirror. She nodded with each word, making sure I understood. I looked down. I fingered the smock hem and stared at the tips of my scuffed boots beneath it.

I was lifted from that chair and found myself in another place, one with a barber pole that spun off to the side of the front door. *A place for men and boys.* The barber ran his fingers through my hair. There were no neon hairdos in the window, just a sign that read, "Free shave and shampoo." I couldn't read yet, but I had asked Mom what it said as we walked up, and she read it to me.

Mom said to him, "My son finally needs a real haircut." Mom had me in a summer-thin plaid shirt with buttons tucked into jeans and my cowboy boots on. Same old style

I've always had. She had taken out the earrings she'd pierced me with back when I was six months old, signifying my femininity. The earrings were tiny diamonds her mother had bought for me with her money from working overtime at the mill. She had taken them out in the car on the way there, pulling over to the shoulder when she realized they were still in. Even though I didn't like girl stuff, it was hard for me to get the earrings out myself. She put them in a small bag and shoved them into the glove compartment. Many people commented on how I was such a pretty baby boy. She thought the earrings would help tell them otherwise.

"Handsome little guy," the barber said pumping the chair up higher. He fingered his scissors and made a few quick snips at the air. His white smock inched closer to my body. The metal blades gave me chills. They clicked over and over before he went at it. Maybe it was a tic he had, revving himself up. I got goosebumps like when the last lady sprinkled my hair, but this time it was more exciting. Before I could inhale, in rapid fire, the blades sliced back and forth. When he was finished he used electric clippers around the nape of my neck and around my ears. That made me happy. He spun me around and my eyes met the mirror. It was so short! I could look myself in the eyes. Finally, I was the boy I wanted to be.

Mom came over and stood behind me, next to the barber. She ran her hands over my head. "Looks good," she said. When she stopped and looked more closely, her hand was soft at the back of my neck. She saw the birthmark, the one that was the same as her dad's. It was in the same place and even shaped the same. His was always easy to see because he had been bald for a long time. She tapped her fingers against it and whispered, more to herself than to me, "My dad had the same birthmark." I wanted to see it, but I couldn't.

The apples don't fall far from the tree. That's what people say. And it's true. We had a big apple tree out back, about halfway between the farmhouse and the pole barn. I spent a lot of time in that tree, daydreaming or brooding. In the fall we collected all the apples as they fell to the ground. Most of the apples fell right in its shadow. The deep grass was soft, and you had to be careful to not step on an apple and roll your ankle.

Dad would get up on a ladder and go pretty high, almost to the top, to pick what remained in the tree. I climbed up high too; I had all the branches memorized. He said, "God damn it, be careful. You'll fall and crack your head open." I imagined myself falling and shattering on the ground like Humpty Dumpty with my brains spilling out of my broken skull. I squeezed my eyes shut to get the image out of my head. He's the one who should've been careful. When he said stuff like that, he didn't know what he was doing to my mind. Furthermore, Dad was always the one more likely to break his head open.

We'd put the apples in large bushels we had scattered at the tree's base and Mom and my sisters took them to our back patio. They emptied the bushels into a large aluminum bin. Some apples were already old and had a sour funk to them. If any were too squishy or riddled with worms or other bugs Mom threw them out. Then Dad would go over to the trash and look them over again, sometimes putting them back in the aluminum bin.

After we had a bunch of apples, we put them into the wine press, which was a barrel with a large flat iron head that was attached to a pole, at the top of which was a wheel you turned to lower the flat iron part. The apples would get smashed and the juice would run out into a bucket below. We watched Dad mix in a brewer's yeast and using both his hands on a long wooden spoon he stirred the sweet, pressed apple juice. Sometimes I liked to feed the sour apples to the horses. The fur on their noses and big lips tickled my palms as they took the apples and crushed them in their large flat teeth.

Back then I was attached to Mom like a leaf-eating worm. In a sense we all were.

At Mom's birthday party I sat next to her during dinner at the picnic table. We had the roasted lamb over thick slices of white bread with chewy crust, green onions soaked in olive oil, potato and cabbage salads. Mom placed a bottle of apple cider from last fall on the table. The cider had lost its fizz and turned sour. She poured it into a small bowl and told me and her friends to dip the green onions into it before adding them to the top of the lamb. There were between twenty and thirty people that day. Aunts, uncles, cousins, from both sides of the family, friends; Mom had a handful of close girlfriends. It's sad that she hasn't seen them in a long time. She feels like she doesn't have anything to say anymore. These days, drinking nearly a case of beer a day wouldn't make any sense. You just can't do that sort of thing when you get old, or maybe you can, I don't know. She recently had her hip replaced. At some point she'll be able to walk upright again. She's seventy-eight and still has a bunch of things she wants to do. When she can fly again, she wants to visit Tulum in Mexico. She said she's been seeing a lot of people there on the computer. I suppose that's cute, and I'll have to take her. But not until the pandemic is better, otherwise it doesn't seem like a responsible thing for us to do.

But I remember at her fortieth birthday party, she had a lot of things to say at that picnic table. It was the same picnic table where we gathered while hosting all our events. We used thumbtacks to hold the Schlitz tablecloths in place that we kept in the top of the pantry where all the canned foods were stacked. I was always excited when I saw them brought down and set out to get pinned. I knew something good was going to happen. This was the same picnic table where Bunny and Nina would argue, where my first niece, Kristina, would later sit in her swimsuit with ice cream rolling down her chin. The same table where I'd have many birthdays with different sorts of cakes placed on top of the Schlitz table-cloth. Chocolate chip pan cookies would be my favorite. This picnic table was where we'd host my cousins' birthday parties because our house was the best with its ten acres, fruit trees, gardens, pole barn, and pool. Where we'd sit on the Fourth of July and watch the fireworks Dad's brother brought over that were incredibly large, so large we didn't have to go to a fireworks show. The same table where Mom would lay out my cousin after he was drowning in the pool and give him mouth to mouth. Where Mom and Dad would plan their separation. The table made of soft pine where if you put your mouth against it, for whatever reason, you tasted the forest. Where Nina would sit and cry after Bunny threw a skateboard and hit her in the nose—the blood dried there in the cracks of the warped wood. The table I'd lay on to sunbathe when I was ten years old and I thought getting a tan looked nice so I could look my best for dates with my pretend girlfriends when I thought no one was watching. The place I'd sit on the day of the farmhouse auction and fall apart inside, knowing we'd soon have to move.

At this table, on Mom's birthday, she sat with some of her closest friends and kept telling me to get up and play with the other kids. I watched everyone have fun while I wrapped my arms around her arm, hugging her close to me and burying my face into her warm skin. The cigarette smoke swirled around my head before rising up into the warm June air. What looked like hundreds of cigarettes were in the one big green glass ashtray they all shared. We were still out there after dinner, after the cake, and when the outside lights illuminated the side of the house not far from the picnic table where we sat and the pool lights turned on, showing bright green and blue in the water and you could see all the little midges, moths, and mosquitoes and other bugs jumping into the water at the light beneath its surface.

The streetlamp came on between our driveway and the neighbor's and if you watched long enough, which I did, you'd see bats circling beneath and sometimes they'd come by where we were if the pool was silent and skim for the bugs. But there were still people in the pool enjoying themselves. Mom drank beer, but it didn't seem like she drank because she was sad. She seemed like she was happy. She told her friends how the apple cider was made, what she was going to be canning this year, how she was planning to landscape the yard. She talked about the hazelnuts we picked and roasted and the mulberries that we turned into many things. She explained how to make mulberry hand pies and how she seasoned them with the apple cider vinegar. She laughed a lot. She talked shit about Dad and how he gave her a set of Ball canning jars for her birthday—*that was the best he could do? What an idiot!* But even then she still didn't seem too sad about it. She seemed happy and it made me realize that you can be happy and sad at once. If Mom were a tree, she was the mulberry. The only tree where silkworms thrive, giving itself to make something beautiful.

CHAPTER 6.
BOROWIKI

WE SPILLED THE CONTENTS FROM OUR MESH SACKS onto the cutting board island in our farmhouse kitchen, and I felt the excitement in my gut, like butterflies, the same way people said they felt about falling in love. I feel that way about the mushrooms. I thought about kissing them. Spread on our island, their smell was like the trees, dirt, earth, the beginning of time. I knew when we'd eat them, they'd taste like all those things too, plus better. Dad would always say the mushrooms tasted like steak because I don't think he had any better ideas and he wasn't wrong, but they tasted like everything on Grandpa Regan's farm. They tasted like Grandpa Regan was going to live forever. They tasted like Busia. They tasted like how good it felt to be with all my family in the same room at once. They tasted like how Dad's hands felt when he tickled my back at night before I went to sleep. They tasted like how I cried when Nina would sneak out to go on dates or be out with friends instead of staying home with me. They tasted like how my sisters felt when they used drugs. They tasted like the place where I grew up. They tasted like the land, like my body.

Borowiki means boletus in Polish. In late July Dad and I brought the *borowiki* to Mom. *Borowiki*, or *boletus edulis*, is a cousin of the porcini, which is a very nice mushroom to eat. If you look for them in a field guide, you'll see "choice" printed next to edibility. I don't think Dad has ever had a real porcini, but someday I'd like for him to have one. He always called the mushrooms by the name his grandmother, Busia, called them. I never met Busia, though I knew she was inside of me in the same way Wayne was.

Because we didn't have them at the farmhouse, Dad and I hunted the *borowiki* at Grandpa Regan's farm, about thirty miles south and forty to the east. His farm was surrounded by pine, oak, birch, maple, and hemlock. He had one hundred acres in Medaryville, Indiana. He built the house before he was set to retire from the steel mill and his retirement gift to himself was to work himself on that farm as long as his bones would hold out. Sounded right and though I was just five at the time, I knew I was him too.

Mom sliced most of the *borowiki* into quarters and the smaller ones in half. When Dad and I hunted them, he told me to look near the bases of the largest pines, and specifically under the hemlocks. "See how this one has the branches in triplets, how they fan out like the chickens' feet?" He placed his palm under one of the branches and held it there. The pads of his calloused palms were shiny beneath the hemlock needles. The branch looked like a peace sign on his palm. "See how these don't have the needles going all around the stem but they're sort of flat"—he pointed at them with the finger of his other hand—"and the needles just come off the sides?" I crossed my arms over my chest like I'd seen adults do and held each elbow with the opposite hand. I squinted. "Yeah," I said, but I don't really think I saw what he thought I should see. "You gotta look under these trees or nearby 'em. That's where they'll be." He continued walking, shuffling his boots over the sandy path. "Remember, the *borowiki* have pores under 'em, not gills. We don't want any mushrooms with the gills, these ain't like the meadows. These ones only got the sponge bottom and when you touch 'em they might bruise a little, but that's okay."

"Okay," I said.

"All right, now you're gonna find most of 'em 'cause you're closer to the ground." He always said that, but I think the truth was that he just couldn't see that well behind his thick glasses. And I did find them; I found a whole bunch of them. Nice ones, too, and I knew because he said so. They were young and firm and not riddled with a bunch of holes. "Here's how you check they're good," he said, grunting while he knelt. He pushed his glasses up his nose with the tip of his finger; his hair in the front hung over the rims. "Gimme your pocketknife," he said. I dug it from my pocket. He opened it and ran his thumb over the blade. "Christ. This one's sharp." He looked at me. "Did I give you this one?" Before I could answer him, he said, "Never mind, take mine." And he stretched up, digging into his pocket among the change and wadded-up tissue paper and produced his own. He set mine down then did the same with his—opened it and ran his thumb over it. "You take this one. It won't cut you." He put mine in his pocket. I probably wasn't going to get cut. If anything was going to be dangerous, I knew, it was something he would do. He would get cut. It was always that way. But I said, "Okay," and I took his pocketknife instead. He cut the *borowiki* at the base, then turned it upside down in his hand. He sat back, resting his hams on the heels of his boots, and showed me the bottom. "See here—clean, no holes. Touch it." I did. He watched me. I looked at him. "It's firm, yeah?"

"Yeah."

"That's a good one you found. You done real good. Keep finding ones like this. These ones are young and they're good this way, not too buggy."

"Okay."

After Mom cleaned and cut them, she set them aside. She was going to add them to duck blood soup. *Czarnina.* Mom liked to cook *czarnina.* She had always loved Busia and Busia had taught her, at the restaurant, how to make it. Dad and my sisters loved the *czarnina* too. I didn't love that it was made from duck blood, so I just ate the mushrooms and noodles that Mom had put in it. I was a picky kid sometimes. But the *borowiki* was one of the most important ingredients in the *czarnina.* At least in my family's recipe it was. The *borowiki* gave it the deep flavor of the forest. Busia could never get the *czarnina* exactly how she liked it when she was living in Gary, Indiana. Gary didn't have the same terroir as her home, a village in northern Poland. But it was still good. Everyone loved her *czarnina* and they liked when Mom made it too. The people of Gary lined up after their shifts at the steel mill, outside Busia's restaurant on the corner of 34th and

Broadway that would later become Jennie's Café. Busia's was a long way away from the inn her family once had in Poland, though she still seemed to be a happy woman.

⟶

The inn where Busia grew up, and that her family kept, was in the middle of four hundred acres of green hills in the northern end of the temperate forest. Gardens were everywhere you looked and neatly arranged with cabbages and other brassicas, nightshades, leafy and succulent greens, Jerusalem artichoke flowers and marigolds, potatoes, squashes, peas, and beans. Tacked here and there, against trellises and up the logs of the inn, were vines full of grapes. Those and other vines also climbed with ferocity up the sides of the barn, which was set back from the inn about twenty yards. In late July the garden was mostly yellow. Big sunflowers hung their yellow heads, framing seedy faces. Nearby were small orchards of apple and pear whose fruits would be used for ciders, butters, and vinegars. Two longhouses sheltered draft horses and mules. Pigs occupied one pen that was sectioned off at the far end. The pigs were for fat, side meat, bones, sausages, bacon, and roasts, among other things. The goats and lambs, in another section, were mostly for roasting whole, or for their legs, while Busia's father sold the racks, bellies, and shoulders to the butcher in town. But sometimes the tender racks were saved for special occasions, hung and gleaming, slippery with fat over the spit. The sheep were for wool—warm itchy sweaters and blankets—and their milk for cheese and one skinny cow provided milk as well. Chickens lined cages and roosters roamed free.

Between the longhouses was a large pit about two feet

deep, three feet wide, and five feet long, where embers perpetually sizzled. Every couple of hours Busia fed it from the nearby stack of splintered logs. At each end of the pit were posts with a crank. The crank rotated the long spit suspended between the posts. Busia ran that spit through the animals and tied their legs at each side. She cut thin slices of garlic, layering them under the skin until they were carefully shingled as a rooftop. She used lots of salt to coat the animals, which guests appreciated; salt was an offering, a symbol of hospitality. She spun the animals for hours until the skin was dark and glistened like golden-and-brown-tinted, cracked glass over the rendered fat. The spinning caused the fat, blood, and water to leach out, ensuring a crispy skin with tender fat and succulent muscle tissue. The best part was the skin. When it fractured, the meat beneath was so soft, you could pull the muscle tissues free with your fingers. That meant it was done.

The inn was built from cedar logs bigger than you could wrap your arms around. The dimensions of the inn were forty feet wide, thirty feet deep, and thirty feet high. Knots twisted and turned creating natural designs on the walls. The roof reached near the tops of the maples if you included the attic loft. Busia and her younger sister, when they were little, told anyone who asked that they lived in the castle on top of the hill. Their father, Adam, like my own, said he was king of it. There were six rooms. One belonged to the sisters and another to their father who was widowed. Their mother's clothes were still folded in the dresser drawers; her modest jewelry sat on a table in a small wooden bowl. They liked it that way. Sometimes, to feel her, they took her things and held them or they wore her necklaces or slipped into one of her house dresses at night. They stood at the window like she had, drinking tea made from dried turkey tail mushrooms, chaga, and bark. They embodied the figure they remembered. Lit by a single candle in the window, watching themselves as they looked out, pretending to see what their mother had—the roosters chasing them through the yard, feeding apples and clover to the horses, and gathering chicken eggs into baskets made from sweetgrasses.

A crack echoed. The wind came in from the north—the southernmost end of the boreal forest. The sound waves echolocated white oak, wild apple, gray pine, paper birch, hemlock, beech, mulberry, and silver-tipped maple. The wind pushed the echo into the valleys and bounced it along the surface of whitewater rivers. It spread across fields stubbled with yellow prairie grasses.

The echo stopped and stillness swarmed when Ginivive Skaczkowski—my great grandmother, Busia—stood there, holding a duck by his webbed feet, allowing the blood and the remnants of his esophagus to spill into a porcelain bowl below. The axe had sliced through the duck's neck, shattering the nugget-shaped bones, and stopped at the rings of a walnut tree. The wood splintered under the axe, from where the crack had originated. Before she whacked off his head, she had made a slit at the back of it, cutting a major artery and allowing his blood to drain. It was best to drain the blood first before cutting off the head. The blood for *czarnina* needed to be clean, clear from any undigested food remaining in the throat.

By September, Busia would be gone for America as fast

as the boreal breeze arrived. But for now, July was hot. The height of summer heat brought out the oils of the countryside's life and death. Busia inhaled, smelling the decay of animals, leaves, mushrooms, clay, and rotted, massive tree trunks. In the yard, a few buttercup flowers held on like the duck's body which now jolted headless in her grip. She walked through the grass, crushing the buttercups and if she looked at the right angle against the sun, beyond her shadow she saw the manufactured webs of tiny, female spiders that stretched one blade to the next. She was fond of these webs.

That summer she was nineteen years old. She wore gray slacks held by suspenders over her dad's gray shirt, collarless, with tiny iridescent pearl-like buttons up the front. Her brown leather work boots with cork soles rose to where her knees would someday ache. Her gold hair was a croissant, pinned on the top of her walnut-shaped head. A few strands framed her lean face. Her nose was the shape of an arrowhead and her eyes, a faded gray, were deep set and symmetrically spaced under her thick golden eyebrows. She was average height and rail thin, but stronger than she looked. Her rolled-up sleeves exposed thick forearms.

"Something like you," Dad would say one day, telling me about her. But she was more interesting, I thought.

Moments before, she had scooped up the duck by his legs and held him in one fist. The duck's feet made like they were swimming as she grabbed him. Now, they were a bouquet. Dirt accumulated in the creases of the wrinkled skin over his joints and between the petals of his feet. He quacked. He made a few other noises while his blue tipped wings went up and down, beautiful and shining.

Gentle but firm, she sliced the artery at the back of his neck and drained the blood, then she held his neck over the severed walnut bole she had climbed when she was young, when it was once a tree. With her other hand, she suspended the heavy axe in the air, then let it drop hard and precise, through the vertebrae running the duck's neckline. His head plunked into the bowl, and she held him up, allowing the rest of the blood and contents to spill out.

The large porcelain bowl she used to collect the blood was delicately painted with pink roses and gold trim along the rim. The duck's blood formed a dark red puddle, so dark it was like a bowl of ink for writing letters or making sketches, both of which she liked to do very much. Her slender fingers gripped the duck's legs and he spasmed once more before death set in.

A green glass bottle of red wine that had turned to sour was next to the bowl. She added some of it to the blood to prevent clots. The smell of iron and acid was piercing; she could almost taste it as it settled in the ripples of her own esophagus. Just then, the whip of cool air blew in; it felt good, releasing the shirt stuck from sweat to her chest. She caught the scent of forest. She loved this smell. This meant the *borowiki* were here.

Rivulets of blood ran through the lines of her palms. She rinsed her hands in a pail of water only to stain them again as she picked up the duck's head and cut out his tongue. She put the head in another bowl. She would save it for later and share the brains with her father and sister. The brains when roasted were very good. Then, into another pail she disemboweled the bird, its guts like oil paints of beige and maroon. She reserved the heart, gizzards, and liver. She'd use the tongue, heart, muscle meat, and blood for her *czarnina*. The carcass and feet, once she cleaned them, she'd disjoint with a cleaver, and this would be the soup's base.

Back in the kitchen, Busia chopped a mound of garden and wild herbs: marjoram, oregano, savory, thyme, parsley, gooseberry, woodruff, burnet, spicebush berry, mountain ash, and nettle. She pushed the leafy fragments and berries onto the blade of her knife and used her finger to slide them into the soup. The *czarnina* was on its way.

Hung over the hearth fire was a cauldron, wide and deep. She pulled the duck's tongue from the boiling broth of roasted bones, feet, herbs, twigs, barks, and flowers. She held the steaming tongue between her finger and thumb, unflinching. It was hot, but her fingers, knuckles, and palms were thick from heat and work. She had new scars on top of old scars from years of shoveling manure, pruning flowers, weeding gardens, chopping wood, killing animals, and foraging through thorny bushes. The tongue rested on her palm and the steam danced serpentine into the air. Using a small knife, she peeled away the tongue's thick outer layer. This part was too tough to chew. The miniscule taste buds bled beads of water. She set the mollusk-like tongue on the counter, then sliced it in half. One of the halves she dipped into salt and ate. It was so good. The other she chopped into small pieces. It was not a lot, but still, she added it back in. She was true to her recipe, and where it was scribbled, *half of a duck's tongue*, she meant it.

She worked on a wood block made from her father's walnut grove. Adam was proud of her. He was also proud of his walnut grove. He went on and on to anyone who listened, much as his great-grandson would do someday. Adam had a scripted commentary on the trees' height, usefulness, worth, and how his great-grandfather had planted them. He reminded Busia whenever she worked on it. "Made this block, even the table," he said while rapping his knuckles against it, or giving it a little stroke as if it were a baby goat. She knew, so much so that eventually Dad would know, and I would know too, someday.

On this night, the *czarnina* was a deep ruby color. Duck breast, thick noodles, *borowiki*, sun-dried plums, wild apples, and onions were layered inside the bowl and fresh, chopped herbs were added over the top, making a large green mound just before she served it. The acoustics of the inn calmed when dinner was served. Walnut spoons scraped against walnut bowls, logs popped in the hearth, fat fell into a pan over the embers from a lamb leg spinning over the fire. No one said anything and Busia knew this meant it was good.

This was how she did it. It was how it had to be done. Mom tried to do it the same with the forest mushrooms we brought to her. The *borowiki*, emerging from the networks below, mingling with the trees' roots, acting as conduits, and transcending time from Poland all the way to our farmhouse kitchen; they were the most important part.

From Slavic folklore, the Leshy is the shape-shifting god of the forest. You must make an offering to the Leshy before entering the forest. I learned this from Busia. I learned it from Dad, too. I also learned it from Mom and my sisters. Reciprocity. I learned something about this a long time ago from all of them. I learned we had to help one another, not just our family, or other humans, but the things outside of ourselves, the things of the lands and the forests. The things we could see and the things we couldn't.

On Sundays at Milkweed, after the guests leave, I'm very hungry. I don't feed myself well when guests are here because I'm too busy. All the running around can really make you hungry. By the time Sunday arrives, I'm craving something from home. But not our Chicago home or this home in the forest, but the home I used to have, the one I grew up in and it's even deeper than that. I crave even more than that home, it's like something from the home Busia grew up in, the inn in the far distant forest. It's a deep, deep craving. I know truly, more than all that, it's a need to fill a hole I can't see. It's a want for something I never used to want. *Czarnina* is what it must be. I want *czarnina*, and the want is dire.

Out here there is no easy way to get *czarnina* or anything like it for that matter. It must be made and to make the *czarnina* perfect you need *borowiki*.

For *czarnina* you must have ducks, because after all *czarnina* is duck blood soup. I was never going to be able to kill ducks I raised. And before I knew I wouldn't be able to kill them, one day I got ducklings. I was too far ahead of myself and brought the ducklings back to the cabin. The Dodge Ram's cab had the ducklings in a box, all next to me in the passenger seat. It was truly magnificent to have baby birds next to me in the truck. When I got home and Anna saw what I had done she was pissed. I had only gone out for errands when I found myself at the Tractor Supply Co. A few hours later I was back in the pickup with the ducklings and everything they'd need to grow up right. It wasn't the first time I'd come home with something she didn't know I'd be coming home with. I was like Dad in this respect. If asking or talking about the things I wanted with my wife was going to give me an answer of "no," I just didn't talk about those things with her first. And it always seemed like the things magically appeared without my having any control over it.

Anna's fists were against her lovely hips. "What about George and Bunny's prey drive?" she said. "And what about the wolves, foxes, and bears? And what about killing them?" She narrowed her eyes at me. "Are you going to do it?"

I shook my head. *No, I wasn't.* It was impulsive, a contrast to how anxious I was. You'd think I thought about these sorts of things. But I sometimes didn't and it wasn't that I wasn't thinking. I was always thinking, but what I was thinking was not often right. I knew that. Most of my thoughts and actions were a gamble so much so that Anna didn't really want to hear my ideas anymore.

I couldn't return the ducklings; I had already bonded with them in that hour-long car ride. So, I raised them until they'd be fine to live on their own. I took them to the beaver ponds that were about a mile from the cabin. They seemed to be fine there. I took them the ends of bread after the weekends and other healthier snacks like oats, barley, cracked corn. I'd count them as they swam over to me at the edge, where I stood in between the cattails, lily pads, and irises; they were all there.

Anna was right about killing them. I'd never be able to kill ducks I raised or any other animal for that matter, I guess aside from fish and frogs. Well, and the occasional bug, which I thought I should stop doing because some of them were quite lovely. But she was right, certainly I'd never be able to kill an animal I had raised. I wasn't like Dad in that way. She reminded me how I loved animals and that I shouldn't even be eating them. Honestly, I don't know why I still do it. It's very contradictory to how I feel. I guess humans are like that. Instead, for the *czarnina* I purchased the duck blood from a farmer. Anna wanted nothing to do with it.

When making *czarnina* I followed Dad's instructions and imagined the way Busia must have done it, over the hearth in a large cast-iron cauldron, plenty of forest herbs, mushrooms, and things from the garden. She made the noodles with raw milk from the cows. I'd never be able to make it the same, but I'd try to get close. I'd make sure that I hunted the *borowiki*. I didn't take the gun into the forest even though Dad recommended it. Dad always reminded me to watch for wolves. "Busia's scar," he said like he'll never forget it. He saw her scar a long time ago and it was bad, even many, many years after he was grown, and she was already old then. He told the story as if it involved wolves, but he said Busia said it was the Leshy. She was attacked while gathering blueberries one evening as the sun was setting. That was the last time she stayed in the forest after dusk. The Leshy—or the wolf, or wolves, no one really knew for sure but her—attacked her from behind, missing her jugular yet tearing into her shoulder.

Dad didn't believe in that sort of thing but I've seen enough to believe it. After being out here for several years, I knew Busia was right. If there was a Leshy, we would be hunted for the things we did.

I went to the forest, and I left an offering of bread ends for the Leshy. I placed the bread on a bole at the entrance of the path I took. I left a thimble of salt and a smear of hand-churned butter on a small antique plate. After I left my offering, I walked deep into the forest in search of *borowiki* on one of those Sundays and it was like something from my old pop-up book about gnomes. The storybook mushrooms were out, yellow- and red-capped with white flecks like gouache. When these appeared the *borowiki* were soon to follow.

Busia and I entered the forest. She and I went alone, nearly a century apart but also together. Sometimes the forest felt dangerous but we weren't afraid, not together, not of the wolves or of the Leshy. Like a split in time, side by side, the forest Busia entered was much more ancient than mine. Hers was first growth; mine was third or maybe fourth.

I carried a hook-blade knife with a brush at the end of the handles made for field-dressing the mushrooms. She had something similar. We disappeared into the dense forests. She wore a cape. I wore a mackinaw jacket. Our garments were both red and black. Her cape was red, trimmed with black, a cape she stitched herself. My jacket was checkered. I bought it at Target. The garments were what allowed us to be seen through the forest cover while everything that was alive, aside from us, stood still.

Our forests spread out like cadavers in lecture hall. From a hawk's eye view, the sun came and went, first illuminating the ribs then scapula. The sunlight spread over the hills and river as the chest opened. We walked along the spine, climbing the vertebrae of hills, through the ferns and vines, the organs and veins, muscle tissue and fat. We went deeper and where the sun rested on different shades of greens and the ground, it was warm. I touched a soft mound of moss. From our vantage point, light fractured through the trees, and a ripened lime-colored blanket spread out. To our right was a cluster of spicebush berries like a wild peppercorn, a satisfactory seasoning for the *czarnina*. We cut the spicebush berries at the nodes, leaving us with a cluster and a few ovate leaves. Next to my boot, sweet cicely lit up against the brown, dried leaves along the ground. These were forest glands, the color of parsley but with a stronger taste, more fragrant with a spicy note, and would be the finishing herb. We found sassafras. I held the sassafras between my thumb and index finger, rubbing it. The aroma was of root beer. I didn't love root beer, but I loved sassafras. I clipped four large leaves, which looked like mittens made for a person with a few fingers and a thumb. Sassafras, a natural thickener, was perfect for *czarnina*. I took a few stems to reserve for another day as a braising herb for the moose I had in the chest freezer. There was woodruff, which is like if tarragon and vanilla had a baby. Then there was the spade-shaped sheep sorrel, sour from oxalic acid. We collected nettles for substance (they have such a good flavor, not bitter at all), gooseberry leaves for tannin (these are bitter), and lamb's quarter—a sweeter version of spinach. Busia knew these things from her mother and her mother before her. I knew them because she whispered them to me—and because I'd have taught myself about these forest herbs, though I don't know everything. I just know what I know. We went on, collecting things here and there, gathering herbs and berries while hunting for the *borowiki*.

Our eyes shifted left to right. The forest floor became a painting, a dew-blended watercolor. The storybook mushrooms, fly agaric, were ground ornaments. They would make the brave or starving ill, perhaps even hallucinate. We didn't touch those ones, but we knew when we saw them it meant the *borowiki* had arrived. They always came right after the fly agaric opened to release their spores.

Leaves, acorns, pinecones and needles, moss, saplings, detritus, and the webs of spiders freckled the ground. Sprouting between these items, little knobs like the tips of penises emerged. We laughed. This was it. We took our knives, cutting the knob at the base. We held the mushroom in our hands, looking it over. This was a treasure, a *real* treasure, right between our fingers. The sex organ of the forest. The forest's penis in our hands.

We collected birch, pine, and chestnut *borowiki*. These mushrooms had slick caps and beneath were sponge-like pores instead of gills. Their smell was of soil, pine, resin, funk, and whatever trees they grew near. When touched, some turned colors, the way a sensitive person blushes. After they were cooked, the bite was substantial, so much it could be mistaken for a thymus gland or veal cutlet. I know Dad said we had to be careful at what color they bruised. These would be fine.

Happy with my collection, I came out from the forest along the path. I checked the bole and the bread was gone. The butter was gone and the salt was spilt but it looked like some had been used. I closed my eyes for a moment and I saw the face of Busia, a face I didn't really know, shadowed beneath the hood of her cape.

In the *czarnina*, the forest mushrooms accentuated every

other ingredient, giving it a depth of its own. They were a natural form of MSG. For my *czarnina* I added the duck blood to the duck stock. The fresh *borowiki* I cut small, and sautéed them, adding them to the base along with the spice-bush berries, sassafras, sweet cicely, nettles, gooseberry leaves, handmade noodles, fermented and pickled wild strawberries, dried blackberries and blueberries, and other things that I can't tell you about because it is a secret. And when I sat down to eat it, I got full and knew Busia would be satiated too but it wouldn't be the same. Because after all that, I still had a hole inside of me.

CHAPTER 7.
WOLVES

SOMETIMES THE WOLVES HOWLED LOUDLY. THEY sounded like the background of a spooky Halloween movie. The howling was just like that, like how the movies would have us believe. In the movies if you heard wolves howl it was certain you'd see them later, and sometimes you saw them attack the person who heard them. It's not like that in real life, though Dad thought it was.

On the cabin's porch, under a solar lamp, I read and wrote. I listened to the owls, the wind, the crunching of leaves under critters' paws. Distracted from the work and enjoyment of reading and writing, I looked at the stars. But of all those sounds, the wolves were the apex. The howling came from either the south, beyond where the logging was, or from the north on the other side of the river where the trees were older. The howling never seemed to come from the east or west.

Most of the time, it sounded like there was a pack of

wolves. Other times it sounded like there was just one. That's how it was this night, like there was only one wolf. I heard the howl and I stopped writing for a moment. I couldn't stand the thought of a wolf without a pack or a young wolf who had lost their mother. I felt like claws were tearing through my heart. Moms were safety if you were lucky—my mom was. And that night the singular howls were louder than I'd ever heard them. The wolf was crying for another, I felt certain. And I didn't often hear such cries after I'd already gotten into bed, but I did this time. I heard the cries and I couldn't sleep. I thought of Mom, and the wolf's mom and I began to cry.

I cried silently so Anna wouldn't hear. Anna slept through the wolf's cry and mine. I scooted over on the bed, closer to the window. I wanted to get up and look out, but after the storm a few nights before or whenever it was, I didn't want Anna to catch me. I didn't want her to think I was getting paranoid, always looking out the window, waiting for danger. But that was a silly thought because she already knew I was a paranoid person.

While I listened, my body began to tingle, which meant sleep was near. I was crying myself to sleep and felt ashamed about it. I was ashamed that I was supposed to be a grown woman but I was still, in a sense, crying for my mom, for some safety of the past. Crying at the thought of a lost wolf.

I thought of lobster mushrooms, trying to take my mind off it; I thought of chanterelles, *borowiki*, and morels. I replayed all the mushrooms I'd ever hunted out here and knew I would sleep soon. There were times I could go back pretty far. It was like time travel; you know, memories are like that. I liked remembering what I was thinking and feeling each time I hunted mushrooms. And when my eyes began to dry, I closed them for good and I remembered these things like it was a game. I remembered about our first season out here and the morels I found. Morels were my favorite mushrooms to think about before bed because I'd dream about them and even if they were sometimes stressful dreams, they were still fortunate dreams. Behind my eyelids I saw their winding structures and I drifted off.

✧

The following day I slept till 1 PM. I cried a bit then too. I might have been depressed or was distraught over the wolf or missing and worrying about Mom. She wasn't feeling well. She was alone. Nina, who lived with her in the apartment below us in Chicago, our other home when we are not at Milkweed, she was a traveling nurse because other places needed nurses badly due to the pandemic. I couldn't be there and I worried about Mom all alone.

I got up to use the washroom but only when my bladder was screaming at me, when it didn't seem healthy that I should hold it anymore, but after I released myself I went back to bed. Because of my hypoglycemia I got up three different times to eat. Aside from that, I stayed in bed most of the day.

The sadness and crying might have been hormones. A month before, I had been pregnant for eight or so weeks. The pregnancy wasn't viable, and I had to have an abortion. The truth is that sometimes women must have abortions when they don't want to. This was the first one I'd ever had, and it wasn't because I wanted it. Anna and I were both heart-broken. We had maybe gone too far thinking of names, imagining how things would be with a baby. It left us gutted. She cried a lot at the time it happened. I didn't. In a sense I think I felt like that wolf. Alone.

I didn't get out of bed that day until 5 PM. When I did, we went down to the river with the dogs. They were still our children. We were still a pack. We went down because we figured since this land, "our" land, occupied two-thirds of a mile of the Sturgeon River, we ought to swim in it. Sometimes we did that. I had fished it plenty by then too. Perch, crappie, brookies were in the river, but not a whole lot of them. I caught a little perch once and tossed him back. I'd also caught a few chubs, but I didn't keep those either. Someday, I hoped I would catch a big brookie or a few nice perch. I'd like to fry them up in the cast iron over the fire. I'd use bacon fat to baste the fish with lots of herbs. After the fish was cooked and the skin was blistered, I'd peel it off, remove the bones, and put the fish on fresh slices of bread. I'd use the bread crust to wipe up the salty grease from the pan. There's nothing like fish cooked over open flames. This was how I read about it in *The Nick Adams Stories* by Hemingway, and I wanted to do it exactly the same.

We went down to the river, chasing after the dogs, and I remembered the first time we came down to the river to swim. I couldn't believe this place was ours, that we could live here, that there was a river to fish and swim in. I could barely put together how I'd gotten it and felt so dang lucky. Getting into the river the first time, we baptized ourselves though we didn't believe in that sort of thing but I don't know what else to call it.

It was mostly cold in the water so we waited for the first

warm day to submerge ourselves. Being between two lakes, and so far north, it was colder than most places. Because we had to wait to get out here until most of the snow melted, we just needed to be patient each year. I learned being patient from Mom, but I wasn't skilled at it. Not even now. Anna had more patience than me. Each spring I couldn't wait to get out here. I'd leave from Chicago as soon as I could and sometimes when I got here there was still snow in the backyard and the river was high from the snowmelt. Anna didn't mind waiting another week or so. She said she'd rather wait until all the snow was melted. She liked the warm better than cold. I liked the forest better than anything else.

But that first time we got in the river, the water was so cold. We jumped in anyways because we could. Our bodies were cut in half by the water, a beautiful sight. Anna's especially. She's a perfect hourglass shape; I don't care that much about bodies but it was impossible not to notice perfection when you saw it.

I came up from the water with my eyes closed, imagining myself as Nick Adams. The water mirrored the sky. Our torsos combined with the landscape. Little bugs with large pads for feet balanced on top of the water, hopping along the surface with little effort. They took flight when George jumped in and some minnows changed course to bypass him.

The water was refreshing and reminded us we were alive when no one would know the difference since we were so deep in the forest. Except for Dad, he would know. He called me every day, and I know the reason he called me every day was to make sure I was breathing. He was worried about the wild animals or fire or hypothermia or us starving to death.

I'm more worried about people than any of those things but I worry about those things too, just not in so much of the systematically sexist way he does. I don't think he'd be so worried if I actually once *was* his little boy.

Before we'd gone to the river that day, I'd talked with Dad on the phone. He was certain at any given moment a wolf or bear was going to attack. Or he thought we'd get lost driving, or get stuck in the mud, or the truck would break down and we'd starve. He asked me if I'd been keeping his cowboy gun in the truck. "I'm serious," he said, and I didn't say anything back and we were silent for a moment.

After Anna and I got out of the river we dried off, pulled on our clothes, and walked the narrow path along the riverbank where cedar trees grew big and branched over the running water. The largest one had been struck by lightning and cracked in half. It became a natural bridge to the other side, where seventy more acres of our property extended. We still hadn't set foot over there, and I didn't intend to. Maybe someday we would, but it wouldn't be to forage or cut wood or really to touch it at all, just to admire. I thought it'd be nice if things were left alone. I wanted everything about it to stay exactly like it was supposed to, without our footprints. Exactly how it was before white people ever got here.

We walked west and the river went the opposite direction. If you paid attention to where the river went, it was impossible to get lost out here. Out here I knew that when the sun was on my left in the morning I was facing south, and the opposite was true of north.

We walked along the riverbank and I couldn't help looking for something to forage. Lots of times I found it, whatever it might be, and sometimes I'd find new things I never knew about. I would pick something that looked edible and take it home. I would look through my field guides, seeing if I could identify it.

That day I saw something I knew well. Out of the pine needles on the ground grew what looked like narrow, wiry brains. The light caught the rippled edges of the morels. I adjusted my eyes like you do when looking at an autostereogram. First there's nothing; then there's everything. There was a damn carpet of them. They tipped this way and that, like "poorly performing penises or the hats of gnomes," I said. Anna laughed, liking the latter description.

Every spring, since I could remember, I've dreamt of morels. They were always within my reach and just as I grasped for them they vanished, my hands clapping instead but it was still a wonderful dream. That day, I turned my towel into a satchel and collected many of them.

On the phone call with Dad he had said, "You need to take the gun with you when you go into the woods. Actually, as soon as you step outside that cabin. And you got to keep in it your glove compartment whenever you're out. Or put it in that holster I gave you and keep it on you." There were nearly four hundred miles between us. Dad wanted to lasso me, pull me back to his hip pocket. I got it, he wanted me to be safe. What I didn't get was him insisting my safety would come from me handling something that was quite unsafe. I wasn't anti-gun, don't get me wrong, that's not what I'm saying. But you know, accidents happen. And I guess his instructions would be sweet if they weren't so sexist, like I said.

He thought it was hard for me to protect myself and I

think the most frustrating thing was that deep down I knew he was right. He expected me to shoot a wolf or a bear or whatever, which I would never do unless I absolutely had to. The animals out here were skittish. They didn't need to be shot. I felt lucky when I saw one. I don't mean to sound ungrateful that I have a dad who loves me. I understand. He didn't want to place that call and have his daughter not pick up ever again. It had already happened once. He couldn't imagine it happening again. I get it.

Shortly thereafter he switched the subject to fires. He told me that as soon as it got warmer out, I'd need to burn a creosote log because it would clean the chimney, and that I needed to make sure I was outside when I did it. I told him I loved him and had to get going before he could remind me about having a boat to get out by river in case of a forest fire. He was insistent upon those things.

～

I shouldn't have showed Dad the pictures I took of the wolf pack the morning they came through. They came through after a large chunk of the forest nearby was taken out on semis. I was outside on the porch with my morning coffee when I heard footsteps in the leaves. I looked and that's when I saw them. They were beautiful, with dark fur like eyeliner around their eyes. They looked hungry and fast. When the logging had started it seemed the wilderness had moved in on us but that wasn't the case. Their homes were demolished. The wolves walked along the same path to the river I took for fishing. The path where at the entrance I left bread for the Leshy. Clearly, they were on to me, arriving shortly after the time I would have already been down there. Maybe it wasn't the logging that brought them closer—maybe it was me leaving crumbs. I took up my camera and attempted to get a few photographs, but the wolves were too quick, and the photos ended up blurry.

Some people around here said the wolves were watching us. That they watched for routines, and we'd better not let the little dogs out by themselves or go out much on our own at certain times of the day. Some people said the wolves would wait until a routine was established and know just how they would take us before they'd make their move.

I imagined that the wolves watched us from the edge of the forest. They lined up, their pack eyeing ours when the sky turned from pewter to black. The wolves—a judicial monolith of knowledge.

They asked one another, *Don't they look sad?*
Or tired. Why are they so tired? the gray wolf pressed.
They don't do anything but chase sticks and balls.
And fat! the red wolf, the leanest of them all, noted.
They smell too. Not like us, the oldest one said.

The wolves smelled of pine and forest resin and the pheromones of a thousand microscopic invertebrates. They had stunk with the death of the logs they jumped, with the spores of black fungus crusted to their privates, and putrefied intestines of prey creatures caked between the bark of their paws.

The oldest one continued, *They don't hunt either. The demons feed them.*

The wolves called us demons and if you saw what our species did to the forest, you'd know. They watched George lift his head. The hundreds of thousands of small hairs on his snout prickled. He let out two large *grrrruffs*. Then lazily, as if his head weighed one ton, he dropped it down between his front paws. His big, floppy jowls spread out. He looked like a rug.

Ha. He can't even detect us.

Suckers. They cackled.

And on that evening when we were in the river, the dogs and ourselves, I bathed away the funk of sleep. I washed the tears crusted to my hair and eyes from the day and night before. I washed myself of the worry. I was in the best place I could possibly be for what I wanted to do, but for some reason I still wanted the feel of the farmhouse. It was almost as if I were no longer the child, but the mother who had lost her pup. It was most definitely that a child was missing.

CHAPTER 8.
MULBERRIES

MOM MADE HER OWN VERSION OF *CZARNINA* AND SHE
put mulberries in it. She put mulberries in a lot of stuff. I loved
collecting them with her. We had two mulberry trees, one in
the front of the house, near the ditch where the hazelnuts grew
wild, and one in the back, near the large garden by the barn
where Lucky would be laid down for a long time. Oh Lucky.
Mom had brought Lucky home to me one night while I was
sleeping. She found him at Dad's union hall. They were there
because Dad was giving one of his last campaign speeches
for his run at being the president of U.S. Steel Local 1042.
Mom said she was sitting next to her friend Phyllis when the
dog came up and curled into a ball beneath her chair. The dog
chose Mom out of about a hundred or so people that were
there in the audience. And she didn't even really love dogs.
He didn't have a collar on, and when Mom asked around no
one knew anything about him, so she and Dad put him in the

Oldsmobile that night and brought him home. I'd wanted a dog for a long time. We always had cats and dogs that lived in the barn and other animals and I loved all of them, but I really wanted a dog for myself. That night I had fallen asleep on the floor watching the Christopher Reeve *Superman* movie. That was the only Superman there was back then and he was an incredible superhero. I wanted to be like him.

That night I had the same dream I always had, the one with Nina and Devin in the yard and the Indigenous man on the horse, but instead of being cut off at the kneecaps I woke up when large droplets fell from the marshmallow clouds, pummeling my face. I opened my eyes to a small, wet, brown snout and pink tongue coming at me. I buried my face into my pillow, laughing with excitement. Lucky dug his tongue into my ears, hair, and eyes.

He was a funny dog and made me laugh a lot. He liked to give millions of kisses. He was so affectionate, but almost as if he was compulsive and had to constantly lick. He was cute, sort of like a Chihuahua but a little bigger and quieter than a Chihuahua. Maybe a cross between a corgi, Jack Russell, and Chihuahua. He didn't bark so much like Chihuahuas normally do. I couldn't believe Mom brought me a dog, that she even brought him home to me as a surprise. I sat up with the blankets around me. Lucky got up on my lap and curled into a ball, resting his chin over my calf. We sat there on the living room floor in the dark with the moonlight coming through the big picture windows and the kitchen light on, trailing into the room while Dad stood at the threshold of it.

"I can really have him?" I asked Mom.

"Yeah," she said. "We already named him, Lucky."

I told her I liked that name.

"He's Lucky," she said. "He came right up to me and knew I'd bring him home to someone who'd love him."

"Yes, I do love him," I said, and put my palms over his protruding ribs. "He's hungry, I think."

"You have to put a collar on him and learn to walk him in the yard. Without a fence he can't get out. The street is too busy, you know."

"I know," I said. Even though we lived in a rural part of Indiana, cars went down our street pretty fast. It was called Old Lincoln Highway, and had been the old, main highway there before US 30 was built, and even then, US 30 was old. We were about a mile from that highway. I wasn't allowed to ride my bike on Old Lincoln Highway because we didn't live in a subdivision like a lot of other kids did, and it was just too dangerous. Mom had told me about a little boy we once knew who got hit by a car while riding his bike and he didn't have a helmet on. She said to me, "He's turned to a vegetable." I imagined him like a carrot in the hospital bed with tubes attached to him. It was not a pretty thing to think about.

The same thing happened to Lucky. He got out one day when Mom was grabbing the mail. He was too small and quick and bolted out the door and went straight for the road. A car hit him and didn't even stop. Mom rushed out and got him. He wasn't squished, but he'd been thrown into the ditch. The impact was so hard he was already gone, and I suppose it was good that it was a quick death. We were in pieces about it. It was a very traumatic thing to happen and

Mom was as upset as I was. When I think about it now, she might have even been more upset than me.

We put him in a small wooden crate Dad had saved in the garage and dug a hole beneath the mulberry out back. I picked the mulberry tree because I thought it was the prettiest tree and it was one of the bigger ones. I didn't want to put him by the mulberry in the front, by the road, and remind him of what had happened for the rest of eternity. I didn't want him lying underground hearing the whiz of the cars going past, speeding on to nowhere important. *Where did people even have to get to that fast?* It didn't make any sense.

We lowered him in, backfilled the hole, and I put a cinder block over it as a tombstone and with chalk wrote *Lucky* in my bad handwriting that Mom helped me with by putting her hand over mine and drawing out the letters. After Lucky, I brought home other dogs I found while out with Dad, but she never let me keep them. Back then she'd tell me my strays had snuck out, that they mustn't have wanted to stay, but when I got older I knew it was because she let them run away. And now that I'm an adult I think it was because she loved Lucky so much that it was painful for her. She didn't want to have to go through that again. She didn't want me to go through it either. I cried for a long time after Lucky was gone.

⁓

The mulberries got ripe in June. It was always the mulberries and strawberries to show up first. Both have tons of seeds all over. I liked mulberries better than I liked strawberries and Mom did too. We went outside with two wide, woven baskets with short sides. We didn't use narrow, deep baskets because if too many berries stacked on top of each other, the ones on the bottom would be mush by the time we were done. We used woven baskets because Mom said the berries needed to breathe. There were all sorts of bugs on them too and she told me not to eat them till we washed them. But I looked at them and I didn't see any bugs, so I ate them anyways. The mulberries fell all over the ground and Mom said I shouldn't pick those ones as much as I should get the ones in the trees. I didn't understand why with all these seeds we didn't have an entire forest of mulberry trees in our front yard. The birds liked mulberries too. Sometimes I saw mulberry saplings growing out of our other trees where a bird must have pooped, and it got caught in the bark and began to root itself and after several years a nice stalk of mulberry with several leaves would grow right out the side of another tree altogether.

Mom liked to make mulberry preserves that we'd spread over toast in the mornings, and she'd make mulberry hand pies like her grandmother use to make. Her secret ingredient was to add a splash of the sour apple cider for brightness. "I used to pick mulberries with my dad just like you're picking the mulberries with me," she said while holding me at the waist and lifting me to get the ones I couldn't reach. Mom and her dad picked mulberries at her grandmother's house, but her grandmother on her mom's side. Back then she didn't see her dad a lot because he was always gone, out drinking or gambling or both. So, when she got the chance to be with him, she took it because she loved him very much. Usually he would get his paychecks and then be gone until the money was spent. He'd come back to my great-grandmother's, Grandma Hubbs's, house, where my grandmother, Mom's mom, lived in a camper out back near the barn where the sheep were, while my mom and her sister had a room in the house with Grandma Hubbs. And sometimes her dad would crash on the couch even though he and her mom were divorced.

Grandma Hubbs had a small farm in Lake Station, Indiana, close to Lake Michigan. She raised sheep but not a lot of them. It was more of a hobby farm than anything else. They had a few chickens and minks and a couple other animals. Her daughter, my grandma, worked in the steel mill driving a tractor and would do so for fifty years. When I was little, I remember her always in her pajamas. She wore her pajamas to work and everyone at the steel mill called her "Pajama Grandma," and even after she was retirement age she kept working, all the way until she was something like seventy-five or more. She liked the overtime pay and saved lots of money over the years. A child of the Great Depression, she didn't believe in banks and kept her money stashed all over the house in places like teddy bears, mattresses, and the walls. Plus, she was careful from her experiences with Wayne, who when he ran out of his own money tried to steal hers to pay off his debts at the bars and card houses.

Wayne would take Mom out to the forest behind Grandma Hubbs's house. Once a year they'd go out in late February, when it was still very cold, with a couple of metal pails and spigots and a small hand-crank drill. He showed her how to tap the maples. She was there to hold the pail while he drilled. Then he'd hammer the spigot in, and she'd hang the bucket over it and put on the tented lid so that not too much snow would fall in. Her hands got cold and white, and she winced while shaking them out.

"Cold, huh?" he asked her.

"Yes, Daddy," she said. He put his big hands over hers and blew into them. He told Mom she needed to not think about being cold. Being cold was nothing. He had spent his whole childhood being cold in Canada and it wasn't anything to worry about. He was proud of his French Canadian background.

Wayne told Mom that up there, the Laurentian Mountain range was stacked with tall pines. Their branches drooped beneath the heavy snow, frozen with silence. The only sound would be the crunch of snow beneath your snowshoes. A single-room cabin was what they stayed in: Wayne, his father, and his father's father. He slept on the cold floor, which in the mornings he would be stuck to fast with frost. A large potbelly stove was in the center. He'd hover near it, but his father told him not to: "You get too hot and then you get too cold later." His father opened the iron door of the stove. The embers crackled as he added more dried logs, one at a time. Each log immediately began to pop. On top of the stove was a steaming water kettle. They kept it full of water by melting ice in a pail next to the stove, then ladling it into the kettle. The steamy water added moisture to the dry air, but they also drank it, pouring it over whiskey in enamel mugs, which in turn kept their hands warm and their insides warmer. Wayne was too young to drink, but a little over a century ago a kid might as well do adult things even if he was only ten or so years old, so he did. Alongside the stove were three rows of twine nailed between two large logs. Their socks hung at the ends, drying out from the snow. Meat, which they'd heavily salted, hung in the center.

They left the salted meat hanging until it was leathered.

He told Mom that if you stood close to it you could smell the iron from the muscle and the caramelization that encased the outer layer as it dried. When it was dried, the venison showed the flavors of what the deer ate—berries, grubs, shrubs, mushrooms, and cedar. The black bear's muscle tasted like salmon. When her dad told her of this she imagined the hulking bears, fur so black it was indigo and silver in the white light of the snow, thrusting their large paws into the icy river, grasping at fish. Wayne told her about other animals too, like otters, beavers, squirrels, chipmunks. How he liked to hunt squirrels with the small gun his father gave him. She imagined the otters snacking on mussels, sliding along the banks, rolling and playing with one another. And when he told her about the squirrels, she had to not think of it because their fear of being hunted, she imagined, was too great of a thing.

Wayne spent his childhood winters in the frosted mountains. At the height of winter, the forest felt alive even though it was dormant. His mother and grandmother stayed at home and did things that kept life moving. They cooked, taught the other littler kids (brothers, sisters, cousins) to read, washed clothes, sheared sheep, milked cows, knitted. The pelts Wayne and *the men* were out to get was part of their livelihood. If they were vigilant, they brought the money they made home and didn't spend it all on booze and gambling. For the most part, they stayed true to their promise.

Wayne even got his own fur cap made from a raccoon he trapped. You know the sort of hat, with the tail in the back. He didn't let his father see, but he cried when his father killed it. He really wanted that cap though. Once he had it, he wore it with a sort of bravado. It made him feel like a character from a storybook. That was how Mom saw him—larger than life. He was the little boy in plaid shirt, dungarees, thick boots, fur cap, and a small shotgun slung over his shoulder, emulating his father. He was sweet and gentle and had a magic way about him.

That day out in the woods, tapping maples with Mom, he wore a raccoon cap, maybe not the same one but one that looked just like it. He had on a big scarf Grandma Hubbs had knitted and thick gloves lined with soft wool. He took off his gloves and put them on Mom. After they tapped the maples but before they went back to the house, where Mom could smell the fire already coming from the chimney, her dad sat on a log and lit a cigarette. She sat on the log next to him. He lit the cigarette and blew out a large cloud of smoke, larger than it would have been because it was so cold out. He smoked unfiltered cigarettes and Mom would too, someday, starting out by stealing his. He reached his hand to the inside of his jacket and pulled out a flask. He took a swig.

"This is whiskey." He held it out in front of her. "Would you like to try some?"

"Yes, Daddy," she said.

"Okay, I'm gonna let you try some. It's going to burn your throat, a nice burn, but don't spit it out." She took a sip, much smaller than he would have done at her age. The whiskey was strong but she didn't make a face though she wanted to. She handed the flask back to him and swallowed, afraid of it burning her throat but it wasn't so bad. It got her warm inside and she liked that part.

"When it gets a little nicer out, we'll come out here and pick mulberries for Mummum." That was the nickname he gave to Grandma Hubbs. "Would you like that?" he asked.

"Yes, Daddy," she said to him, and he put his arm around her and gave her a quick hug into his side.

⟶⟍

That following spring Wayne was true to his word. While they were in the forest he said to her, "Mulberries have at least fifty seeds in this one little nugget." He held a single berry in front of her face. "I'd be willing to bet on it." She stared down her nose at the bulbous berry, pocked like the moon, textured with ridges and valleys. Each seed's nucleus was surrounded by an electromagnetic field of pulp—a small universe between his fingers. She was enraptured. Mulberry pie, mulberry jam, mulberry juice, mulberry seeds for more mulberry trees. Of all those things she was most interested in the mulberry pie. All these images passed through her brain while her eyes followed the shadows of birds, passing over the ground. "Yep, more's gonna grow," he said, "because the birds love these berries. They shit 'em everywhere." He told her silkworms thrived in mulberry trees, and that's how silk was made. He looked at her staring, cross-eyed at the berry. He knew she at least got the gist of it, and that was enough.

Out in the forest, Wayne reminded Mom to stay away from all mushrooms. He got sick from one once and after that didn't care to know any more about them. Out there, he pushed the wicker basket in her arms, filling it with as many mulberries as it would hold. After they finished, she was careful not to tip the basket, steadying herself as she stepped over every bole or big rock in her path. "So many mulberries in here," she said to him, which translated to *so many mulberry pies.* "Yeah," he said. "All right, come on." Mom could tell he was itching to get out of the forest, and since he didn't have his flask with him that day, it probably meant he needed to get out of there and tie one on.

They brought the mulberries back to Grandma Hubbs and then he disappeared that evening. He was gone for a couple days. When he got back to the house, she and her sister ran to their bedroom door when they heard him come in but only watched through a crack. It was never safe to say it would be okay to greet him after he'd been gone on a bender. He was all black and blue in the face, so they stayed quiet.

Grandma Hubbs patched him up while Grandpa Marcus, her husband, was on the night shift at the mill. He was a metallurgist.

Mom and her sister peeped through the crack in their bedroom door. He slumped on the couch, looking defeated. His head bobbed around like it was floating in water. Lit by the glow of the fireplace's flames, Mummum used a wet washcloth to dab the blood beneath his nose. She pressed gauze to his cheek. Mom and her sister saw little more than their silhouettes in the otherwise dark room. Mom would always remember this night and ones like it, how Grandma Hubbs patched him up. How Grandma always helped him when he was in trouble, even though he was no longer her son-in-law. The moon shone through the sliding glass doors, and on this night, they saw him and Grandma Hubbs kiss for the first time. The first time they'd seen. Their hearts beat rapidly, as a baby rabbit's when you hold it in your hands. They were young but they understood enough. Barbara looked as if she would start sobbing at any moment. Mom clasped her sister's upper arm and said, "We ain't telling anyone." She dug her nails in a bit to signify the importance of what she meant.

"I know," Barbara replied. "I know," she said again.

And they didn't tell anyone. Mom didn't tell anyone, not for a long time.

Even back then as she and I picked mulberries together she didn't tell me all that. She waited until I was much older, of course.

That night, after spying, Mom and Barbara got themselves ready for bed. It was easier for her sister than for her to find the sandman. Barbara hopped into bed and pulled the quilted blanket up around her ears. Mom had set every single knick-knack they owned out on the plywood floor. She used a torn piece of dress that didn't fit anymore to dust off the knick-knacks' surfaces. Then she polished each one. On a stack of their schoolbooks was a short cup that held their pencils for school. She and Barbara loved to smell the fresh shavings of the cedar sticks. They pressed the tips hard in their notebooks, noting what their teachers said. Along with their school supplies were the nesting dolls. Mom put all the knick-knacks back in place on the nightstands, bookshelf, desk, and dresser. The nesting dolls were perfect, the pencils sharpened, the notebooks shelved biggest to littlest, the ballerina in the box, the glass of water, the two dried marshmallows that she and Barbara were saving in case they wanted a snack. Now that the room was cleaned and organized, she felt better about what they saw. As she finished up, she used her fingers to dust the lamp that she had forgotten to polish, the one that had cherubim flying around at its base, holding a tulip that nestled the bulb. Then she turned out the light. She got into bed. Finally, she closed her eyes but only slept halfway. She was conscious of lying down, that she felt if she could sew her eyelids shut, she would. She turned on her side and stared at the crucifix that once hung in the front hallway but was now on the wall at her side of the bed. One night not long ago, Grandma Hubbs put it in there saying she couldn't stand him watching her anymore. Mom didn't think anything of it at the time. But now, instead, she thought of the transfer of maple water to spigot that her dad had showed her. She thought of how fast the maple sap released itself from the tree. She thought of the mulberries. She thought of the hand pies. She thought of all the things she'd do with the mulberries and the maple sap. At the very end of all her thoughts she imagined herself like a reed, drifting down a river, which finally put her to sleep.

⌒⊶

Mom would go on to dust, polish, fold, wipe, align, scrub, and dry things, compulsively, for the rest of her life. She'd make sure you did it too. *Everything. Has. To. Be. In. Order.* Back then she did it to save her dad, to save herself, her sister, and her mom out in the trailer. But someday when she'd finally tell me about it all, she'd tell me she might have thought her mom knew all along. And with all the things she *needed* to keep in order, she didn't call it OCD, but instead she'd say that she was superstitious. She told me she thought that if everything was perfectly placed, then everyone would be okay. Her dad would be okay. Barbara would be okay. Later, after she had us—we'd be okay. Everyone she loved would be okay, including herself, if everything would just stay in order.

⌒⊶

Once Mom and I brought the mulberries inside, she plugged the sink and filled it with cold water. I stood on the footstool so I could reach. At the sink we dumped our baskets in. There were a lot more bugs than you'd have thought. I imagined a bunch of those little black and tan ones crawling around my stomach and along my throat. I asked Mom, "But when I poop, they'll come out right? Like the birds?" She laughed at me.

"You're silly," she said. "The bugs will dissolve in your stomach."

"But how?"

"Because your stomach has acid in it that makes the food so you can digest it."

"But sometimes the animals poop and Dad says there's worms in there."

"Yes," she said, "but that's a different thing."

"What if mine has bugs in it?"

She pushed the berries around in the water. "There're not too many bugs. You probably didn't eat too many. Don't think about it."

"Will I get worms?"

"No, you won't get worms."

"Not even a few?"

"Not even a few." She took the berries out and placed them into a strainer that was on a towel to catch the water that ran from them. I was anxious. All I could see were the bugs. "If you're worried about it, drink some tomato juice," she said.

"Why?"

"Because the vitamins in it will help you."

"I don't like the tomato juice."

"Do you want the bugs to go away?"

"Yes."

"Then drink it."

Mom poured me a small glass of tomato juice and sprinkled a little salt and black pepper over the top. I drank it. It was good with the salt and pepper but I suspected she was tricking me into drinking the tomato juice.

"With half of these berries we're gonna make pie. The rest we're gonna dry and add to the *czarnina*."

"But why do you put fruit in the soup?"

"Because that's how you do it."

"But it's sweet."

"That's okay. A little bit of sweet things is okay in soup. It's okay in a lot of things. Most things you eat have a bit of sugar in them, even if they don't taste sweet. Busia put plums and wild apples in her *czarnina*."

"But why does the blood have to be in it? I think I'd like it better without."

"The recipe calls for it. That's how Busia's recipe is. That's how it was done in Poland."

"But why blood?"

"Lanie." Mom slapped her thigh. "Put some of these berries in the skillet." She set the bowl on the counter next to the stove. I got off the footstool and moved it over to the stove. She added a splash of oil to the bottom of the skillet. I got back on the stool and picked up the bowl and put in the berries into the skillet. There was a large mound.

"I think there's too many," I said.

"They'll cook down. Turn on the flame," she said to me. I turned it on. "Now sprinkle a little salt." I did like she said.

"Mix them gently." I did.

After a few minutes the mulberries bled their juices and began to shrink in the skillet. She put a cup of sugar next to the stove. "In a few minutes add the sugar, and when it dissolves give it a gentle stir and turn the flame down."

"Okay."

After a short forever of thirty or forty minutes, the berries thickened. Mom added a couple drops of vanilla extract and the sour apple cider.

When they were done, we let them cool inside the skillet while Mom made two large piecrusts and flattened them out on two baking trays. We divided the berries between both, and Mom turned up the corners of the piecrusts to hold them in place. "These are called crostadas. It's easier than pie. We are going to bake them just like this."

"I like this."

"Good." She handed me a bowl of egg yolks and added a couple drops of heavy cream. "Mix this and brush it on the outside crust then sprinkle sugar over the top." I did what she said. We put them in the oven, and I sat on the floor in front of it and waited. "You're being very patient. I thought you didn't like pie," she said.

"You said this wasn't pie."

"It's not. But it will taste similar."

"But we picked the berries and everything," I said, proud of that part.

"That's special, isn't it?"

"Yeah."

"Will you eat the *czarnina* then?"

"No. I don't think so."

CHAPTER 9.
WILD STRAWBERRIES

DAD HELD THE WILD STRAWBERRIES UNDER MY NOSE. They were my size; I was small then too. We were at Grandpa Regan's farm where the strawberries grew wild. Raspberries and mulberries were my favorite but I loved strawberries too, especially from the wild, which were much sweeter and also more tart than ones from the store. Mom liked strawberry shortcake. Dad liked strawberries green or white, dill pickled. He also liked them when they were red and freshly dressed in sugar. At Grandpa Regan's farm wherever the land wasn't sand or covered in leaves and mosses and such, the strawberries spread over acres and acres.

Strawberries aren't really berries. Dad told me, "They're not like blueberries or blackberries."

"What are they?" I asked.

"Well, ah, I, ah, guess they're like roses?" If Dad hadn't had so many daughters, he would have finished college with

139

a degree in botany. He told me that once. He loved studying plants. He might have gone downstate to Purdue instead of the local Indiana University campus. He left out the part about having daughters, but I knew what he really meant. He didn't want to say anything that could hurt my feelings. It wouldn't have hurt though, at least not now. Sometimes I wished my parents had had us later and got to do what they most wanted to do. Mom said she would have been a forensic scientist if she hadn't gotten married so early, which also meant if she hadn't had so many daughters. I know she would've been good at it.

"This is the only fruit that has its seeds on the outside," Dad said.

I didn't say anything. I picked a strawberry from his palm and ate it. I chewed it good, between my molars. I took another couple berries from his palm and ate those too. I savored them, pushing the chewed strawberries with my tongue against the roof of my mouth, spreading them over my palate. It was perfect, so aromatic that as I bit into it the flavor filled my nose.

"Better eat these, we don't have a basket for 'em today." We had fishing poles instead because we were going to Grandpa's big pond. Dad said we were "gonna catch some bluegills." I was more interested in the berries. I scanned the ground and saw many of them ripe for picking. I crouched down and opened our tacklebox, which smelled of the stinky bait Dad liked. He said that the fish liked it too. I moved a couple of my shiners, weights, and other tackle around, creating space in the top compartments, and started filling it with the berries.

He crouched down, picking them along with me. He held another one up; the side that had been against the ground had deteriorated. "See here," he said, "bugs got to this one. If they touch the ground for too long, they'll rot, or bugs'll get to 'em."

"Okay," I said, thinking about it.

"Why are these berries called strawberries?" he asked.

I shrugged. "Because they are like roses?"

"No. Think about when they ain't in the wild. What we do at home with 'em?"

"I dunno," I said.

"Yes, you do."

"What do I have you do to 'em when the flowers start turning into berries?"

"I put the hay under them."

"Yeah, you put *straw* under 'em. That's why they're strawberries. We put straw under 'em so the ground and the bugs don't do this." He held the rotted berry under my face again. I took it from his fingers and threw it into the forest.

The wild strawberries were everywhere. Dad said it was because the seeds being on the outside makes it so when they aren't picked, they just keep going back into the ground and more and more keep coming. He said the birds, the deer, and other animals like them, and because almost every animal eats strawberries, and not all the seeds are taken up in their digestive systems, they get pooped out and the berries keep growing.

I like to tell people that story about the strawberries. You'd be surprised how many people don't know why they're called *straw*-berry. I guess it seems too obvious, like a trick question.

Sometimes when I made syrup from the wild strawberries around the cabin, I'd set some out in a little bowl on the post of our porch. I'd wait and it wouldn't be long before the hummingbirds showed up. I spent a lot of the pandemic with my binoculars, appreciating what bird watchers did. I knew why Dad liked watching the birds—it wasn't just waiting to die, like he'd once said retirement was all about—sitting in a chair, watching the birds, and waiting to die. The truth was watching birds was more like wanting to live.

And it was just so sudden, right after I picked what seemed like the last of the wild strawberries, that just like that—a quick snap or maybe it was as long as overnight while I tried to sleep—all the birds were gone. I sat on our porch, listening for them, but it was silent. When the jack pine warblers were here, they sang three to four notes every second, loudly protecting their territory. I loved the warblers. They were pretty birds. I woke up many mornings, or afternoons depending on how you looked at it, hearing their songs.

There were many birds out here. Cedar waxwings, which were lovely. Red-headed woodpeckers that poked the birch trees for weevils. If I was out early enough in the morning, plenty of birds were in the yard, eating the wild strawberries, the insects, the worms, and so on. Our yard was a carpet of strawberries. It wasn't good for us bug-wise, but I didn't mow the lawn until strawberry season was over. I let the berries do what they needed to do so I could collect as many as possible. It takes time to collect many of them because they are so little. The birds would be there in the morning, hopping around like they do, going from plant to plant, picking at the berries, and I didn't mind. I think the wild strawberries made them happy because day and night they sang. And then one day they were just gone.

One night I was on the porch alongside the cabin that wrapped around the north and east sides. At the furthest northeast corner, it opened to the sky. The space was approximately eight by eight feet. Sometimes at night I put down a blanket and pillow, lay down, and watched everything: the Milky Way, meteor showers, constellations, shooting stars, the universe. I could see it all. There were many other sounds to appreciate. I listened to the crickets, bullfrogs, and bats. The Sturgeon River trickled and I closed my eyes, seeing it go from west to east. Beavers and otters played along the banks at night. I heard their splashing. In the mornings, when I went down to the river to fish, I found piles of freshwater mussel shells like the otters had been partying at a Belgian pub, *moules frites* for dinner. Also, at night came the sounds of the squirrels and chipmunks pitter-pattering over the pine needles and leaves covering the forest floor. There was the prancing of deer—forest horses are what I call them. There was the stalking of the wolves, not as stealthy as they thought. The scuttling of field mice, the buzz of mosquitoes and moths, and the occasional single-prop plane way above going to the nearest small airport. All of these sounds lulled me into a trance. My ears were like a dog's, twitching. And because sometimes I was afraid, I tuned in further, making sure I knew every sound so that if something ever was out of the ordinary, I knew to be alert.

And on that evening while at the northeast corner of the porch, not long after the birds were gone, I called Anna to come listen. She came out and stood next to me in the dark. I held my finger to my lips—*shhh, listen*. She looked at me with an expression that said, *what are we listening for?* An owl called out. Anna's eyebrows rose, asking, *this?* Soon after, the bats started up. She looked at me. Her eyebrows cramped. I looked at her with my eyes wide saying, *what can* I *do about the bats?*

At the river things were louder than normal; we perked up as the leaves blew up on a swell of wind. Chipmunks and squirrels, red and black, went from tree to tree. If you watched long enough, you'd see some of the squirrels fly. A wood turtle toddled through the understory and I knew that sound. Even the delicate footprints of the foxes echoed. All these sounds were white noises out here, and I didn't worry about them much unless it really crunched down, expressing weight, only if it was close, only if it was something I hadn't heard before.

From our porch I looked through the trees using night-vision binoculars. That one time when I saw a pack of wolves, they'd passed right beneath me, and I didn't need binoculars. The alpha wolf had acted as if he didn't see me but I sure saw him. I knew he smelled me. He smelled my Shih Tzu, Clementine, who was in my lap. When I heard his footsteps, I set Clementine down and got up from where I sat drinking my coffee, and looked out. I watched him push his snout up into the air. His brown nose wiggled. I saw his colors of red, gray, and white. He was so close I saw the muscles flex along the bridge of his snout as he took in rapid breaths. He moved on and several wolves followed him through the ferns, club-moss, and milkweed lining the yard.

Anna looked at me while I looked through the binoculars. I could feel her eyes on me and that maybe she was a little disappointed in me. She seemed annoyed. She knew I loved this, but she didn't love it as much. She said she did, but she didn't.

Anna was the kind of person that could be fine anywhere for the most part. I was not. I hoped our relationship wouldn't become like Mom's and Dad's, at least not yet. Mom and Dad made it thirty-five years with a bunch of kids; we'd only been together five, and no kids, just dogs. We were still too new at this to be unhappy about the other's happiness and I felt we were too new not to try to love what the other loved.

A few minutes passed and other sounds started up, quieter sounds. It was amazing what you could hear when you tried. The moths kamikazed the citronella candle. Stuck in the hot wax, their wings sizzled against the flame. Hundreds of gnats and mosquitoes banged themselves against the naked Edison bulbs in the sconces on both sides of the glass doors on the porch. The bats echolocated us, awaiting our absence to swoop down and consume the thousands of flying insects they put away per hour on average. The leaves went up again, sounding like waves. The wind ran through our hair. And there were so many sounds, but no birds. The bird songs were gone. Completely. My skin prickled with bumps at the eerie thought of it.

Fifty some yards down the hill, a large splash sounded from the river. I just knew it was a bear. This was the sound I was waiting for and the reason I had the binoculars over my eyes. This was the sound I wanted her to hear. I scanned back and forth, all of it dark and blurry. The sound was louder than the beavers and otters. I adjusted the binoculars again and aside from the bright eyes of owls, I couldn't get a clear view. I put my finger to my lips, imagining the sow standing near the edge of the river, crouched down as the water ran over her massive paws. She'd thrust them into the water, bringing up a brookie, the kind I would like to catch. Her claws dripped and the brookie's gills rapidly opened and closed until ultimately the fish became stiff as she tore into it. While she did, along the riverbank, the chokecherry eyes of her two bear cubs glistened shiny as the ones dangling above their heads. The chokecherries down there were far enough away from the logging that they grew in abundance. The cubs sat upright on their hams, eager for dinner.

Hearing the splash, Anna's eyes opened wide. I was happy she heard it. We listened, excited now, together. It *must* be a bear. I was certain. I hadn't seen one in a while, not since our neighbor had set out piles of corn and molasses mash around his camp. He said it was for the deer, but it seemed more like a trap for bears. I can't say for certain.

I saw a massive bear that day he set out the mash. I had gotten into the Jeep, driving down to a large, wild strawberry patch I had marked on my map. I liked to collect strawberries everywhere I could, not only from our yard. But I had to be careful—they were so delicate. I knew this from when I collected them with Dad all those years ago. I had to collect them in a way they wouldn't smash one another. Sometimes, back in the city, guys sold strawberries like these to restaurants for forty dollars a pint. Half the time they were from Southern France or somewhere else far away and it made sense they were so expensive. Here and now though, they were everywhere, right beneath my boots. I had to be careful where I stepped. I got on my hands and knees, crawling, and gathered them. I didn't worry about anyone thinking I looked strange. There was no one here. No wolves or bears bothered me. I wasn't afraid either. When I was foraging lots of my fears went away.

Ticks, though. Ticks I could not escape. I wore all white from head to toe. I tucked the hem of my white jeans into my white socks and wore white shoes and after I was out of the brush, they were easy to spot and pick from my clothing.

Most of the time I made vinegar from the wild strawberries here. I mashed them up with raw honey and poured our well water over them in a jar, then covered the jar with cheese cloth and let it sit at room temperature for a couple weeks. The berries would fizzle, coming up to the top of the mixture, and then fall back down again. That's when I checked the liquid at the top to see how acidic it was. I used a small, clean spoon to taste it. If it was tart, then I'd strain the berries and bottle the liquid, again with cheesecloth over the top, and let it age. Over time at room temperature the concoction evaporated and became concentrated. Eventually I'd store it and use it later over greens, vegetables, and proteins. Because I cooked for only a small number of people each weekend, my concoctions could last for years, developing flavor all the while.

Making vinegar is something else I learned from Dad. It was a nice way to preserve the berries. Otherwise, they didn't last long, and it was hard to use them unless I picked them just as I was about to serve them. Without a team of people to help, this was a hard thing to do, but I still did it sometimes. Right before the strawberry course we'd sometimes serve our guests, I'd run out to the yard and collect as many as I could. I'd place them fresh over a soft homemade cheese with a sauce of wood sorrel and pine. There's nothing better than a sun-warmed, fresh, wild berry.

Other times, I fermented them in 1 percent salt by weight and used the salty-sweet liquid as a seasoning. The salty berries left over I dried and pulverized to a powder that I used to season homemade butter or other things. Sometimes I just held them in a simple syrup (one part sugar to one part water) and allowed them to do what they do. That was the syrup I'd use for the hummingbirds.

And it was that time, when I went to collect them at the patch down the road, that I saw the massive bear. I crossed over the hill separating our land and our neighbor's, not far from where he left the corn molasses mash. The bear must have heard my engine and becoming frightened, darted across the path. I believed he might have been the father of those same cubs who were at the river. I assumed he was a male because he was so massive.

Majestically, he galloped on all fours, the muscles rippling under his fur. His snout was brown, fading to tan near his eyes, but the rest of him was blacker than anything I'd seen before. He was such a deep black he was also silver, blue, and purple in the bit of sun that was coming through the trees. "Holy shit," I said out loud. I'd never seen something so beautiful.

Later, when I returned with several pints of the tiny, ruby-colored strawberries, I told Anna about the bear. Instead of sharing the excitement I'd felt, she felt fear at the thought of the bear being so close. She wanted me to ask the neighbor to move the mash further away, because that same night we had the dogs in the yard, and we heard the bears fighting. We assumed the noise must have been from them fighting because we heard loud growling and thrashing. We ushered the dogs inside and for the rest of the evening they wouldn't stop barking.

Around midnight Anna was fed up. She wanted me to do something about it. I wasn't sure what to do. *What would*

Dad do? I loaded a full round of bullets into Dad's cowboy gun, took it outside and released the safety. From the porch I fired it to the southeast, well above the tree line in an attempt to scare the bears away. I felt terrible doing it. My eardrums rang. Later that week I got an ear infection in my left ear.

It was real, that sound at the river. Anna had heard it too. I hoped the splashing noises were from the sow. I hoped she and her cubs were eating well. I hoped they had a safe den. I worried about their home and where it might be now with all the logging that had happened. I didn't care if they were closer now, and we had to share with them.

After Anna went inside for the night, I took a walk. I waited until she was upstairs in our room. Once she made it to bed, she usually fell asleep immediately, so I waited until then so she wouldn't know I'd left. She was not as worried as Dad about the wild animals, but she still worried. It was very dark out.

In the southernmost end of the boreal forest the night moved like a skirt. I loved walking at night, watching the aspens quiver, revealing one side then the other—a sequined gown. Birch and beech stood straight. The wind chased away a few clouds; the skirt lifted. There was the Milky Way. I had marked on my calendar that meteor showers would be here soon. Then slowly, from four to ten o'clock, what looked like a slow-moving star was the International Space Station passing way up in the sky.

The stars were sharp and smart. They knew what they knew, which was everything. I imagined reaching up and grabbing the Milky Way's tail and, while holding her like a funnel, tipping the stars into my mouth, drinking the universe. The trees drank her, and they knew everything too.

I plucked a beech leaf from the petiole. I inhaled the acrid oil the leaf left on my fingertips. I licked them, rough against my tongue where my fingers were shiny at their tips and thick with callouses like Dad's had once been. Most of my callouses were from cooking, handling hot things, foraging through thorny bushes, and chopping wood. I had cuts and burns and scars on the tops of my hands. My hands were like what I imagined Busia's had been. The taste the leaf left on my fingers was like a bitter, black fungus. I tasted like the outside, how cattail pollen smells, like the invisible spores and leaf duff. Tasting like the outside was somehow the point of it all. I smelled like so many things, from a long day in the forest, but mostly like the beautiful dankness of it and even still, I'd never be as outside as the underbelly of a wolf or the caked earth beneath a fox's nails, or the crusted blood on the red-tailed hawk's talons, the seed-germinating tortoise, the aphid-ranching ant, the hummingbirds, wasps, bees, and other pollinators that were so important, the beech trees with diseased bark, oaks that sent out messages, deciding whether now was the time to throw their mast. They might wait until the following year when the squirrels would be thinner.

Pointy hemlocks reached up; cones thick with resin like crystalized knobs. In the winter, the maple's sap surged through the xylem and the bats, warblers, and squirrels devoured it. It was 2 AM. The climbing moon wasn't shy, coming to steal the Milky Way's show. Orion, Polaris, and Pisces were still clear. The International Space Station sailed by again. I don't care if it's cliché to tell you that bats flew across the moon in perfect bat shapes like from a comic book. Geese squawked, taking the shape of longbows and arrows. A sandhill crane looped around, sounding as prehistoric as it looked.

The beech leaf was in my hand. I saw from the reflection of the moon the imprint of my thumb on the stomata. I saw it because I knew it was there. If you'd been there, I'd have shown it to you, and you'd have seen it too. You'd have seen the spiraled grooves of my thumbprint mimicking the constellations. You'd have known that beneath our feet the detritus, sand, soil, rocks, roots, and mycelium formed its own underground constellations. The shapes, the ones we could see and the ones we couldn't, were all there and we'd have known—the thumbprint on the leaf, the mycelium, the constellations—they were all the same. If you had layered them onto a viewing slide or looked through a telescope, we'd have seen how they were all the same, fractals of one another. We'd have breathed, and the veins and capillaries running through our lungs would have been outlines of oaks and the cross-sections of sheep's head mushrooms. We were part of this, we'd have known. We'd have talked about how our lives and histories were like this, interconnected. All we had to do was be quiet and listen. After a while, we'd also have known none of this belonged to us or man or *Homo sapiens*.

Being alone I was fine and unembarrassed by myself; I spread out my arms to make like a tree and stood with my face lifted to the moon. I didn't meditate but it was something like that. I knew it was because of the logging that the birds had left. I apologized to the forest, the Leshy, and the birds for the destruction.

When I got back to the cabin, I mouse-snuck through our room, gathering my pajama pants and shirt for after the shower. While the water ran over me, I whispered to whatever or whomever might be listening, and maybe it was a prayer. I asked that the missing birds find a good home. Somewhere they could feel safe. After the shower I got in my pajamas and I went downstairs and added a few more logs to the fire. I curled up on the couch and, staying awake another hour or so, I ate all the wild strawberries.

CHAPTER 10.
A FEAR INVENTORY

FINALLY, I HAD A PENIS, THOUGH THE TIMING WAS all off.

One morning I got up from bed and stood before the floor-length mirror. My belly was rotund, as if I had swallowed a whole watermelon. I grabbed at it. I turned to the side and exhaled, letting my posture fall into the way I held myself without thinking about it, the way that felt most comfortable when I wasn't in front of a mirror. It's always frustrating to let it fall into the way that it is while relaxed because when you see yourself, at least when I do, I think, do I really look like that?

We will never know how we really look. Not really. It will always be through pictures or mirrors or, for better or worse, through the eyes of others. Anyways, I turned to the side. I wanted to get a good look at the profile of this new body. My back had several rolls in it. I had become a stuffed croissant. I know, I know; no one wants to hear about a skinny person gaining weight, but this wasn't that. It was a new body. A body that didn't belong to me. I had back rolls and a rotund belly that stuck out much further than my feet, which I could no longer see when I looked down. I placed my hands beneath this belly and hoped I was pregnant. I placed my palms over my belly button, beneath the mound, over the mound, and counted to sixty each time, hoping for a kick, but there was nothing.

On closer inspection I saw how dark the usually thin blonde hair over it had become. The hair traveled around my navel and down to my privates. Tufts of dark brown hair sprung from around my belly button all the way up over my chest, spreading to my arms, and there was hair on my back too. There was hair in the dimple above my buttocks, in that indented area above the coccyx. Where once it would've been able to hold a cup of water, now it was full of hair that descended into the pies on each side of my anus. I lifted each leg and saw they were covered in hair-like fur. I turned toward the mirror again and that was when I saw the apparatus.

I had a penis. I had a penis flopping to one side, and behind it were long, saggy balls. The balls hung lower than the penis. I had no idea if that was normal. I wasn't versed in that sort of thing, but Dad had balls like that because of his hernia. I never saw them naked, but it was easy to see the shapes of them through his pants when he sat on a couch with his legs spread. Balls that hung to his mid-thighs, somewhere almost exactly between his groin and knees. It was incredibly grotesque.

No No No No No. Not now, god, not now. This wasn't what I meant all those years ago when I prayed for a penis. I didn't want this penis like this now. I would have liked to have gone about it in another way, any other way, but not like this, and not for it to look like Dad's. I certainly didn't want this body with all the hair and flabbiness. I looked up from the penis, over my chest, neck, and at my face. My face in the mirror, it had changed. My eyes met with Dad's, staring back at me.

I woke up. This was the sort of dream I was able to wake myself up from because my dreams were like that at times. The dream gets to a point where it's utterly ridiculous and you must release yourself from it. I looked across the bed and Anna was there, sleeping, her mouth slightly open. I wiped the sweat from my forehead. The area under my boobs was sweating and I placed my hand under my shirt, wiping it away and also just checking that my boobs were intact and there was no hair on my chest. The room had filled with the mushroomy funk of morning breath issuing from us and the dogs. George was at the foot of the bed, Bunny was along-side me, Clementine was between our pillows. I checked my phone, and it was only 7 AM, way before I wanted to get up. I put my head back on the pillow and exhaled. I tossed and turned for another hour, thinking about all I could do that day, and I couldn't fall asleep again. Several times I closed my eyes, thinking of all I knew was out there, all I could forage on a day like this one. The sun was coming up. It was going to be a nice day, but I didn't have the discipline to get out of bed this early. Then I thought about how nice it would be to sit on the porch with a beer and cigarette. That got me up.

I went to the washroom, peed, washed my face, put in my contacts, brushed my teeth, and got dressed. It was still a little chilly, so I put on a pair of Carhartt dungarees with lined legs over my pajama bottoms. I wore a flannel shirt underneath and put a Carhartt beanie over my head. It was one of our days off. Days off weren't often days off because at that moment I was in school full-time, and of course foraging and working on prep for the weekends. But it was a Monday, which meant I didn't have as much prep to do, though I had a class in the afternoon.

Clementine followed me downstairs, where I threw a few logs into the fireplace. Restarting the fire, our only source of heat, was a necessity the first thing on chilly mornings. I wanted Anna to wake up warm.

I took my pocket notebook and pencil out on the porch with me. I liked to write with a pencil. I didn't like how ink went through the page and I liked to use both sides of the paper I wrote on. It was colder outside but the sun hit the porch and I sat in the sunlight. I got a beer from the cooler and a menthol American Spirit from the pack and lit it. I opened the beer and took a swig, setting it on the table next to me. This was how Mom once did it, early in the mornings, before anyone was awake, wanting to take the edge off, a beer and cigarette seeming like the best possible answer. I know it's not. Beer makes you gain weight and is bad for a bunch of other reasons and that large belly was still on my mind. Since I began drinking again, and what with the pandemic on top of that, I'd gained thirty pounds. I'm not going to complain about it because yeah, I know, no one wants to hear about a skinny person gaining weight.

I opened my pocket notebook and for a while I didn't write anything. I didn't smoke from my cigarette or drink from my beer. For a long time, I just sat, tired, staring at the trees. Truth was I didn't feel right drinking a beer and having a cigarette that early, even though I wanted them. I watched the clouds slide behind the trees. I watched shadows change shapes. I thought about Mom and Dad, about them getting old, how it's been difficult for them to do the things they once did easily. I thought about how I was getting old. My body was changing and the energy I once had was diminishing. I've simply been exhausted from years of running myself ragged. Drinking again and still smoking wasn't helping me feel any better.

I thought about big things like grief, and how if I was truly being honest with myself, I'd never gotten over losing my sister Bunny. That no amount of grief counseling or therapy or time could truly make it better. Time was supposed to heal, *but did it?* My dreams of her were more frequent. If anything, I was only becoming more and more like her. I knew what would happen if I did become her. That's why I was where I was and why I did the things I did. Why I obsessed over cooking and food; why I wrote and read with ferocity. She loved doing those things. I thought about how she might have liked to read what I wrote— but maybe *she*, in fact, was the one writing it. If Bunny could ever read my work, I feared I might not be her favorite author, but I would have wanted to be. Or I would have been her favorite author because I was her little sister. And the thing was, the thing I thought about most, was that if she hadn't died, I might not be here at all. I wouldn't have had a restaurant, at least not a restaurant named after her. I might have been the one who died instead. For a long time, ten plus years, I had quit drinking and a large part of the reason why was because I knew what could happen to me if I kept drinking the way I did, the way she had. It would end in death.

Almost everything I've done since Bunny died has been to cope with this grief. I've built my world around it. I do so much because I never want to slow down. It's a coping mechanism. People tell me how impressed they are by how much I do but I tell them it's because I'm ill, in a sense. It's because I literally cannot face what I feel. I keep frantically busy and moving so that I don't feel what I would otherwise feel. I don't do well with idleness. I'm certain too much idleness someday would land me in jail. Like Bunny.

It's not like my life has been bad, I know. It's just a strange thing that some people have, that life is difficult to deal with no matter your circumstances. I know for some people it's easier. They don't worry about things much or remember things. If you don't remember things, I think maybe it's because the things didn't matter much to you. My friend Jesse said that once to me. Now I believe it to be true. Maybe everything matters to me too much. I remember nearly everything.

In all this time of grief and darkness, still, it's not always dark. There is a lightness to it, which comes in the form of dreamy, fantastical thoughts. Sometimes I think that somehow Bunny will come back or she's still out there somewhere. That if I do just the right things, arrange my life and the world in the right order, she will reappear. I can't get the farmhouse back, but I daydream about recreating it, slat by slat. I daydream that if I rebuilt that farmhouse she would be there because I believe somehow, she's already there. I believe she's still there.

Sometimes when I'm visiting Dad in Indiana I drive past that old place. It's run down now. The fruit trees are gone, the hazelnut and crabapple trees in the hedgerow have been cleared and the space bushhogged and there are no rows of cedars or peonies, and the paddock, the fence, the swimming pool, the pole barn—it's all gone. But if I could go there, buy it, and rebuild it exactly the way it was, with the same shag carpet, wicker furniture, artwork, wallpapers, tables and chairs, and blue tile in the bathroom, the puzzle-like kitchen tiles, then we would all be there again, back before we moved and Mom made Dad sell our things at auction, when there were kegs floating in large bins and a lamb roasting in the driveway and the antiquated, rusty farm equipment in the yard. When I die, if there is a heaven, and if I go there, then it will be that farmhouse exactly as it was in 1984. Death's white light is the lamppost in the drive. I arrive at the mailbox. I walk toward the light. I look to my legs, and I'm wearing Dad's boxers, the same ones I used to wear. My legs are those twiggy things they once were with mosquito bites and the poison ivy, but it doesn't itch because this is heaven. And I'll be that little boy again but with a real boy penis this time appropriate to my age with the little strawberry-colored nub that floats up in the tub while I'm in the bubble bath. My hair will be short and parted on the left. Bunny will be at the top of the drive, and she will pick me up and carry me into the house and I'll smell the lavender shampoo in her hair and beer emanating from her pores. She will be my big sister again. My best friend. Mom and Dad and Kelley and Nina will be there too. The barn cats, horses, pigs, cow, chickens, rooster, pony, they'll all be there. It will be Fourth of July and family and friends will be in the pool, Mom will smoke unfiltered cigarettes with impunity with her best friend, Mrs. Petrovic, and we'll all eat roast pig and lamb. I'll meet Dad's grandparents for the first time ever. Busia will bring the *czarnina* and Jaja will bring the wine. I'll look as if I'm too little to drink but I'll drink anyways because in heaven you're any age you want to be and in whichever body you want to be, and it will be fine for me to have a drink with my great-grandparents.

Then I think everything will feel good. But I don't know. I always want the things I want and work very hard to get them and then once I have them, I don't know if I want them anymore. Maybe I won't like heaven.

Out on the porch, a mosquito landed on my arm and I brushed it away. It was getting warmer out. My body felt itchy. There were lots of bugs. I liked them, though. The flying insects, different types of butterflies and moths, wasps, large bumblebees that drank from our yellow nasturtium flowers in the garden, they were all often covered in pollen, and I was happy they liked the flowers I planted. I loved the pollinators.

I continued to stare out into the forest. I thought of other pollinators like Mom and Dad. I'd like to believe they will both live to one hundred years old. It's unlikely, though. Dad has already lost three out of four siblings. He and his brother, who is ten years younger than him, have outlived everyone else. And while that younger brother is already in a wheelchair, Dad is still out in the garden. But it's hard to think about. When I look into Dad's eyes, I see fear. Mom has had many health problems over the last ten years. She's stubborn as hell, though. When the Grim Reaper comes for her, she'll tell him to fuck off. When I look into Mom's eyes, I see fight.

Regardless, the death of my parents is bound to happen. It's something we prep ourselves for a long time to experience. The shortness of life when compared to everything else is a very scary thing. A blip. I feared it. And once death happened to me, I wondered who I would inhabit, or where I'd go—maybe back to that farmhouse, or maybe into another me trying this all over again. There were plenty of dead people inside me already. There were plenty of other versions of me inside of me too.

My dream had been strange. It was like Dad had emerged from inside of me more strongly than ever this past year, and now I had fears I'd never had before. Fears of the worst possible scenarios, things that were extremely unlikely to happen. Things I had never worried about before, or if I had it hadn't been debilitating, whereas now they kept me from sleeping. My whole life he'd been tilling my brain like he did Grandpa's fields. His seeds had turned to sprouts.

I had learned in Alcoholics Anonymous, while doing the Fourth Step—which reads, "Make a searching and fearless moral inventory of ourselves"—that almost every behavior I had ever displayed was based on a deeper fear. That every action, good or bad, I'd taken had come from a need to stifle those fears. The idea behind making a searching and fearless moral inventory was to get it all out, to recognize what those fears were, and by getting it out knowing that there weren't any fears that couldn't be overcome.

I wasn't in the program anymore, clearly, but that didn't stop me from thinking about it, sometimes longing for it. I had felt safe there, unafraid.

I sat for a while, still staring at the trees. I thought about everything I was thinking. I finished my beer and got up to get another. I got another cigarette. The sun got higher, and a shadow fell over my chair, but I stayed there as it got warmer out. The chill of morning didn't usually last long this time of year. That was one of the beautiful things about the Upper Peninsula. The weather was perfect summer weather, never too hot. Perfect, if you didn't mind the bugs.

I decided to write a fear inventory. If I wrote it down, as I once had, then maybe the fears would go away or lessen. Maybe I could sleep better. Maybe I'd be better in general, getting it all out on paper. Maybe I wouldn't be so fearful. So I began:

I'm terrified by all that I fear:

—How easy it would be for an intruder to break into the cabin. A big guy, or multiples thereof, many big guys, because of course it'd be guys. Ladies don't just break into cabins. Would we be here or would we not? Would they be coming for us or just looting the place? Or more simply with intent to vandalize? They'd pour gasoline around the perimeter and strike a match or throw a Molotov cocktail through the window, blow up the place. They could or would have guns, depending if it was premeditated or a crime of opportunity while out on their snowmobiles, when no one else would possibly be out here because it's nearly impossible to pass when there's snow even with a machine designed for such terrain and weather. Crimes of opportunity are around every corner. There're many places to hide a cadaver or two.

Would the intruders come through the basement or one of the windows or just through the door? Bust it open? There are no deadbolts. I've locked myself out and easily slipped back in with a credit card and ID. IDs are usually better for this sort of thing, being a little bit stronger. But the intruders wouldn't have either. Their IDs were probably confiscated by the authorities after a second or third DUI. Having not completed the AA meetings required to get the slips signed for the court, they would be without. And there is no easy way to get a credit card if you have a few other cards that are already maxed and expired. Bust it open is what they'd do. They wouldn't be afraid of making noise because there is no one out here to hear them.

Because of this horrid thought, before bed I pushed a small table in the loft to the top landing of stairs, then stacked two chairs on top of it and several behind it. I figured them having to climb over that would give enough time for me to get the loaded cowboy gun, which was on the dresser behind the picture of Anna and me at the wedding shower her family insisted on throwing for us.

—All the ways I could die out here. Wolves and bears, though they are the least likely but I can't shake it. More likely is cancer: brain, throat, lung, breast, I could go on—the possibilities are endless. They say not having children puts you at a higher risk for one or the others, mostly breast. Is that true or just some sort of propaganda to get humans to procreate? It's hard to know these days what is real and what isn't. I drink one cup of green tea every day steeped with shaved bits of chaga and turkey tail fungus. These are said to be cancer-fighting agents. But then I also smoke cigarettes so it gets cancelled out. I don't smoke many, but still.

During hunting season, I could get hit by a stray bullet. Hunters wouldn't be expecting me to be searching for mushrooms even though I wear the DayGlo beanie. If they're firing a gun with a larger caliber, a bullet could reach me somewhere they didn't even know I was walking. That would be terrible but could be a much faster end than cancer or a crime of opportunity.

Among the many possibilities when it comes to dying, there're also falling asleep at the wheel, heart attack, and stroke—Bunny was killed by one of those. There's high blood pressure—Dad's got that. A logging machine with the long saurian neck busting through the windshield while I drive past. The tall piles of logs tumbling down on me as I rumble over the washboard path. A head-on collision with *King Tom* or *Whiskey Bent* or the guy who's best in the bush. I shouldn't assume that's a guy but come on, I probably can—though women can and do drive logging semis.

A multitude of forest fires. Or a fire in the cabin caused by the creosote build-up in the chimney, just as Dad feared. A propane gas leak, asphyxiation. Drowning in the river. Mis-identifying a poisonous mushroom. Some unknown allergy. A poisonous spider bite though I don't think we have many poisonous spiders out here, but you know what I'm saying. Exhaustion. Appendicitis. The chainsaw could slip while I'm cutting firewood, hit my leg at a major artery, and I bleed to death. Bleeding to death in general—the hospital is more than an hour away.

—How we'll never catch up financially. I fear something will happen, any number of things, and we won't be able to operate and certainly won't have the money to refund people. The pandemic set us more than a year behind. There were lots of necessary refunds, and many other related expenses for that matter. We will be hosting guests for another year and a half before we can make any more money and we'll continue having to sell reservations, popups, and classes well into the future to keep going. This is what I fear most about that: something will happen to me, any of the above, and there will be no way to make people whole. We'll have to sell everything and still won't be able to get people their money back. Gambling addiction runs in my family. I fear it's got me by the balls, because why else would I be doing this? Even with many years of Michelin stars behind me, the restaurant industry is a gamble. Though I don't gamble like lottery or casino type of gambling.

—If I've become Dad, would I be as dangerous as him? I worry about it more and more with each passing day. I've always had anxiety, but I am inheriting his anxiety and his fears. They're different than mine; they've always been more intense. I fear fear, and I'm anxious about it.

—Late-stage capitalism, the crumbling economy and infrastructure, globalization, plastics and microplastics in everything. Billionaires going to space for no good reason. Wildfires, dwindling freshwater reservoirs. Melting ice caps, rising sea waters, dying ocean life, overpopulation. And logging, the destructiveness of which I witness daily.

—That I'll never be able to sleep well again. It used to be so easy when I ran the restaurants full-time. I fell asleep from pure exhaustion yet now it's somehow that the exhaustion is the very thing keeping me up. My brain is on fire. When there are guests at Milkweed it's nearly impossible to fall asleep, even if I go through all my mental lists of wild edibles. Recently I began using a mantra: "It's okay, you're okay, it's okay, you're okay." I'm mostly worried about keeping them safe among the wilderness. There are so many things to worry about when you host city slickers in the wild.

Then there was the other night when I fell asleep just as the light was showing behind the curtains. I woke up from the beginning of a dream I couldn't remember to the buzzing of my phone on the nightstand. I didn't want to look at it. My bladder was full, and I knew if I made it the twenty feet to the bathroom, if I gave in to the sweet release, which would be heaven, I'd be up for another hour staring blankly at the ceiling, listening to every noise that happened in and outside of the cabin. Listening to the footsteps of strangers milling about, starting the coffee, sitting on the porch, chitchatting, reading, working remotely, their stomachs grumbling for the breakfast I would soon get up to make for them. The wooden fence gate around the small yard would open and close as people came in and out to hike or do their morning jogs. That sound was a trigger for the dogs. I imagined people in their rooms, wearing the robes we've provided, stretching, yawning, bright-eyed, excited about what they'd do today in the forest—hiking, kayaking, archery, bocce ball, reading, enjoying nature—and the food they would eat and the drinks they would have (all of which I am happy to provide). I thought of my prep list. I had to roll out the handmade tortilla dough and cook it on the cast iron, bake bread, cut the pasta for lunch, prep the sauce, shape roses out of fermented wild apple leather, bake deer-shaped crackers, pop out owl-shaped butters, rehydrate mushrooms in stock, pick berries from the yard, wood sorrels, nettles, flowers from the garden, the list went on.

When guests were here, I spent most of my time in the kitchen and Anna gave them activity suggestions and set up some of the games for them. She reminded them not to play with the bows and arrows if the dogs were in the yard. Some people are cat people and not dog people and it's surprising the things you must inform them about dogs. Most people went on hikes. They collected every mushroom they found and brought them back to me like cats with mice, laying the presents at my feet. Like I said, I'm not a mycologist so I didn't know all of them. I got out my mushroom identification books, along with the old one from the library where Dad had the names written in Polish next to the common names. I looked with my guests for the unidentified mushrooms and sometimes I showed them how to do spore tests on my black apron or white apron to see what would happen. This helped us determine the edibility. It was a sweet activity we did together.

I turned on my side and that didn't help my bladder. It's just so small. I rested there for a moment and opened my eyes enough to see a missed call: *Mom (2)*. Shit. It was 6:49 AM. That meant it was 5:49 AM by her. She'd always been an early riser, but this was a little early for her, especially since she hadn't been working. I closed my eyes and when I did, I saw her lying at the foot of our back stairs. I shook the image from my head then saw her on the floor of her room as she called, struggling to get a hold of me, struggling to get up, her arm was broken. She called because she didn't know what else to do, even if I was six hours away. I was convinced something serious had happened.

Mom had been prone to falling and hurting herself. She's a seed now. I'd love to tell her she has another twenty years but it's not likely. I really hate the idea of this. Sometimes I wonder how I will survive it, but I know people who love their mothers survive their mothers' deaths every day.

Either way, I couldn't fall asleep again. Not now. I propped myself up on my elbow and called her back. In the bed, Anna and three of our four dogs crowded together. Our bedroom was warm. My breasts and armpits were sweating. That was a new thing that started to happen to me. I think because of my age, I was more warm than cold and odd parts of my body were often sweating, sometimes for no good reason.

I called Mom back.

The phone rang once before she picked up. "I'm sorry, so sorry. Didn't mean to call you. Accident. Just taking the dogs out."

"Are you okay?" I asked, the first words of the day cracking from my throat, over my dry lips.

"Yes. Good. Just taking dogs out. Accident. So sorry." She apologized over and over. I was pissed but I couldn't be pissed. Butt dials happen. I call people with mine all the time. I hear a voice coming from my back pocket. Sometimes it's people I've never met and have no idea how their number is in my phone.

Mom knew it was early and that Saturday mornings were the busiest day of my week. She knew I needed all the little bit of sleep I could get, and she knew she had woken me up. And she knew because I'm her daughter that there was no way I was going back to bed. *Fuck.*

"Okay. Good, you good?" I asked.

"Sorry. Yes."

"Okay, love you, bye."

"Love you too." I set the phone down and stared at the ceiling. My bladder was pounding. Then from the other side of the bed, oceans of dogs away but so god-damned close, I heard a voice and turned over. Anna was on her side with her phone in her hand, facing me, but watching the screen.

"You've been up this whole time?" I didn't even realize.

"Yes," she said.

"Did my phone wake you up?" I thought maybe the buzzing that woke me up got her up too.

"No, my feet are screaming." Anna has arthritis in her ankles. Her feet get swollen and it's hard for her to walk. She's only thirty-two, but there will be wheelchairs or bionic ankles in our future. I'm not sure which way it will go. I guess it depends on our healthcare system in this country, another thing to worry about, because god knows we don't have the finances to fix her up. Back in the day, we got married earlier than we meant to for insurance purposes, and we still pay lots of money every month for the minimum coverage. I rubbed her shoulder, knowing it wasn't going to do anything to help her.

"Can I get you anything?" There was nothing I could do but I asked anyway. One because I love her and two because that's what you do with your partner. I wouldn't get up for my bladder, but I'd get up for her if she needed something. I'd be pissed about either one, though.

That's just how I wake up in general. I'm not a morning person. I'm a little pissed, inside and out, until I've had my first cup of coffee, but I try not to let anyone know. Anna knows that about me, as do others close to me. But I think that my being pissed is part of the reason why Anna fell in love with me—one time she said she figured that if people were pissed about things, it meant they were also passionate about things too. It's not completely true, but it's also not false.

I gave in to my bladder and went to the bathroom. I used to wet the bed and my pants. Of course, I was much younger then, but those things stick with you for life. Did to me. I'll always fear wetting the bed. Anna was curious when we were first together why I got up four times within the first hour of laying down for the night. I told her if I woke up in the middle of the night and needed to use the bathroom, I'd be up the rest of the night. It was an anxiety thing, and that's mostly true, but under the anxiety was the fearful child who wet the bed. At home, at my cousins' house, at friends' houses, I woke up in my onesie pajamas, the kinds with the zipper along one side from the ankle to the collar bone, soaked down the back. That pajama outfit when wet was itchy. Wetting the bed is something you don't forget.

—Cyberwarfare, government spies, malware. All my passwords were recently breached in a data leak. My email has been hacked. There's identity theft, misinformation, and all the online forums where people claim the use of free speech to hate each other. Social media might be the most problematic of them all.

—There are the undeniable fears of the past. I have in my memory bank the orated stories of my family's history, all the various traumas, ailments, afflictions, anxieties, addictions. Some of these are public knowledge, having been written out and made public in the newspaper: my aunt who stole my grandma's money, my alcoholic uncle who for once got sober and was ironically killed by a drunk driver, my sister who died in jail. Then there're the ones that are supposed to be secret: adultery, illegitimate children (some born of rape), incest. The whispers about the uncle who raped the aunt. The

170

other uncle who beat his children. The uncle who tormented my sisters and tried to abuse me.

There are fears that are bankable, reliable, recidivist— the repeat offenders, the cycles of abuse: mental, emotional, physical, sexual, fiscal. The ones you need therapy and a good deal of soul searching to break.

—And the real killer: grief. I'd say that's something to fear, the worst of them all. I fear it, very much. Grief is the one that settles in your marrow, links to your DNA. That's the one that tears you apart. I wouldn't ever rule out dying of a broken heart. After Bunny died, I felt like I could never have a healthy relationship with anyone, ever again. Abandonment. I thought anyone just could or would *go*, whether on purpose or accident. They'd just go. How could I let myself love someone when eventually they'd be gone? Despite myself, I have. I worried about what would happen to them, and what would happen to me when something happened to them. Or the other way around. I knew the rest of my family felt the same way. After Bunny died, we didn't hug or kiss as much, it was like invisible barriers formed around us. We didn't spend as much relaxed time together. There was always this thing, no matter what. It felt impossible not to have it. Even if I wanted to let it all out, there was still the wall. The best I could do was write about it. Tell strangers, you, how I feel and what grief is like, though maybe you already know.

My family will read this and they will know, though I think they already do. We just don't talk about it. I mean we do, but not about the deep-down stuff. There's nothing like it, though. Nothing. Grief may be the worst thing I've ever experienced and at the same time the only thing that keeps me going. I have lived through it, but it scares me half to death.

Animals or pets die, grandparents die, and that grief is understood. We're primed for those early on; we experience them as some of our first bouts with grief. We all expect our grandparents to die. Then there are incidents with goldfish from the county fair, other pets, the ones we treated like family—Lucky.

We know someday our parents will die too but that isn't so easy to think about. Siblings die, friends die, spouses die, even some people's children die. My parents had a child who died. I had a sibling who died. I've had friends die. And among all those faces of grief there are also stillbirths and miscarriages.

—There's the death of others by homicides, suicides, school shootings. Mass shootings. Shootings in general. There are many ways to die and many ways to grieve. It's all heartbreaking.

—Guns are scary too. Of course, many people really like guns. They think guns are good. "The right of the people to keep and bear Arms, shall not be infringed," and all. Anna and I have guns, sort of a lot, but I rarely shoot them. I'm afraid. Though once I knew how to do it just right. Dad's friend Rick said, "Your boy's a good shot," or something like that, referring to my five-year-old self.

Dad loves his guns. He owns thousands of dollars' worth of guns, collector's items, guns from the Civil War, Korean War, Vietnam War; AR-15s, AK-47s, sawed-off shotguns. He loves his guns and he's always voted Democrat. He's a Blue Dog, union Dem and never has he worried they would take away his guns or ammo. Now, he's not a great shot any-more, but he truly loves handling them, sighting them in, target practice, hunting, clay pigeons. He used to love to scare other men with them, threatening to blow their brains out when they brought my sisters home past curfew. The man just loves his guns. He's told me, and I know this is something he thinks is very special and meaningful, that I will get all his guns when he passes. I've prepared myself for that enough that I know I don't want anything. Things like settling estates don't always go pleasantly, so if I get his guns that's fine, but if I don't get anything that's fine too. What I want is him. That's the most important thing, and that is something I can't have forever.

When we moved to the wilderness, Anna's stepdad, the auto salvage magnate of Somewhere, Indiana, brought us one of his old shotguns. It was a nice shotgun but just a bit older. I can't remember who the maker of it was. It was a 20-gauge. He brought the ammo along with it in a tattered box. When he first got here, he told us the cabin and being out here in the forest was nice and all, but that he wanted to get us something from his trunk. He went back out and I couldn't see what he was doing until he stepped from around the CR-V. I could see it then, a shotgun wrapped in a brightly colored plaid flannel blanket. He brought it up to the cabin and I took it from him on the porch. He handed it over like there was a baby inside. I walked through the doors with it. He and Anna followed me. It felt ceremonial. He said we were going to need it, "two girls out here, looking like y'all do, pretty. Some bad guys could have bad things in their mind and come on out." He loved us. This was how he knew to help protect us. It was the same with my Dad. The transfer didn't happen in the same way with the guns or ammunition, and Dad didn't say the same things, but he was thinking them. He blamed his worry on the bears and wolves but truthfully, his fears were also about the men who could be out here. They both knew bad things could happen because in their lives they had either been those bad guys or knew those bad guys or fought those bad guys or any combination thereof.

—And then there are viruses too. Viruses that have begun because of our encroachment into the natural world and the manipulation of it for power, money, greed. Viruses that cause pandemics like covid where more than a million people died from what perhaps could have been more preventable. All the funerals no one was even able to attend. All the deaths. That we have lived through it with these broken hearts is unbelievable.

—In addition to all these fears, there's millions more and if I thought about all of them, I'd never sleep again. Most fears are speculative. Things that *could* happen but are unlikely. But they've happened to others, and I know because I've seen it or read about it or maybe it was a past life, either way, I felt it hard. And those things that have happened to others, those people's fears that they may have overcome because they've been through them, are still my fears. I fear them for myself. I fear them for others. Some fears are inescapable. And there are fears out there I don't have but someday I might.

⌒

And after all this inventory of fear, I concluded the most important thing I must do is outlive Mom and Dad. I put down my pocket notebook and pencil. I sat for a while longer. I had another beer and cigarette. I felt like I could go back to bed. It was 10 AM. I could sleep two more hours and get up again at noon. I had garden work to do.

I watched the trees, thinking how as long as they stood still, they never seemed as restless as I felt. I thought about what trees I could plant for my family out here. We didn't have any black walnut trees up here. I loved black walnuts, but I didn't think that was the answer.

My next thought was immediate. Beech and oak! I'd plant as many oak and beech trees as the loggers had taken out—more so. I'd plant them and with each tree I'd bury one of my fears. I decided I'd give them all away. The oak and beech trees wouldn't be afraid.

CHAPTER 11.
FISHING

THE MUSHROOMS WEREN'T POISONOUS, BUT I DID A
spore test anyway. Dad would have wanted it that way. Even
if he knew a mushroom was a verified, safe, edible mushroom, he'd still say, "Watch out now." He'd want me to boil
that mushroom three times for ten minutes each. Eat only
an eighth of it. Then wait twenty-four hours to see if I had
any side effects. Then and only then should I consider using
them. With all his nonsense he'd even made me a little afraid
of some mushrooms that I knew were fine.

I did the prints anyways because I liked doing them.
They were beautiful. Sometimes the spores on my black
or white apron ended up looking like a work of art. They
showed up white, pink, mauve, brown, and other colors too.
After the first time Anna saw the prints I did on my aprons,
she liked it very much. She got me black construction paper
and white construction paper so I could set mushrooms on it

with their pores or gills or ridges, depending on the type of mushroom, facing down. The spores fell out, and if she liked the print, she would set and frame it. I don't know how she set it. I didn't ask. Once I knew if it was edible or not, that was where my task ended and hers began.

Dad always wanted to know what I was doing out here. There were things I did that I just couldn't tell him about. I kept him updated to the best of my ability, in a way that kept him from having a heart attack. I gave him pieces of information, the necessary stuff. But like the time I saved George from the river, I talked to him that night, and left out the jumping in the river part to rescue the dog. He would have told me never go into that river again. I sent him pictures of mushroom prints instead and he said, "You done real good. Keep on doing that with every mushroom you find." It wasn't realistic, but I was careful and anxious myself, so, you know, I wasn't going to eat any mushroom or serve any mushroom I couldn't identify. Dad was living if not in me at times, like in my dreams, then vicariously. He listened as well as he could when I told him about my days. And he reminded me to take the gun every single time and I said, "I will," but that was a lie.

⌒⌔

Before I did the prints that day, it was 10 AM when on the porch I grabbed a mesh sack, two reel rods, the tacklebox, one net, a netted hoodie to prevent mosquitoes from biting my face, a single can of bear spray and one can of bug spray, the ends of a bread loaf, and a bit of salt.

At the bottom of my tacklebox I had a tofurkey and sauerkraut sandwich I'd grilled the night before with pepper jack cheese, mustard, and a remoulade I made with wild capers. A cold Reuben was a wonderful snack in the forest. I wrapped the sandwich in wax paper and secured it with a rubber band that didn't squeeze it too tight. The sauerkraut was home-made and extra flavorful. I made the sauerkraut by using the green cabbage our local farmers grew. I sliced it thin and added 3 percent salt by weight of cabbage. I massaged it hard until the cell walls were broken and the salt and water from the cabbage created their own brine. I allowed it to sit in that brine, packed airtight in a jar, covered with cling film, and after anywhere from ten to fourteen days I checked the flavor. When it was tart, had the proper salinity and crunch, I stored it in smaller jars in the refrigerator. I didn't pasteur-ize it with heat unless I was going to keep it on the shelf. Without the heat process I found it kept a more pronounced tartness and crispy quality. The capers I used for the remou-lade were a mixture of green elderberries, unripe blueberries, and pine flowers that I fermented with 1.5 percent salt for two weeks and then stored in a light vinegar brine. In the remoulade I also used harissa, mustard, hot sauce, egg yolks, and wild berry vinegar that I emulsified with canola oil to create the thick base. Then I folded in the wild capers along with pickles that I'd made from other wild ingredients like beech leaves, thistle stems, and milkweed flowers. It was a delicious remoulade.

The mesh sack with the bread ends and salt went over my shoulder. I'd put the sandwich in the bottom of the tacklebox with the bear and bug sprays and all the other things: hooks, weights, bobbers, flies, and worms I'd found under logs that I stored in a small container with soil and a few holes poked into the lid. There were also little, shiny ornamental lures that looked like small minnows, extra fishing wire, nail clippers. And two beers.

Yeah, I've been drinking again if you didn't catch that earlier. I'm an alcoholic, as you may know, which I wrote about in my first book. Addiction is not an uncommon thing to write about. And if you didn't already know I was alcoholic, you might have thought as much from reading here about my family history. Addiction has got many people gripped by their sometimes long, saggy balls. Lots of people count their sobriety by days and hours. There's an app that will track it down to the minute if you want to follow it that closely. As of this point in time, while writing this sentence, seven hundred and twenty-one days (due to leap year) is the amount of time I've been unsober—though I haven't been drunk that whole time, I've only gotten drunk about three times in all those days, and I haven't blacked out once. The times I've gotten drunk were because I ate psilocybin and that kept me awake and drinking. Now, I have a few drinks every day. Probably more than the two-drinks-a-day maximum for women that is suggested by professionals, but I don't know. Knowing what I know about drinking and family history, this is playing with fire.

You probably wonder what happened. Everything and nothing happened, that's sort of how things like this go. One day your shoe comes untied and the next day you're having a glass of whiskey. So, it went:

The date was in June 2020. The next day would be Mom's birthday, so it's an easy date to remember, but also you don't really forget these sorts of things.

I was making the bed in our four-sided wall tent that

peaked at the top like a very small A-frame house. The tent was twelve by twelve feet on a wooden platform that was fourteen by fourteen feet. It was one of the accommodations for our Milkweed guests, though in 2020 we didn't have guests because of the pandemic. The tent was a nice structure. The walls were a thick canvas, there was a screened window that zips, and the roof had a small chimney hole that had fireproof material around it. There was even a wood-burning stove that went inside of it, but when we had guests, we didn't encourage them to use it unless it was below forty degrees Fahrenheit. Later, we'd even take it out of the tent due to potential hazards. All I can say is we've learned along the way.

After I made the bed, I stood there for a while. I didn't quite know for how long.

Anna and I had slept in the tent the night before because I liked that room, very much. The room also had a full-sized bed with mosquito netting around it and, basically, the whole thing was dreamy. Anna was good at decorating things; she'd made it more than pleasant. The bed's frame was new, topped with a fresh mattress. At that point, the room had only been used five or six times the year before, 2019, when we had our first season. The mattress especially, was satisfying. Without guests in 2020, we'd been spending a lot of our time doing things like that—testing out the different accommodations, keeping the place up, caulking, keeping out mice, organizing leftover items from the previous owners into "keep" and "donate" piles, starting gardens—learning what did and didn't do well in the soil, which was mostly sand. The earth here wasn't like the Indiana soil where I'd grown up, where all you'd have to do is till, lay out some manure, and then plant seeds. We cleaned the basement, scoured the walls, filled holes, chopped wood, patched screens. We did all sorts of things that we wouldn't have been as free to do otherwise given time constraints. But we were also restless. *Or maybe it was just me?* I needed things to do. We had been three months into a pandemic and out of work for the most part. Anna was immune-compromised, so we had to be careful. People were protesting elsewhere because of the terrible death of George Floyd. Everything felt uncertain. Keeping in motion was the only thing that felt certain to me.

So there was the pandemic, but also a racial reckoning nationwide, even worldwide. I felt ashamed of how privileged I had been, and still am. I had been living in a liberal bubble, thinking people wanted the world to be better. Though of course I wasn't completely blind. I'd already been feeling the trauma that came with the four years of our president at the time, who we feared could be on his way to re-election. I'm sure others saw it differently and that was because there were now two different worlds. I knew in 2016 that things weren't anywhere near as good in this country as I'd thought they were. But in the spring of 2020, the talons dug in. I was unbearably sad. I was experiencing the slow-burn trauma so many of us were as the pandemic raged. I hated how I felt so bad when I knew so many people were worse off than us.

Not long before that date I'd had an unviable pregnancy. The possibility of becoming pregnant again seemed like not only a bad idea, what with how the world was, but also becoming less and less likely. I was over forty. I mean, I was a middle-aged white woman with pretty much everything she ever wanted. *Really, a child though? Was it even right to pass along my genes?* At times it felt like a crime against humanity to do such a thing. Wanting a child felt selfish.

Maybe it was that hole I thought I needed to fill? If I could create the same magic at the cabin that I'd loved about the farmhouse—the birthdays, holidays, experiences of nature I'd had—I thought it could bring me closer to what felt like home. The idea that I could try to do that for someone else seemed exhilarating. And I know people will say that I do this for our guests, but I don't know if it's the same. The truth is, child or not, the hole will always be there. I believe it is how I am wired.

Anyways, I had gotten solar panels put in that summer, and with those, along with the batteries, propane, septic, and deep well, I was nearly set for the coming of the end of the world. I felt good about being prepared. I was off the grid, deep in the wilderness. I wasn't so much living as I was secretly prepping. As a joke, Anna tells people I'm a nihilist. It's not always a joke though. She also says I'm on the autism spectrum, obsessive-compulsive, anxious, depressed—so yeah, it's not always a joke. Although not everyone understands, that's also just sort of how alcoholics can be. Alcoholism is an umbrella and often many of those things fall beneath it. I would still say that I'm alcoholic more than anything else. I still believe that when in AA they say that belief in a higher power could fix these things, these maladjustments to life, these terrible obsessions and behaviors associated with it, *these fears*, that they're right. Over the years I've tried hard to pray and make that happen for me. Sometimes it worked. I went through stretches where everything rolled off.

Where I wasn't so often afraid. AA is a great thing. It saves lives. At one time, it saved my life. I wouldn't be here if it weren't for all those years I didn't drink.

I'm not sure how long I stood there in the tent, staring at the pillows, thinking a million things at once, my thoughts fluttering back and forth like the aspen leaves. That was when I decided I was going to have a drink. If I'm being honest with myself, I had already been thinking about it. It wasn't like a light switched on. At the beginning of the pandemic Anna started drinking whiskey. She'd never really been a whiskey drinker. It was always wine before, but we didn't have the same easy access to wine anymore, and we had not been in Chicago at all for the first month or so of the pandemic. We had gone to her parents' house, at the junkyard, and her parents at the time were snowbirding in Florida. Us being gone allowed space in our two-flat so Nina, an ICU nurse, could stay in our apartment and not have to be as close to Mom, who was seventy-six at the time and still got chemo infusions once a month.

The whiskey triggered me. The amount Anna drank at the beginning of the pandemic triggered me. I thought this was going to turn her alcoholic. She had it in her family like I did. But she had it under control and it wasn't her fault. It wasn't. It was just a trigger, making me think more and more about drinking myself. And I'd tried to bury the thoughts, but I couldn't.

I was sleeping most of the day. I'd lie down for a nap that would last five hours. I had kept myself so busy and when I suddenly wasn't I didn't know what to do with myself. Even though we kept in motion it felt like not enough. Feelings started to come up, things I hadn't really felt in years. I wanted to feel any other way than how I was feeling at that moment and that feeling was of having lost control.

I'm not using any of that as an excuse. What I'm saying is simply that I couldn't think about things anymore. I needed to numb myself. I felt Anna was sort of slipping away. Sometimes I think I decided to drink to get her attention. I'm always thinking—it's just not always right.

The moment I decided I was going to have a drink, I didn't call my sponsor, which I knew I was supposed to do. I had been sober for more than ten years for Christ's sake, I knew what to do. I just didn't do it. I hadn't been going to meetings—there were none anyways, aside from Zoom. Our connection was poor, being in the middle of the forest. If I had really wanted to stay sober enough, though, I could have gone to town to get better internet access to the meetings. There was always a way. Many people became sober during the pandemic. Either way, I didn't say anything to anyone. I didn't even tell Anna what I was going to do until I did it.

I went into the cabin and grabbed a squat whiskey glass, plopped in two ice cubes, and poured Lillet over the top. I went to the kitchen and peeled a thumb slice of orange rind over it, watching the oils spray from the skin as the sun came through the window onto our small bar area. The slice fell from the peeler and the ice snapped. I did this in front of Anna while she watched the news on her phone. It was that easy. I guess a part of me wanted her to see what I was doing and stop me, but she was having her own trauma. At that time neither of us were talking much or expressing anything about what we felt. We both assumed things were falling apart so we let it be that way. For many months we'd been living in the same space but in two separate, lonely worlds. Only at night did we collide before falling asleep with what seemed like a hundred acres of dogs, blankets, and life between us. And that's how it happened. It was that easy. It was that hard.

～

Though it was 10 AM, knowing all that I knew about these sorts of afflictions, I packed two beers into my tacklebox. I didn't want to get drunk. I wanted to feel normal and thought that's how you did it—do what normal people can do, like have a beer while fishing. I was testing myself. I guess I also still wanted to feel a bit numb. It's the same thing Mom said she wanted to feel when she used to drink in the morning. She asked me recently how many beers I drank a day. I said two, which was sort of true. She asked me if I ate breakfast first, and I said sometimes, yeah. She said she hadn't seen me messed up but thought something was wrong, that's why she asked. I said, "Maybe I'm just doing it like you used to do." Then she said, "Well, then that means there's something wrong." That's the thing with me, with alcoholism, something always might be wrong whether I'm sober or not.

Before I left the porch for the river, I stopped. The warbler was on her eggs. That was the good thing. My prayer or whatever it was had worked. The birds were back. They seemed happy. We might've had even more birds around us now. The loggers weren't as close but were several miles out, by where the ramps grew and I worried what that meant for the following season.

The warbler mom was a gem. I don't know if it was the

same warbler that I'd followed with my binoculars from the year before, but either way, she liked this spot on our porch. I hoped she felt as good above me in her nest as it smelled here in the summer, like wild carrot and milkweed flowers, pine, and sunbaked wood. It smelled good the way good moms could make you feel. It was how Mom made me feel.

I had seen the warbler mom land on the rim of her twig nest and drop tiny berries into where her babies were, their mouths wide open, and some of the berries had little bugs on them and green worms that moved over the surface by bringing their entire body into a high peak then lengthening out again. Truth was I couldn't see her babies or the little bugs and worms, but I imagined how it was happening.

At the pin cherry tree, before I went into the forest, I placed the bread ends and salt onto a bole covered in a velveteen moss. Then I walked into the forest. It was cooler there. Ferns reached my kneecaps. The clubmoss parted around my ankles. Where the blackberry thorns were they tore into my jeans, but I wore thick denim so the sharp tips couldn't get through. I set down the tacklebox and poles in the brush, stopping to tuck the ankle hems of my jeans into the elastic bands at the tops of my socks. It wasn't a cute look but a good way to prevent ticks. Ticks are creepy bugs. I liked the idea of living purely in the wild—camping out every night, foraging and fishing for every meal—but then I thought of all the ticks I'd have and it wasn't so romantic anymore. But if I had to—which someday I might, who knows—I'd do it no matter the cost: ticks, wolves, bears, coyotes, and all. They'd get to me anyway. So would the mosquitoes, land mollusks, moths, and biting flies. If I still believed in god, I'd ask god to make me a dryad, the mythological nature spirits that lived in trees. I'd pray like I once prayed to be a boy. God didn't answer me then, but maybe would change me now?

Before I fully descended the hill to the river, I looked to where I could see our bedroom window, checking if Anna was watching. She was probably still sleeping. If she wasn't sleeping, I didn't want her to see me leave the bread out. I didn't want her to see where I was going. She never minded the oddness of anything I did, but she'd have something to say about the bread and salt. She'd say I would be attracting predators. I turned, descending the hill, and Dad's voice started up: *don't go down there without the cowboy gun.* I shook out his voice and went on down the hill with my poles, net, sack, and tacklebox.

The forest was layered. From the pin cherry tree down to the river were beech, followed by birch and maple mixed with elm. Past that I crossed into pine, fir, spruce, and a thin grove of young hemlock.

The first time we made this trip to the river, back in 2019, I stopped and said to Anna, who was right behind me as we followed George, our Newfoundland, to the sound of the river, "Don't you smell cotton candy?" I looked up at the trees, some bleeding resin and others covered with a black fungus. I had put out my hands, palms up at the splendor. I inhaled again and said, "Oh my god. It's the trees." I inhaled deeper, closing my eyes. "These trees are candy!" I exclaimed.

Anna didn't feel the same. "Stop being neurodivergent!" she yelled, and continued, "George is going to jump in the water and we have no idea what's down there!" She was right. Back then, she was more anxious than me. We had no idea what the water would be like even though I had a feeling it would be okay. And it turned out that it was fine. That first time it was nice, and each spring when we got back to the cabin, we took a trip down to the river to see if anything had changed. Sometimes trees fell into the river or sometimes the river was higher than other times depending on how much snow had fallen during the winter.

On our first visit back in 2020, the second year out here, it wasn't fine. The largest cedar tree along the river had been struck by lightning and was half-submerged but also resting as a bridge to the other side. The river was higher because there had been a lot of snow that winter and the melt filled it. When we got here, there was still snow in the backyard, in the spots where it stayed shadowed for a long time throughout the day. But the river was quiet, even with the higher level of water. We didn't think about it having a strong pull because we had been in it before. You can't always tell what's under the surface; it was stronger than we knew and though the river flowed faster and higher, it moved quietly, without much texture, swirling softly around the fallen cedar's branches.

George jumped in as he always did. When he got to the middle where he couldn't touch the ground anymore, the current proved its strength, pushing him toward the cedar. He struggled against it. We watched for a moment. He's a water rescue dog. *Surely he would be fine.* The current pulled him into the fallen cedar's branches. As the branches touched the top of his head, we saw the fear rise in his eyes. Anna got nervous. I knew what would happen and gave her a stern look. If she screamed, it would only scare him more. I might have yelled at her, "shut up," before she said anything.

I began to undress. I took off my boots and jeans. It was fifty-five degrees that day, gray and cloudy. When Anna would later recall this story to others, she'd always talk about how I jumped in with my sweater and beanie still on. I intended to go in with just my underwear but when I saw George was about to go under the tree I immediately jumped in, sweater and beanie and all.

The river was like ice water. There was still snow where trees shadowed the riverbank. My sweater clung to my body and got heavy. When I got to the middle of the river, the current slammed me into the tree faster than it had George. I grabbed one of the cedar's branches as my legs were pushed under it. I held the branch tight. I paddled hard with my legs to get from under the cedar and maneuvered myself behind George. With one hand I searched under the water for his large bottom. I pushed him as hard as I could out of the current toward where Anna stood at the river's edge. Before she could grab him, he found his footing, got out, and shook off.

I used the branches like monkey bars, climbing my way out. One of the branches took off my beanie and when it fell into the river, it disappeared. After I got out, Anna rubbed my shoulders as I shivered from the cold. We quickly ran back up the hill, me still barefoot, hugging my boots and jeans to my chest. I called for the rest of the dogs. They didn't like water as much as George and had watched the whole incident from the sidelines. They all obeyed and followed behind.

I took a hot shower and put on warm pajamas. I drank a hot mug of jasmine tea and fell asleep on the couch with George's heavy head on my lap. The next day I had a fever and the skitters. I worried I might have covid but Anna looked up the symptoms of hypothermia. I had a mild case.

~

It was probably 10:15 AM when I got to the river and walked along it for a little bit. Right away I found three midsized *borowiki*. They were young and fresh. I sliced them at the base like I'd been told to all my life and added them to the mesh sack. According to my observations from the years prior, I knew the boletus would begin soon as the fly agaric came up. They'd start in the lowlands and by mid-August they'd make their way up the hillsides to the path. With all the logging over the past couple years I worried they wouldn't be down here, but a few had appeared.

The caps of the dark brown *borowiki* were covered in morning dew; the sun hadn't got to them yet. The pores on the underside were the color of a cultured cream or fresh churned butter. After I cut them, I turned them over, inspecting the slice in the stem for holes. Sometimes there were none, like this day. These were fresh and very young. If there had been a few small holes that would likely have been from beetle larvae. Even if there were a few holes the *borowiki* were still good. I'd slice them thin, making sure the beetle larvae were no longer present. I'd dry them or something of the sort, powder them, and later use it as a seasoning for sauce, or else mix the powder with salt. Sometimes I fermented them in 1.5 percent salt, using the liquid that came from them, salty and sour, as a seasoning. I suppose they'd be fine to eat with the larvae if there were just a few, but I didn't like that idea.

Other times, if the mushrooms were already mature, they

might be riddled with holes or gouges in the underside and sometimes even the cap where slugs or other creatures had gotten to them. When I saw *borowiki* in that state I didn't collect them because the cleaning would be too much. I left them so they'd release more of their spores. There were animals too who would still like to have them. Sometimes I'd step on them to really make sure the ground took the spores, but mostly I left them. I held up my mesh sack in the sunlight and admired the ones I had. These three *borowiki* were exceptional.

I found a nice spot on the river to settle. I climbed the lightning-struck cedar that reached across the river. Because of the situation with George, a few people had suggested I bring the chainsaw down here and cut it to pieces, sending the cedar logs down the river or hauling them back up to camp. Cedar is a softwood. It's easy to split. It burns quickly and doesn't give off much smoke like pine does. It would be nice for camp, but I didn't listen to them. I wanted it to stay where it fell. And because I did, I had this spot where I sat, away from everyone in the middle of everything.

The river wound downstream to the southeast. The sun was higher over the branches now and about to come over the water and eventually onto the back of my neck. Other logs and branches were in the river where lightning had struck in the past. The roots of the cedar dangled in the water with bits of dead leaves and soil hanging down and new things growing from them. The river went past faster than it looked. It pooled behind the splayed branches, which broke the surface in some parts. Dad said if I didn't go fishing first thing in the morning, even earlier than I was out here now, I'd need to find a shaded spot. I used the cedar like a bridge, sitting on its thick trunk, and figured the tree and the branches would cast a long enough shadow over the water. The pines on the other side of the river helped with shade. I sat with my legs crossed and my ankles under my calves. The tacklebox was to my right and the net and mesh sack to my left. I sat facing the way the river ran, along with the current. Before I did anything else, I ate the tofurkey Reuben.

I was satisfied. I pulled a cigarette from the breast pocket of my flannel shirt. I know it's not cool to smoke anymore. One day you do it to look cool and the next day you're addicted. Now smoking is just a crazy thing to do. You must admit that if you smoke, you're aiming for a slow death. I can't see it any other way, which is causing me a lot of anxiety, because despite everything, I quite like my life. I love it, to tell you the truth.

I placed the cigarette between my lips and before I lit it, I tied the rig to the line, placing a shiny fly at the end. I added one of the worms. I loaded the thing up. I didn't completely know what I was doing but I did what I thought needed to be done. *What would get the attention of a fish?* This seemed right. I pulled the rod back over my shoulder and, flinging it forward, I let my finger off the reel trigger so it would go far. I'd seen Dad do this. I'd done it with him. I remembered how Mom's stepdad used to stand in the yard and do this all day: cast, reel in, cast, reel in. I didn't really get to know him. He was alcoholic too, so I heard. I don't remember much about him aside from the casting. I don't recall ever talking to him. I do remember him telling me, and my boy cousins to "shut up." I remember his bathroom smelled like rotten tobacco and that I'd rather have wet myself and cried about it afterward than used his toilet.

The fly and worm bounced on the surface once, then sank down and were carried out with the water. I held the pole for a short while, waiting for the indicatory tug. When I realized nothing was going to happen, I opened a beer and lit the cigarette. This, I figured, was being normal.

The other side of the river, across this narrow, natural bridge, the land was untouched except for by me, maybe hunters who'd come before me, and definitely the true hunters and gatherers before us. This river, the Sturgeon River, had been used by many people though, and there were few to zero sturgeon left. On that other side of the river, seventy acres of land was also "ours." As far as I knew that land hadn't been tread on by Libertarians or lumberjacks or maybe any other person for a long, long time, which was for the best. I was probably wrong, though I wanted to believe it. That side was all trees—birch, cottonwood, hemlock, pine, and elm— climbing up the rise of the hill, with lots of cedars too, a large grove of them like a true cedar swamp was somewhere on that side. There were no paths, nothing. Old trees and young trees created a canopy so thick very little sunlight could enter.

The river mirrored the trees, rippling downstream. I watched how the simple, pinnate, compound, and palmate leaves trembled out from their fibrous petioles against the wind, just vibrating, making things feel calmer than they were, making me feel calmer on the inside too. A calm that felt eerie simply because it was calm. I looked behind me, feeling many eyes on my back. Like the wolves and the bears, the Leshy was probably sleeping or resting in the cool shadows. I concluded the eerie feeling was probably because I was out here, in the morning, drinking a beer in a way that I thought was somehow secret.

The current pulled my line far away and caught under something. I reeled it in knowing it wasn't a fish. The fly was still attached, though I had to tug it a couple times. The worm was gone. I opened the tacklebox to retrieve another beer. I crushed the first can and put it in the bottom of the box. I lit another cigarette. I didn't want to smoke or drink too much so I only had one cigarette to one beer. Never two cigarettes to one beer.

Now the sun was higher, warming the top of my head. I wore an electric lime-green beanie for high visibility. It wasn't hunting season, but I had to be careful. I heard gunshots all the time. I took the beanie off and placed it in the tacklebox. The river glowed and the cedar leaves spiraled on the water. It was dizzying. I should have had more than just one sandwich. After a few more tries, still not catching any fish, I moved further east, where there was more shade and another fallen cedar. I walked along its trunk. I balanced with my gear, feeling self-conscious, and I thought if anything the Leshy must pity me. The wide cedar bowed under my weight, but I felt steady enough.

I sat down, bending my knees and crossing my legs the same way I had done before. I cast out the line again. This cedar, a little fresher than the last, smelled better than any candle or oil that had its name. Feeling the effect of the beers, I lay down, holding onto the pole. The cedar moved gently like a hammock, powered by the water beneath it. I closed my eyes a little. *There was no need for religion or god when we had trees.* Then that voice, not Busia's or Wayne's, but instead maybe the one that comes along with the night terrors said, *Yeah, but the loggers. Soon there won't be any more trees here, which means no god.* I might have dozed off for a bit, thinking or dreaming of Dad and the many fishing stories he'd told me.

My line tugged. I had the handle of the pole between my arm and chest. I felt it pull. I opened my eyes. I sat up, nearly losing my balance with excitement. I reeled her in. A tiny fish smiled and frowned at the end of my line. Her skin was stippled with scales of silver, blue, and yellow. Globes of water flew from her tail as she pulled away from me. I reeled her in and grabbed hold of her with my net. She was a little longer than the length of my hand. I spread open the net. She looked wonderful. I gently removed the hook from her cheek and considered who else was under the water with her, who was still swimming, a mother perhaps, thinking she was right behind. I leaned forward and opened my palms, gently dropping her back into the river. A bit shell-shocked, she rested there for a moment before swimming quickly downstream.

CHAPTER 12.
CHANTERELLES

CHANTERELLES WERE DANGEROUS, IN A WAY, LIKE some men. Every time we hunted chanterelles it seemed like something bad happened. Like Mom, I too was becoming superstitious.

It was a warm August day. We were about to go to the county fair, a thing I adored. I counted on it and counted down to it. The fair was a defining event of summer, a punctuation of time as important as mushrooms, holidays, my birthday. I was in the yard with a bouquet of purple and white clovers in my fist. My legs were bitten from mosquitoes. I was trying to not scratch them because Mom told me not to. "That'll only make it worse," she said. She and I walked over to the paddock. I didn't have on shoes and the hard weeds and grass poked at the undersides of my feet. The ground was cool because a few days before it had rained. In some low spots the ground squelched under my feet and felt nice on my toes. I steered clear of the rooster who was on the far side of the barn, away from us, thrusting his neck back and forth, jabbing his beak into the grass. I wondered if he was eating bugs like crickets and grasshoppers. "Do the roosters eat bugs too?" I asked Mom.

"What do you mean, too?"

"I ate bugs."

"When did you eat bugs?" she asked me, wondering what the hell I was getting into.

"I eat bugs when I eat mulberries."

Her eyes got wide, remembering our conversation from before. She called me silly. She smiled with her smile that was missing teeth on both sides.

"Yes, they eat the worms and other critters," she confirmed.

At the paddock Mom rested her foot on the bottom slat of wood along the fence. I watched her and did the same. She rested her elbows over the top slat and pressed her palms together looking around. I did the same but with the bouquet of clovers. "Okay, here they come," she said. My sisters came out from around the side of the barn. The shod hooves of the horses clip-clopped. The horses whinnied. The buckles on their saddles clanked. My sisters tapped their heels against the horses' bellies and they sped up.

I didn't know it then, but this was going to be the last time they'd show their horses together in the 4-H. Mom would say they didn't want to do things like that too much anymore. That they were growing out of it. At another time in the future, I'd try to use that phrase and tell Mom I was growing out of school, but she didn't listen to me. But I didn't think Mom cared too much that they didn't want to do it anymore. She didn't seem to care about what they wanted anyways, or maybe it was because she didn't love the fair like Dad did or I did, though she was good at riding the rides.

Mom's best moves were on the Tilt-A-Whirl. She really whipped it. We spun so fast my head felt like it was going to fly off. From the sweat and elephant ear grease on Mom's face she looked as if sprayed with glitter. Her brown hair was scraggly from a grown-out perm. I thought the color was pretty though. Not "mousy" like her mother sometimes said. She said to her, "Sandra, it's mousy, you should dye it." Sometimes there's no use in listening to what others think.

Mom *really* swung it. Back then she was heavy and leaned over every curve. She said that was how you got to do it. She hollered, "Lanie, lean!" each time a curve came and the cart began to tilt. We flew across the slippery plastic seats from one side of the cart to the other. I was banging into one side or squished into Mom on the other. She felt good next to me like that, gravity pushing me into her soft extremities. My sisters, on the sidelines, waved every time we passed them. A big wave, all three at once, then a *whoomp, whoomp, whoomp*, the wind cut past our ears. We were happy, laughing and Mom didn't need beer that day, I don't think. Flying around like that, all you could do was laugh. I pushed the stuffed lion I won in the ring toss way up under my arm because losing him would be like losing this moment and I wanted to remember it for the rest of my life. Mom swung it hard all the way around. I swear to god I thought I was going to fly right out of there.

The county fair was a kind of midwestern circus. Instead

of lions and tigers and strong men, there were cows and pigs and farmers. Instead of elephants climbing onto boxes or clowns barrel-rolling, there were monster trucks with fat-limbed wheels stretching over squashed cars. The same kinds of tattooed men who drove the monster trucks also operated the rides. The air smelled like the buckets of pork blood Dad had in our barn. If you've made blood sausage before, you know this smell. Dad and I made it sometimes. I held the cold, slippery intestines while he stuffed in the ground muscle, suet, grains, blood, salt, pepper, and red wine vinegar. That smell though, you don't forget it. I could hear us in there, in the barn. His boots clobbering over the dirt floor and the soft clink of my cowboy boots against it. On the other side of the corrugated walls, the chickens clucked and skittered in the yard. I didn't have to imagine hard to see them. At the far end of the barn, the pigs grunted. I knew what they were doing too. In this barn we performed. I was the tiny clown, and he was the lion tamer putting his head in her mouth. He reminded me to keep away from the pigs, but I still climbed up the side of their pen and reached over to rub their proboscises.

When we got off the Tilt-A-Whirl my knees buckled. Mom giggled from the rush and dizziness. My sisters waved us over to them. "Was that fun?" they asked me. But I didn't have an answer. They knew.

⤝

But before the Tilt-A-Whirl and all that, back at home, Bunny appeared from around the barn on her horse, Strider, named after Aragorn from *Lord of the Rings*. She loved that series. My sisters had American Paint horses. Maybe that seems fancy that they had horses and cared for them because that's an expensive hobby, but back then you could be a steel worker and still afford horses at the auction if that's what your kids liked to do. Strider was blonde with a white diamond in the middle of her forehead that ended in a point between her flaring nostrils. Kelley appeared on Ranger. Ranger was the color of black walnuts after the husks were removed, with a shiny black mane and a large white spot over her right eye. And finally, Nina came around on April. April was all white, with a constellation of black freckles beginning at her nose that spread like the Milky Way over the rest of her body. But you could only see the freckles if you were up very close. Otherwise, she was pure white. The horses whinnied, and April lifted her freshly shod front hooves, paddling the air, and came down into the dirt with a thump.

Mom held me up and I held the bouquet of purple and white clovers through the parallel slats of two by fours, beneath the barbed wire and above the electric fence. Dad had built a fence suited for a fortress because he was always afraid the animals would get out. He imagined us in the yard and the horses stampeding or the hungry pigs making dinner of us. If the pigs had us for dinner he thought he would later find bones, fragments of our former selves, maybe a piece of jewelry, left in the piles of shit he grew the mushrooms on. And that's when we'd truly become the mushrooms.

Nina brought April to where Mom and I were at the fence. I offered her the bouquet, partly for the horse and partly for Nina. The thousands of hairs on April's snout tickled my knuckles and her big teeth delicately nibbled the clovers from my fist. "God damn it, careful!" Dad shouted. He went on, "She could bite your hand off." Dad imagined me bleeding to death after the horse bit off my fist. I knew that was what he imagined because he would grumble things like that preceded by the phrase, "God damn it," or something of the sort. Horses biting off hands or heads, pigs shitting us out, us falling and cracking our skulls open, the list goes on. Nina rolled her eyes and pulled April away, galloping off toward Bunny and Kelley. They tugged their horses' reins, guiding them into a triangle. Clip-clap, clip-clap, clip-clap, in unison they stamped the ground. I was anesthetized, first by the towering beasts, and second by my sisters. They were so cool with their hues of gold and brown hair that was very long, darker at the roots, and streaked with sun. They were lady centaurs in flowy blouses, Levi's jeans, and cowgirl boots.

Mom set me down on the grass. I had on a pair of dad's boxer briefs cinched at the top that hung down my legs like culottes (don't ask). I'd scratched at the mosquito bites around my ankles until they became scabby bumps. Mom looked at me and said, "Go put jeans on," but she knew I wouldn't do it. I didn't like jeans, so she'd have to put them on me if she wanted me in them. But I would wear them occasionally, unlike dresses. A dress for me was something I wouldn't let her get through the farmhouse's front door.

Anyways, when you lived in the country, bugs were nothing. I was used to the mosquito bites. I wasn't afraid of wasps either. I knew they wouldn't get me unless I made them mad. You couldn't be afraid of bugs or spiders, not even the black widows, of which there were few. Daddy longlegs aren't spiders, but they look kind of like spiders and you couldn't be afraid of those either. Those will never bite you.

Ants, millipedes, centipedes, silverfish, beetles, potato bugs, moths, butterflies, crickets, grasshoppers, cockroaches, all of them were around. The first time I stepped on a bee, on accident (it was always on accident), I cried, but that was probably only because it scared me more than hurt, because once Bunny stepped on a bee on accident too, and we had to rush her to the hospital because she was allergic. Mom and I were in the bathroom when it happened. I was naked, about to get in the tub, and my sisters started yelling. They were out in the yard, and we could hear their voices come in through the tented vent in the bathroom's block windows. At the hospital, Bunny got a shot and some Benadryl. She was out later that day. It was scary because before we got to the hospital, she was acting like she couldn't breathe. She was always the most dramatic of us, but I think she was for real that time.

And on that day, getting ready for the fair, in my room, Mom shoved my bumpy, bug-bitten legs into brown corduroy pants. These pants had an elastic waist, and I didn't mind them as much because the elastic made them more comfortable. They were too warm for the summer, but it was the only thing she could get in me to cover my legs. As it turned out, the scabby bumps I kept itching turned out to be poison ivy. That was just the beginning; I'd get poison ivy every summer after this. And eventually, someday, I'd become immune to it. Nowadays I can roll in it naked and be fine.

Mom got ready too. I sat on her bed and watched her change out her earrings and necklace. Mom had some jewelry she always wore and some that she changed out. She wore a lot of jewelry though it wasn't too fancy. Mostly her jewelry was nostalgic. She was like that. She said jewelry helped her remember people. She kept on certain pieces because she said that she could never take them off. I thought that's what people did, but when I got older, I knew it was really because of her superstitions, her OCD. When she was through changing and looked very nice compared to me, we went outside and stood in the gravel driveway. My sisters had already left with their horses in a trailer that they towed with the Ford Bronco. Dad let Bunny drive and Mom was unsure about that but went along with it. Dad had to stay back to finish the lamb with Mr. Petrovic. They were preparing the lamb for St. Sava's, the Serbian church, which was sponsoring the bingo hall at the fair. Mr. Petrovic was Serbian and many of Dad's ancestors had originated from that area before it was split up so he assumed he was both Serbian and Croatian. He had friends from both sides, and I guess that was a big deal back then because one didn't like the other because of the wars. When my sisters were younger and Mom was pregnant with me, they all took a family trip to Yugoslavia, such a big family trip that our extended family went along too. I've seen the film reels. That was when my cousin got the tick in his belly button.

Mr. Petrovic was my godfather and for some reason he always had his shirt off. If he wore jeans or pants it didn't matter. The pants were dirty, like car grease or maybe olive oil had gotten them. I'm not sure if he was a mechanic at the mill or what. His glossy skin was darker than Dad's and very pretty. He smelled like cigarettes and alcohol. And because he was always a little drunk I couldn't understand what he said. When he hugged me or lifted me up, it hurt. He was rough but also kind. I wasn't afraid of him like I was of Uncle Georgie.

Mrs. Petrovic was Mom's best friend. Soon after this summer in 1984, she'd get lung cancer and die. Mom, who'd smoked unfiltered Camels for thirty-seven years, would quit cold turkey the next day. Mr. Petrovic grew grapes in his yard. Some grapes were for wine, and some were sweet grapes such as Concord for snacking and jelly. He and Dad made wine together. They made it how Dad and Jaja, Dad's grandfather on his dad's side, made it. It was natural wine. They threw burnt hay on the top of it to stop the ferment instead of chemicals. I was too young to taste it. Dad only served it to me warm on the nights I had a cough. I remember the burning hay part though. Dad and Mr. Petrovic had barrels stacked on top of barrels. And before Mrs. Petrovic got sick, she and Mom would sit on the bench in the Petrovics' yard and watch the boys while smoking their cigarettes.

In their yard, I played beneath the willow tree. I swung on the branches, determined to be like Tarzan. The goal was to fly from the branches all the way into the pool. I imagined myself flying from branch to branch, then doing multiple flips and landing a perfect dive, like Greg Louganis. But the last time I was there the swimming pool wasn't ready yet, so there was a green layer of film over the top. Little weeds and things grew from it. Frogs, flies, gnats, and other bugs scuttled over the surface. Dragonflies flitted above.

~

Mom and I waited, sitting on the tailgate of the pickup truck. Dad and Mr. Petrovic wheeled Dad's metal rotisserie box out of the barn and into the driveway. Dad had built the rotisserie himself and he was exceptionally proud of it. He was a welder—that's what he did at the mill. We all knew he had built it because he told us. The rotisserie was a silver, spray-painted metal box. There was a motor and chain on the outside of it that made the pole spin. The coals were placed on the bottom, and on the pole about two feet above the embers they'd have the animal. On this day it was lamb.

The metal box had a lid that they would close after they removed all the embers. The whole thing was on wheels and had a hitch on the front so that you could tow it. They wheeled it out of the barn with the lamb inside, plus two other whole lambs they had previously cooked the same way and split up into large pans wrapped in foil that they had kept warm in the barn's heating boxes. Dad had the heating boxes from the restaurant they used to own. There were also two large pans full of *cevapcici* that Mr. Petrovic had made using lamb legs, bellies, and shoulders that they'd gotten from Mr. Elich, Dad's friend, when they picked up the whole lambs. Dad had ground those parts and mixed them with pig muscle and fatback he had frozen after killing one of our pigs that spring. He said it had to have the pig 'cause otherwise it'd be dry. The *cevapcici* was heavily seasoned and spiced. Mom said that Mr. Petrovic made the best *cevapcici* she ever had.

The men loaded all the pans and things into the bed of the pickup truck and covered it with a tarp. They put the rotisserie's hitch on the ball tow of the pickup and I rode with Dad to the fair while Mom rode with Mr. Petrovic in the station wagon.

This was the day of the fair's official start. My sisters were late getting there. Mom, always on time or early, said they should have had their horses there yesterday, but Dad said it didn't matter. Dad was mostly late. Mom was a morning bird getting up at five or six and Dad was a night owl, staying up anywhere from midnight until two in the morning. If he could, he slept till noon. I was more like Dad in this regard.

In the pickup Dad talked about the chanterelles we'd collected the day before. We'd forgot to bring them in with all the excitement of the fair and they were still in the cab, wilting. "Don't worry, they'll be all right. Mushrooms can dry out a little and they stay good." But I was worried. "They'll be all right," he said a second time because he could see I wasn't satisfied the first time. "We can go get more if these ones don't work out."

The day before, Dad and I had gone to Deep River, a park of several hundred acres about a mile away from the farmhouse. I loved Deep River. Deep River was full of old white and black oak trees, way too big to put your arms around, maybe a couple hundred years old; plus there were maples, cottonwoods, elms, black walnuts, buckeyes, hickory, and willows. There was a river but I always thought it was a joke being named Deep River because it wasn't deep at all.

I found the first chanterelle. I was worried I wasn't going to find any because we had gotten so many about a week before when we were at Grandpa Regan's farm. Even at that age I felt like the world had some sort of reciprocity thing going on and that there was only so much luck we could have without giving something back. I think I got that from Mom. Maybe because we kept taking and not giving was why every time we got chanterelles we had to pay in some way. Like the time I got caught in a sand tornado at Grandpa's—I still was sore on my shoulder and hip from where I had been picked up in the tunnel and thrown into the pile of hay. And that same day Uncle Georgie tried to do something bad to me, though he was prevented from it. It was things like that that were always happening with chanterelles.

I'd found the first chanterelle buried under a few leaves, just the rounded edge of the brilliant golden mushroom peeked out. Then we found several more and several more until we had about a pound of them. It was a good find. Dad said, "We done real good." I liked walking through Deep River's forest. There were odd tree knots and dens, wily bushes and branches. I thought the forest was enchanted because when I was in it, I knew I was under some kind of spell. I thought if I could live here instead of the mile away at our home, I would. "Don't you think we could camp here?" I had asked Dad while clipping a mushroom at the base.

"They don't allow camping here."

"No one would find us," I said, holding the chanterelle in my palm. It was so beautiful. He thought about this for a moment but then said, "We'll go camping on Grandpa's farm."

I wanted to go camping a lot. Really bad. I wanted to have a tent and fire and cook things over it. At that time I hadn't gone camping before, ever. To this day, I have never camped with either of my parents once, ever. But I sure didn't want to camp on Grandpa's farm—not where Uncle Georgie could be. "I don't want to camp too much. It's okay," I said, lying.

Dad said I always had to be careful in the forest, but Uncle Georgie being in a forest made it seem like the scariest a forest could ever be. Though at Grandpa's farm I did learn how to use Dad's cowboy gun. He taught me how to use it with his finger over mine on the trigger and I blew an empty beer bottle to smithereens. At least I knew how to do that, I figured, which made camping at Grandpa's seem less scary. Though I'd have to figure out another way to be in the forest, on my own terms. I promised myself I'd figure it out.

But that was the day before, and this day while in the cab of the pickup I had a bad feeling too. Already we had forgotten about the chanterelles in it. I was feeling suspicious.

It wasn't long after we got there, when in the Lake County Fair horse barn, the suspicious feeling left. After all, I was just a kid.

I felt good in my elastic-top corduroy pants, snap-buttoned shirt, and boots. I was going for a cowboy look and thought I was on point. I wore a ball cap with my hair tucked under it. I had slowly been building the courage and would eventually tell Mom I'd want it all cut off like a boy. Furthermore, my sisters were almost real cowgirls, and I pretended I was their little brother, and everyone more or less went along with it.

I loved my sisters. I told Dad they were princesses. Meanwhile, on other nights, he and I would pretend we were sword fighters, wielding large knives from Mom's drawer— but only the dullest ones. We dueled. Dad was the villain. That's because sometimes he was the bad guy. He made my sisters eat cigarettes if he caught them smoking. He would wait up for them, watching out the picture window from the living room while the stars slid over the glass. Sometimes he'd fall asleep and the beams from a passing car would reflect on his face, jumping him from sleep and he'd grumble. He waited, holding his 20-gauge shotgun across his lap like he was holding a baby. If they got home after curfew, he'd pop from behind the gate and put the barrel against the driver side window. It worked; even if my sisters didn't want to, the boys would force them to get home on time. Each time a boyfriend was switched out, it was the same story—my sisters would stay out late, breaking curfew, and then Dad would do his thing. Dad didn't treat my sisters like the princesses I said they were. Sometimes he called them sluts. Sometimes they even got hit.

My sisters would tell me I was lucky. Because I was the littlest and his favorite, Dad wasn't hard on me like he was on them. Instead, Dad would take me on special trips. I was his buddy. We went to the store, or hunting, or foraging for mushrooms. We were pals in a way they weren't. I was his boy.

Dad may have hunted their boyfriends, but it wasn't bad as it sounds. He loved his daughters and did things for them too. He put them in *Tamburitzas*, a Slavic dance troupe. They went overseas to perform. They all learned to play musical instruments. Bunny painted. They had horses. He was good to them.

Dad worried like crazy. He called the hospitals and police stations looking for them if they were an hour late. He said if he was ever mean it was because he worried about them. That was true. He tried to be a protector. He tried to protect my sisters from a world that he thought was pretty messed up. He even protected their friends. He didn't trust other men because he was one himself, so he knew plenty.

And after a bad thing happened this night at the fair, he might have even done something awful. It was hard to say for certain but I imagined quite a bit of it.

Dad was tall and strong. I was pretty sure he could beat

up most other dads. Forty years old at the time of my birth, he was on average ten to fifteen years older than the dads of other kids my age. He was filled out like a man. The other dads were still scrawny and bulging at the Adam's apple. At one time Dad had been a good boxer and held the title for the city of Gary's middleweight division. At least, that's what he said. I don't know for certain. With Dad you never really knew. He lied a lot. Not big lies but little ones, the kind that weren't necessary.

～

That evening at the fair it rained on and off. For a while the rain would stop, the sun would flex, but a couple minutes after the rain would start again. The sky turned gray, then dark gray, and buckets of water fell. It seemed like every time we took a step, another bucket came down. Dad said I shouldn't ever let the rain make me sad.

He could tell I was out of sorts that day, that something was on my mind. He said, "Don't worry about the rain, makes the mushrooms grow. No rain, no mushrooms." He pushed down my ballcap. "We should find them again in a couple days," he said, taking off his own broken-in Pittsburgh Steelers ballcap, wiping the sweat from his face with his forearm.

Dad didn't usually wear ballcaps, but he liked that one. It made sense to him. He was proud of the steelworkers and proud of the unions. In our front yard there was sometimes a sign that read, *Proud Union Home.*

He had said that about the rain earlier over lunch. We'd sat under a tent and the rain fell over the sides. We were all there: Mom, Dad, Bunny, Kelley, Nina, and me. Dad told me if I got to bed on time the next few nights, he'd take me to hunt mushrooms again in a couple days. That sounded satisfactory. I'd have liked to collect mushrooms every day.

For lunch we ate the roasted lamb Dad and Mr. Petrovic had made with steamed sweet corn. Mom had *cevapcici*. If you wanted, you could take some raw green onions for the lamb, but I didn't love them raw unless we had the apple cider vinegar for them. Dad liked to char them and soak them in oil, and I liked them that way best, but they didn't do it that way here. On my plate was lamb shoulder. The muscle tissue was long and soft. The silky fat between the muscles glistened when I pulled it apart. The skin was thick, crisp, and chewy. On top, flakes of salt and pepper were crystallized and with each bite I felt the seasonings crunch between my molars. The salt melted on my tongue with the fat and the pepper stuck in the spaces between my teeth. A fleck of peppercorn stuck between my two front teeth, which made it look like I had a gap in my teeth and Nina laughed at me. At the time I still had baby teeth. Later, when my adult teeth came in, they would buck until I got braces.

That lamb was extra delicious because Dad and Mr. Petrovic had made it. I'll always remember it. They were in the barn for a long time, and I recall hearing the chain on the side of the metal box spinning the lamb, making a constant hum, accentuated by an occasional clicking noise. Beneath the lamb, the dusty coals burnt orange and red. The coals hissed and popped when the fat fell to them and smoke danced up around the lamb as its skin crackled, becoming browner and browner.

Dad with his mouth full said, "In a couple more days

we'll go hunt mushrooms. Probably get another pound of chanterelles. *Borowiki* too. Not long before there'll be some meadows in the yard."

"Okay," I said and took my steamy corncob and pressed it onto the cube of butter on our table. I spun it until it became greasy. Bunny helped me. "Nice and even," she said. "Got to get it from top to bottom."

But still, rain did make a person feel sad, though the thought of hunting for mushrooms, carrying my own pocket-knife, and being in the forest made me feel better about it. I liked to think that sometimes things that made you feel sad would have a happy ending. I ate my corn and imagined being in the forest, finding mushrooms and slicing them with my knife. The images floated across my mind: mushrooms, pocketknife, forest. I knew I would wear my red hoodie like Elliott wore in *E.T.* I wanted to be just like Elliott. Just as lucky and just as sad. I was determined to wear that red hoodie until it became threadbare. The pocket edges curled up, the elastic and hems stretched and frayed at the hips and wrists, and the elbows wore out. Then Mom would throw it out one day when I wasn't looking.

That whole day I was soaked to the bone, itchy, warm, and covered in sawdust. On the far side, away from the rides, were the stables for the farm animals like goats, pigs, cows, sheep, and chickens. We were nearby in the stables full of girls and boys and their horses. The whole place smelled like if you took the Midwest and arranged it into a bouquet. Beyond this smell came the scent of elephant ear fry-grease, vats of butter for the boiled sweet corn, peanut oil for egg rolls, cheese curds, veg-etables, and corn dogs. The food vendors served these and all sorts of other things out of trailers or from under tents. My favorite was chicken fried rice from Lee's Wok. It wasn't the best fried rice I'd ever had, but there was something about the fair, and my family all in one place, that made it the best. The rice was speckled with once frozen peas and perfectly cubed carrots, wispy bean sprouts, chopped chicken thighs, sinewy pieces of leg, and potatoes. The rice wasn't overly brown, which I liked; you could see the yolky color of the scrambled eggs and dots of black pepper. It was served in a white-and-red-checkered paper boat with a fork rising from the steamy mound.

In the corner of April's stall, I sat on a stool. I was on my second boat of fried rice. I could eat a lot for being small. In the next stall, Kelley was on one side of Ranger and Mom was on the other. Mom brushed Ranger's tail while Kelley brushed the mane. The lighting was dim from dusty, naked bulbs that hung from wires laced through the rafters. A whip of rain-infused wind snaked through, misting everything. The smell of corn came in with it—fresh corn, like it had only seconds ago been plucked from the stalk. Baby sweet corn was my favorite. From our garden, I snapped the young ears, stripping back the thin translucent husk, eating it right in the field. If you've never had it like that and get the chance you should. It was sweet and you could eat the whole thing, core and all. It tasted sweet, grassy and green, fresh, of the plains.

Nina walked around April to where I sat. She stood in front of me, bent forward and opened her mouth for me to give her a bite. Reluctantly, I did. At the fair, I had an agenda that went like this: Lee's Wok fried rice, 4-H, pet every animal, pig races, demolition derby, Tilt-A-Whirl with Mom, win a stuffed animal, Gravitron, but nothing that went upside down.

Nina was chewing when she walked into Ranger's stall. She took the polished saddle, worn but shiny, beautiful dark brown leather with big brass buckles, which jangled hanging from the wall and tossed it over Ranger's back. The muscles quivered under Ranger's fur. Nina pulled the strap under Ranger's belly, tightening the saddle, and fitted the brass needle through the grommet on the other side. Nina gave Ranger two smacks on her hams. Ranger triumphantly tipped her head up and blew a puff of air from her nostrils, her lips ruffled. Bunny was in the other stall with Toni Petrovic. Strider was just about ready, and I already knew Bunny felt confident she'd be the one bringing home the medal.

The fair hummed in the background. I heard the clicking sound of the one rollercoaster that had an upside-down loop. It scared me. I imagined everyone raising their arms at the top before they rushed down the incline, building speed. We'd walked past it earlier and Mom asked if I was sure I wasn't going to get on it with her. "Looks fun," she said trying to entice me. It did look fun for those people, or her, but not for me. I also heard the echo of the ranch hand's voice for the pig races, announcing the line-up. The piglets had clever names based off famous people, like Dolly Pigton and Bacon Reagan, and silly names like Elpirga Porkbelly. Stringed *tamburitza* music floated out of the dining hall, where there was now a bingo game. Since the hall had been sponsored by St. Sava's, aside from the lamb and abundance of *cevapcici*, there were yogurt and cucumber salads with thick cuts of red onion and tomatoes, plates of stuffed grape leaves, along with sour cabbages, pickles, spicy peppers, and potato dumplings, towering along the red, white, and blue tablecloths. The melodies from the stringed instruments came to us and my sisters mentioned they ought to go in and say hi. The announcer called out, "B13, B13." I heard the muffled voices of the men behind the thin, shoddy wooden walls of the ring toss, bottle stand, dart balloons, duck pond, and Whac-A-Mole. The carnies coaxed the kids, holding enormously overstuffed Winnie-the-Poohs, E.T.s, bears, and lions around their shoulders, the way Dad plopped me over his sometimes. It was exceptionally romantic.

Not that far away, but farther than what I could hear, past the games and animal barns, past the parking lot, at the edge of the field and forest, Daniela Petrovic, Nina's best friend, was being sexually assaulted.

All those things happened at once, when suddenly, next to me the sound was terrifying, like a china cabinet crashing to the floor. I saw it before I heard it, but it didn't register right away. Ranger had bucked her back legs for what seemed to be no reason at all. Nina was thrown backwards from the impact. Ranger's back hooves had hit her jaw, landing Nina on the sawdust floor. Nina covered her mouth with her hands without touching it. Half of her teeth were broken. We didn't have to see to know. Blood flowed from her mouth and coagulated on the woodchips beneath her. Mom scooped her up. Mom was strong and Nina, though nearly a full-grown woman, was like a child in her arms. Her child. I'd seen Mom do this before. This wasn't the first time she picked her up like nothing though they were the same height. Mom just lifted her like a few sacks of flour. Her back arched beneath Nina's weight. It was a known fact that when something bad happened to your child, the adrenaline surged, and you could do almost anything. Mom *was* Wonder Woman.

Bunny, Kelley, and Toni followed Mom out of the stalls. I dropped my rice bowl in the commotion and was pulled in their wake. Nina was loaded into the back of the Oldsmobile station wagon. Bunny and Toni sat, one on each side of her. Her head rested in Kelley's lap. They'd sifted her teeth from the stall's floor and now held them in the palms of their hands like prayer crystals. Kelley used a towel to catch the blood still dripping from Nina's mouth. I sat in the middle between the back bed where they were and the front bench seats where Mom drove. Nina wasn't audibly crying, because that would hurt too much, but tears rolled down her cheeks. I kneeled on the seat, watching. Kelley told me to turn around and put on my seat belt, but I didn't listen. Mom sped along, keeping one eye on the road and the other in the rearview mirror. She said, "*shhh, shhh*," over and over even though it was already quiet. Bunny brushed Nina's hair back from her face. She felt sad. I saw it in her eyes, she loved Nina and she felt sorry too, almost like she was the one who'd done it. Bunny and Nina fought all the time. About everything really, but mostly clothes, and sometimes Bunny played tricks on her. Bunny looked at Nina apologetically. Her eyes said she would take it all back if that would make Nina better. Part of Bunny was relieved that it wasn't Strider who'd done it— then she'd really feel like it was all her fault.

At the hospital they fixed Nina's jaw but couldn't save her teeth. For the next couple of weeks, it was hard for her to eat, but she got plenty of chocolate shakes and fruit smoothies. Mom would hand me a small basket, telling me to go out to the yard and fill it with wild blackberries from the hedgerow. Mom would blend the berries with fresh milk and honey. I would get a little cup on the side. Mom made chicken broth and her friend Soo Young brought over her Korean beef bone soup, so clear and clean you'd think it was water. That was Nina's favorite. Mine too. Because so many teeth were gone, in photos from the next couple of years you'd see Nina smile with her lips pressed tightly together.

Nina wasn't mad at Kelley or Ranger. She said it was her own fault for walking behind the horse. That was what horses did sometimes. They got scared and they bucked. Ranger loved Nina, but it was instinct. She said she knew it, even had a bad feeling in her gut about it, but she did it anyways and the premonition about it came true.

I, on the other hand, figured it was the chanterelles.

No one got a medal. My sisters withdrew from the 4-H and took their horses home.

꙳

That night, after Nina got home from the hospital, back at the farmhouse, Daniela sat with my sisters in Bunny's room. The door was shut. They talked quietly and I tried to listen, sitting at the top of the stairs, pretending I was playing with my new spongy pink action figures. The figurines had all come together in one bag from the toy store. I had them laid out and was examining them with my ears alert. Nina had moved from the couch to Bunny's bed, which was bigger than hers. I knew without seeing that she was lying there, nodding in and out of sleep, trying to hang on to the conversation but in much pain. I sensed something was wrong and couldn't hear through the shut door, but Daniela was telling them what had happened. After I'd heard the story as an adult, I would remember back to this night and imagine them in there. Daniela wiped her eyes with her shirt sleeves. Her mascara was smudged, and her long dark hair made a curtain around her face but for her eye and cheek, where a blue bruise began to throb. And without it having to be said—because three sisters this close in age could do such things, even if one was partly incapacitated—they agreed to tell the castle's king. Of course, this was against their best judgment, knowing his temper. *But what else was there to do?* Something had to be done.

The farmhouse became a pressure cooker. First the air became hot. I felt it and so did my action figures. I made them fight because what else could they do? This could only be settled with a man down. I used a big guy with a square head and big muscles to swipe out the bottom half of a slender-legged one with a robot torso. I was too small to know exactly what was going on, but somehow, I also knew exactly what was going on.

The air boiled. They were telling Dad. I stopped playing with my figurines and ran to the living room, intuitively clinging to Mom's thigh.

The steam came down around us. Dad slammed things, dashing from room to room. Tearing things apart, looking for something or other that could hurt a person. Daniela got under the covers with Nina and cried. Dad hollered, screamed, and yelled, so many things I couldn't repeat them and I wasn't afraid to cuss. I just couldn't do it justice if I tried. More important phrases stood out like Mom yelling,

"No!" or pleading, "Because someone could get killed!" or "He'd get killed!" or "Jail!" or "Girls without a father!" He screamed, asking himself if he should take his gun, jackknife, brass knuckles, or baseball bat? His dangerous thoughts rolled out. His eyes were black marbles, demon-like.

I had never seen Dad so mad, but I was little, there was still time. For my sisters this was not new, but even they thought this was worse than other times. They lined themselves on the stairwell, in ascending order, from oldest to youngest, watching him. Daniela and Nina had gotten up. Nina held a frozen ham hock against the discolored tissue over her cheek and jaw. Daniela had a bag of frozen blueberries over her eye. It was a spectacle. Dad yelled about his castle as he walked past them on the stairs and me in the living room, barnacled to Mom. The outline of the brass knuckles showed through his pocket. He had his cowboy gun strapped into a leather shoulder holster with the gun resting under his armpit. He stomped out of the house yelling about how he was the king. And when he was fully gone, skidding out of the gravel driveway in the pickup truck, the pressure was released.

In the decades since that night, this is how I came to imagine what might have followed. Dad drove with his hands on the pickup's wheel at ten and two. The muscles in his forearms bulged from the tight grip. Mr. Petrovic had tears in his eyes but was not crying. He held each elbow with the opposite hand, slightly rocking back and forth. A cigarette dangled from his mouth, and he smoked it without removing it from his lips. He inhaled and let the smoke roll out of his nose like a bull. The ash of it became long and fell on his oily pants. He didn't do anything about it. And it was raining again. The windshield wipers slapped side to side. Dad put the butt of his fist against the windshield and wiped away the steam that rose to it from their skin. Dad cut the lights shortly before the far side of the fairgrounds, where the trailers for the carnies were located. They parked several blocks away from the edge of the forest where the incident had occurred. And that was where they waited, in the tree line, with night-vision binoculars, watching for the man with the snake tattoo, Dad with his brass knuckles and cowboy gun and Mr. Petrovic with his bat.

They were familiar with hunting. They had been hunting partners. Parental partners, godfathers of each other's children, wine partners, friends—best friends, meaning this was natural. Though this time they hated why they were there, waiting in the forest, watching. But like other dangerous men, the heat of their madness, the rage inside of them, aroused them. They felt that primal longing to hurt a man for vengeance. They waited quietly in the rain, with bandanas over their mouths and nose. They waited under the trees and when the man they were looking for exited an outhouse, they ran forward like medieval soldiers—bat in the air and brass knuckles over Dad's fist. They ran, caught the man, covered his mouth, grabbed his legs, and carried him back into the woods. I imagine they did what they thought they must do.

There was never a thing about it in the news as far as I knew. Dad seemed satisfied the following morning, eating breakfast as usual in his boxer shorts and dingy white T-shirt. I'm just telling you how I imagine it happened, because once Dad took me to look for mushrooms in that patch of trees near the fairgrounds. He said we should find some good chanterelles there, firm, young, and fresh.

CHAPTER 13.
LAYERS

"The layers. That's the most important part," Dad said. I was driving in his Ford F-150 at the time, heading out to fish. "Busia was famous for her burgers," he said, using his hands to show the layers. "There's ah, ah, the bun." Sometimes Dad still stuttered. His gray, thinning eyebrows arched. He put out his right hand. "Then there's the mustard and pickles." He added his left hand on top of his right. "She cooked them in the suet. It was like she deep-fried them in the fat. She used only cast-iron pans. Seasoned real good." He did the thing again, layering his hands, the right on the left this time. "Then she put the patty on, then the ketchup,"—using his hands—"then she added onions, thin as sheets of paper. You could see through them. Then she added the top bun."

"Did she toast the buns?" I was curious, making mental

notes, drawing the burgers in my mind with arrows of ingredients pointing to the layers I imagined.

"She was open from seven in the morning until three or four in the afternoon. She didn't have to stay open any later than that. I'd count the cash at the end of day. She'd make around sixty to a hundred dollars. *Just in burgers.*" He paused for a moment, looking at me and making sure I was taking it all in. I had my eyes on the road, but I was. He continued, "Each morning there was a line down the block. Mostly mill workers but even some of the firemen and police officers having breakfast or taking burgers for lunch. All the Eastern European guys who worked at the mill came to Busia's. She could talk with a lot of them. She spoke Polish, Lithuanian, a little Russian. Most of those languages had similar roots. That was real nice for the guys at the mill. She was like their Busia too. Everyone called her Busia."

"That's nice," I said, seeing it unfold. I knew where Busia's had been in Gary. I knew that corner at 34th and Broadway. I knew what those Eastern European steel workers looked like with their thick foreheads, long straight noses, high, pointed cheekbones and rose-petal lips.

The restaurant had been converted from a several-story house. The restaurant was on the ground floor and there were apartments above. Back then Busia's had windows on both sides of the street, opening to the side of Broadway where traffic and people flowed. To the other side, the windows opened to a lot where there was a garden. The inside of Busia's was bright. The walls were white; the tile on the floor was black-and-white checked. The bar was white Formica with silver trim and the tabletops matched. The red, candy-colored stools and booths matched one another too. It was a burger shop, one that you might have found on a movie set. I knew it even if I hadn't been there. I knew how it looked when I saw all those pieces of furniture covered in dust in our pole barn's attic.

I saw it that day too while Dad told his story; it was as if I was seeing it through his eyes. The line of patrons zigzagged down Broadway and around the corner onto 34th and then down about another block. At the time, U.S. Steel provided thousands of jobs. Those workers were in this line, either on their way in or on their way home. As soon as my great-grandfather, Vincent, had put in the last vinyl-covered pine booth, lines formed. At seven in the morning Busia's doors opened and the people had eggs and ham, smoked fish, pierogi, *czarnina*, *borscht*, and burgers.

Busia worked in the kitchen. She was the chef. Even after four kids and all this work, she looked peaceful. She had a right-hand mate, Xena, a nice Polish girl who took the South Shore Line in from Chicago to set up early, the same Xena who would work there when Mom became the chef of Jennie's Café. There were two waitresses, Irene and Soo, and two busboys, young men to be more exact. They showed up with Irene and Soo, every morning at 6 AM to get the place sparkling, coffee made, tea bags set, napkins folded, silverware polished, booths and stools wiped for a second time, the floors and booths having been swept and mopped from the night before but that was how Busia wanted it. They took orders, filled waters, cleared the tables, refilled coffee mugs, became friends with each other and my parents, knew their customers—their home lives and the gripes about their supervisors. They were what made Busia's, Busia's.

At that time, the bubble around that corner was Busia's world, and everyone else was living in it. Busia and Vincent lived above the restaurant. There was a duplexed house on the other side of the garden lot that one of their kids would buy someday. Across the alley was a small clapboard bungalow, where Busia's sister lived. Then next to the bungalow was the Sciaras' house, where Dad's best friend, Frank, and his family lived. All of them shared the vegetable garden where the bean, squash, and tomato plants twisted around corn and sunflowers; cucumbers and melons wrapped their vines along trellises, shading the pergola to the other side where grapes hung. The only thing missing was an orchard.

Then Dad said, "It was a *lot* of burgers she sold. Imagine that, making one hundred dollars a day when the burgers were only fifteen cents apiece?"

"That's a lot of burgers," I confirmed. "Why were they so good?"

"It was all about the layers," he said definitively, setting his hands, palms down, on his thighs.

⌒✕

Mom and Dad are like the milkweed when the pods turn brown, splitting at the seams and spilling out the furry seeds. The seeds, they look furry. And I'm trying to catch them, wanting to put them back together, neat and precise. I want to put them back like how I remember them in '84. I want to hold them like the stuffed lion from the county fair, tucking them beneath my arm. I want to care for them like they cared for me, making me feel safe in our farmhouse even if it wasn't always safe. They're both scared of leaving us, I can tell, but they know we'll be all right. They've done a decent enough job. We'll get by but somehow I already miss them.

During our working season at Milkweed I don't have time to dilly-dally. When I can, I try to go down south to see Mom and Dad, if only for one full day and two nights. They are more than worth the six hundred plus miles round trip.

One Sunday after our guests left I went back to Chicago. I visited with Mom at home and Dad in Indiana on Monday. Then I drove back on Tuesday. I got to Chicago on Sunday night around 10:30 PM and Mom had waited up for me. That was late for her. She'd saved me half a rib-eye and four pierogis from Gene's Sausage Shop in Lincoln Square. I made pierogi all the time, but I never ate the ones I made. It seemed like too precious a thing with all the time it took, though by now I was decently quick at making them. The ones from Gene's were stuffed with a mixture of mushrooms, which was so good. I liked them very much. I was touched Mom waited up for me and we talked together in her kitchen while I ate. She wanted to take care of me. She knew I worked hard. I had come home to check on her hip and how she was feeling. I wanted to take care of her too.

Mom and I have one of those old Chicago two-flats where there are many built-ins and crown moldings. Mom and Nina live on the first floor. Anna and I live above. When I got home I went straight into Mom's apartment. I ate the dinner she had saved for me and recapped our weekend, detailing our Milkweed guests and the things I cooked. I told her about my troubles with sleep. She said she'd take me to the store in the morning so we could buy melatonin. Sometimes you need your mom to do things like that with you. I was lucky to have her.

Mom was having all sorts of health problems. When the pandemic hit, I begged her not to go to work. At first, she didn't see what the big deal was and insisted on going. I explained that since she was on a chemo maintenance shot, she was immune-compromised and it wasn't safe. She was worried about being off work. She worried about how to occupy her time. She was worried about money. She was seventy-five in March 2020. The human resources department at her job understood her health status, so it wasn't hard for her to get the time off. But then all sorts of other unfortunate events began to happen. Maybe it was the lack of movement, because when she didn't work, she wasn't as active. Blood clots formed in her lungs and she had to go to the hospital to be treated. Another time Nina's black Lab accidentally knocked her down and her arm was fractured in the fall. Not long after that she got a UTI and went to the hospital again. Then one day she had terrible trouble breathing and couldn't get up from where she had gone to lie down for a nap. We took her to the hospital again and it turned out her heart was beating arrhythmically. All this happened in just one summer, one thing after the other. Then her hip started causing her pain. It was amazing she didn't end up with covid once, which was for the best because that might have been the one thing that could have taken her out.

The pain in her hip got worse. It had been bothering her for years, but now we worried it would have to be replaced. The doctor said that with all her other health issues, even a common surgery like a hip replacement would be dangerous. When she called me on the phone to tell me about it, she was in good spirits. She said she was happy the doctor was honest with her, and they were going to help her figure out other things to try. Before long, though, the pain became overwhelming. She could barely stand long enough to cook her own meals. She told the doctor she didn't know how she could live like this. When I took her to doctors' appointments, she needed a wheelchair. She needed the surgery. Several years later her hip is now new. She can walk without a walker, cook her own meals, go to the store, visit with people, drive. Proof that the women in our family can take a lot. Stubborn women. Strong women.

I ate the ribeye and pierogi and before she went to bed, we made plans to have coffee in the morning before the store. I gave her a hug and thanked her for the ribeye. This visit was before her hip surgery, just shortly before it got too painful. After the store I was going to drive to Indiana to visit with Dad, then when I got back to Chicago, in the evening, Mom and I would have a late dinner and I'd have coffee with her again the following morning before I'd drive back up to the cabin. I had to keep my schedule tight on these visits and rarely saw friends when I was in town because there was just not enough time.

In the morning, after coffee with Mom and shopping for melatonin, I immediately drove to Dad's house. I got there and Dad met me in the driveway. The first thing he said was, "Wind's not coming from the northeast, should be good, might catch some fish here at midday though it's always better at dawn or dusk." He reminded me the fish liked to feed better at night or early in the morning, but early in the morning was never an option for us.

Dad and I headed out in his Ford F-150 single cab with extended bed. I drove. Dad sat shotgun. We headed south on

Route 421, towards Grandpa Regan's old farm. We disappeared underneath tunnels of old oak, maple, and willow. It was a beautiful drive. Before us were massive farms of corn and soy. Plumes of smoke from the steel mills clouded the rearview mirror. The road was freshly paved and every so often an old tree was set at the front of a long drive which led to a farmhouse set way back from the road, and at the horizon full of corn, where the green and blue met, I remembered how easy it was to love Indiana; then the feeling passed.

Fishing with Dad never turns out as planned. We don't catch much. He's always like, "I gotta good spot for us." And then I learn we've been to this new spot a bunch of times before. That day we were at the big pond near the birch grove at the back of Grandpa's farm, even though it hadn't been his farm in thirty-some years. We were trespassing and I wasn't worried about it. I was up for breaking the law. I'd choose this spot any day, not for the fish but the memories.

Dad has told great stories about catching hundreds of fish over the years. I just haven't really seen it happen. And as with most of his great stories, he couldn't remember he'd already told them to me, so he told them again. He's a compulsive man, and not only about fears and worries, but stories too. He probably has thousands of dollars' worth of fishing poles, rigs, and tackle. Lots of guns too, and knives. If you ask me he hasn't invested his pensions wisely, but I wasn't going to say it to him. He had a boat made for fishing too. He wasn't really a fisherman anymore even though he was loaded with the gear and apparatus. The truth was we were together, so the fish didn't matter.

On the way out we stopped at Portillo's. I got a fish sandwich. Dad got a hotdog. We each got our own chocolate shake. I slurped down the last bit of my shake when Dad told the story about the little boy who was fishing on a pier with his dad and saw a boat pass full of people having a party. A *sexy lady* (his words not mine) was laid out over the nose of the boat, sunning herself. Then Dad told me how "the boy yelled, 'Daddy, that man caught a mermaid.'" Dad laughed, liking to tell this story. He'd told it to me a bunch of times and each time I pretended like I hadn't heard it and laughed for him, knowing that this was what must be done. He's told this story so many times over the years that he's forgotten that the boy and his dad were the two of us.

Dad, who used to stand six feet, was only as tall as me now. He had to sit down every couple minutes to catch his breath. Occasionally his legs gave out under him and he stumbled a little, but he didn't seem to care. He'd make a little hopping motion, then carry on, tying rigs to poles, attaching bells too. He teetered a bit at the pond's edge, and I stood up with one hand out toward his back in case I had to grab onto his belt loops to prevent him from toppling forward. His balance was shot. I knew he fell about once a week and he never told me about it. I talked to him nearly every day, but he left things out too. I learned that from him, lying by omission. Sometimes in the summer months when he wore shorts, I saw the bruises on his shins. Before he turned around, I casually stepped back as if I wasn't concerned about him falling and he just continued doing his thing.

It wasn't long before the bell at the end of the pole closest to him rang like an old-fashioned phone, the operator under the water pulling on the fishing wire. Dad grabbed the pole before it disappeared into the deep end of the pond. He instructed me to get the net, which I already had behind him. For once, it was a fish. We were excited. Dad reeled him in, saying he "didn't think there'd be any fish left in here," a slip of the tongue, I suppose. I wanted to say, "Tell me again why we came here then," but I knew why. It didn't matter. It was as good for him as it was for me.

He got a good hold on the pole, reeling it all the way in. The fish flicked his tail back and forth. I scooped him into the net and Dad said, "What in the heck is this one?" He groped around in the net and got a good hold on the "slippery sucker." He held the fish in his large hands like he was praying. Dad was smaller now, but his hands were still large. He opened his palms, slowly, like he had a gem inside or something of the sort. We looked the fish over. Hell if I knew what it was. Dad thought for a minute more and said, "Drum fish. I don't know if this is any good to eat." Quickly, I searched on my phone. He and I just wanted to eat a fish we caught together for once. There was no signal and I held my phone up to the sky. I shook the phone like that was going to help. I *was* my father. Then I got the information: "highly underrated," I read, adding, "I say we should keep it." But it was hard to say if I was even looking up the right fish.

Dad scrunched up his weathered face and the hair on his head, just like the milkweed seeds, ruffled in the breeze. "Na, I'ma toss him back in." He looked at the fish apologetically. He looked at me like it wouldn't be right to kill this fish.

"Yeah, you better put him back," I said, feeling sorry for the fish too.

"Yeah, I'm gonna."

Dad opened his shiny palms. His fingers were thick, and

his nails looked like the shells of mussels, bruised and dark. The fish sprung from his hands back into the water.

After Dad let the drum fish back and we didn't catch anything else we created an adventure. Instead of mere trespassing, without speaking about it, we decided to break and enter. We wanted to see what was still in the old barn. We put the fishing gear back into the bed of the pickup and got out something else.

Dad told me not to do it but waited patiently while I squeezed the bolt cutters against the chain until the link snapped open. He knew this might happen—after all, he was the one with bolt cutters in the bed of his pickup. Dad hadn't been in this barn for thirty-five-some years and it was sure to make him feel many things. That was as long as it had been for me too, if not more, and I was already feeling things. Dad told me that the guy who bought it after Grandpa died had probably auctioned off everything that was in it. I think he just wanted to tell himself that so he felt like he hadn't left any other memories behind. I had a suspicion it would be untouched; I mean, the Dodge truck with refrigerated bed was still parked out there, covered in moss.

I pushed the corrugated doors to the side. It took the two of us to heave it along the rusted track. We covered our eyes with our forearms against the dander that blew at us as the doors opened. Dad was next to me where the paddock once was, now falling apart. The clover, maple, and oak saplings came up around our ankles and calves.

We took a few steps forward and entered the dark barn. We'd always been cautious returning to this place, but I assured myself and him we wouldn't take anything that wasn't ours. *Or was it all still ours?*

A crack in the ceiling let in a beam of sunlight. Dad stood beneath it, a handsome old man. He was no movie star like Grandpa had been, but still. His face was round where it was once angular. He was creased over, a *papier-mâché* version of himself. His hair had a yellow-ish hue where it would otherwise be white. His eyebrows were thin and gray where they used to be thick and dark and the hairs strong as pine needles. I hadn't seen his face this clearly in a long time. When I thought of Dad when he wasn't next to me, I realized I pictured him as the forty-five-year-old man who used to bring me here all those years ago. I didn't see the face of the old man in my memories. I should start, I realized, looking at him in the light, to memorize his face. I should start seeing both his and Mom's faces, of all the ages, of all the times I could remember. That could be a new thing to think about while falling asleep.

Everything looked the same but also different, smaller, dustier, and older. Things had been moved around, some things had been cleared out. Dad whispered to himself, "Shit, they sold all the restaurant equipment."

But I found the burger press that Dad always said he wished we could find. "I'll be damned," he said. "I haven't seen that in a long, long time. Got to get it out of here, you need that." We took it and I planned to use it, making burgers like he had told me Busia did, fried in suet and all, with all the layers as he said.

On the way home in his pickup, the burger press on the seat between us, I asked him to tell me the fishing story about when he'd taken the Sciaras fishing. His stories never stuck to just the one thing and I liked how they would go on and on. The story began in 1958. I pictured how he might have looked then. Like I said, I thought of him looking forty-five but sometimes for these older stories I pictured him like he was in the photographs from his and Mom's wedding album when they both looked so incredibly young and handsome.

Based on those wedding pictures, that's how Dad would have looked that day of his story. He would have been just a few years younger than he was in the album. Mom and Dad might have already had their first date by then.

The story goes that he was outside the house of his best friend, Frank Sciara, the house that was kitty-corner from Busia's, laying on the horn. Dad was impatient. He wanted to get to the water. He tapped his fingers anxiously against the two-toned Chevy's steering wheel with the engine running, waiting for Frank, Frank's sister Lulu, short for Luella, Frank's other brother and sister, and Frank's grandma and grandpa to come out. All six of them plus Dad squeezed into the Chevy, the fishing poles strapped to the roof. They drove north down Broadway Avenue in Gary past the billboards, dime stores, and movie houses with marquees advertising *The Blob*, *Cat on a Hot Tin Roof*, and *Dracula*.

Dad drove them to a fishing pier on Lake Michigan, where lots of men fished. Many of the men wore waders and fisherman's beanies, just like you'd imagine. The guys in the waders went out with a big net, one guy on each end, as deep as their chests. And once the net was full, they gave each other a signal by nodding their heads and looking at each other in a certain way that meant turning around and coming back to shore with enough smelt to fill gallons of buckets. Dad said it's not like that anymore. There's just not that many smelts anymore.

Smelts are a small lake fish, easy to gut and clip off the head, or better yet, keep the head on. The skull gives it a little extra crunch. Dust them in flour, salt, pepper, garlic powder, and paprika and shallow fry them in butter. Dad couldn't stop himself from reciting the rhyme his grandfather Vincent would sing-song to him and his brother when they were small: *Fishy fishy in the brook. Grandpa catch you by the hook. Grandma fry you in a pan. I'ma eat you fast I can.* He told me his grandfather was in a wheelchair by then in '58, but when he was little his grandfather would bench press him and his brother while reciting the rhyme. His grandfather was once a strongman in the circus.

How I described preparing smelt, that was how Busia cooked them—with the head on, dredged in flour and spices, then fried. For a special treat she'd use salted pork renderings instead of butter. They'd come out crispy and she'd salt them a bit more. They ate the smelts with pickles and hard-boiled egg yolks blended with oil.

Grandma and Grandpa Sciara didn't speak much English, but they knew enough. Dad put worms or slugs or minnows on the hooks. He handed a pole to each family member. They'd have better chances if they all spread out a little, he told them, pointing where each person should stand. He'd brought some old shrimp scampi from Busia's to use as bait for catfish, and when he tied it to Grandpa Sciara's line, they caught a big one. Dad held out his hands two feet apart, recalling the story.

By the time they packed up he counted five big catfish in

total. That was dinner enough for several nights. As soon as a fish was reeled in, Dad rushed over with his net or snagged it from the line in his calloused paws and smacked the fishes' heads against the pier's rail. Lulu and Frank winced at Dad's eagerness to end the fishes' lives so fast, and he said, "What? It's better this way." Dad tossed the many fish in his trunk full of ice. That day Dad caught four crappies. Frank got six. Lulu got two bluegills. Grandpa Sciara got one big catfish. Dad told them they all "done real good."

Dad and Frank had become best friends because they were boxing partners at some point when they were younger. Frank would have been a good lightweight, Dad said, but got scarlet fever when he was younger. After only about a year of boxing, his heart couldn't handle it anymore, so they went fishing together instead. Some nights Frank sat with Dad and Busia while they ate stuffed cabbage and fried fish. They spent a lot of time together, at both of their homes.

Dad gave all his crappies to Busia. She gutted them, saving the innards and heads in a jar. She had a couple of quarts of innards and heads packed in dry ice. When she had enough, she defrosted what she already had and combined it with fresh stuff. She added lots of salt and mixed it together. Then she packed the fish guts, heads, and salt down into a jar. She placed a weight on top of the mixture to hold it down, then covered the top of the jar with a lid. She left it to sit on the counter near the stove so it stayed around seventy to seventy-five degrees. As the fish fermented, carbon dioxide built up in the jars and each week she burped the jars so they wouldn't explode. And each week the scent got better, going from muddy lakeshore to caramelized popcorn. At the end, after half a year or more, this concoction became a fish sauce she'd use to season vegetables and meats. When she used it on the pork and beef that she stuffed in the cabbage, Dad said it was a hundred times better than anything else he had ever eaten. She added a couple drops to her *czarnina*, which was the secret no one else knew about except for me, because one day Dad remembered and he told me and now when I make *czarnina*, I use a homemade fish sauce much the same as Busia's.

Before frying the crappie, Busia ran her knife precisely down each side of the fish's spine, through the skin and flesh. With a flick of her knife, two fillets appeared. She dusted the fillets with dried corn she'd milled into a fine flour and sautéed them in pork fat and butter.

After the dishes were done, Dad often sat at the table with Busia and opened the book of mushrooms he'd checked out from the library. He dog-eared all the pages that featured mushrooms he had spotted in the forest. He and Busia sat at the kitchen table under the warm glow of the kitchen light and as he pointed at each one, she would recite its name in Polish. *Borowiki* for boletus, *kurka* for chanterelle, *grib-baran* for hen of the woods, also known as sheep's head. Dad wrote down the Polish names next to the pictures or drawings. Dad never returned that book so I have it now, the binding cracked and all but worn away complete with the check-out tag from the Gary Public Library, with all his dog-ears and notes.

Outside Busia's, in the garden lot, were patches of cabbage and lettuce and crocks filled with dirt where herbs grew. The tomatoes were lopsided and bumpy with long gray cracks. But it didn't matter they weren't beautiful; these tomatoes tasted sweet and succulent. The membranes around the seeds were translucent, chubby, and glowing, holding a world inside—an ovary. "*Capriolo*," Grandpa Sciara said one night inside the Sciaras' house, where Dad was having dinner with Frank's family. Dad and Frank and all the other Sciara kids were seated with Grandma and Grandpa Sciara around the dining table, the seven of them. Dad never really thought about where Frank's parents were, but they weren't around much.

Dad asked Frank, "What'd he say?"

Frank said in Italian, "*Uovo*," meaning egg. "Fish eggs, you know. Roe. Eggs."

"Got it," Dad said, impressed by the comparison.

Grandma Sciara always wore a house dress. It was from the fancy boutique downtown, the crème de la crème, Black Stone. She was dressed lovely for a regular meal, meaning not a holiday or a birthday or some other special occasion. Dad loved her cooking almost as much as he loved Busia's, especially the *ragù*. He told me the reason it was so good was that "all day, wearing her nice outfit, she'd have the pot simmering and she'd be stirring and stirring adding little pinches of spices or herbs here and there. She added the red wine Grandpa Sciara made. He used the grapes that she grew in the garden, grafted from vines she brought with her from Italy to Gary."

Grandma Sciara, like Busia, like great-grandmothers almost everywhere, brought her memories to America in the form of food. For the *ragù*, she cooked the tomatoes so long she never had to peel them. The skin dissolved into the sauce along with everything else until it was a thick, beautiful, almost translucent potion of tomato and spices, like a savory marmalade, rich and sticky from the natural sugars and pectin, it glowed vibrant as the stained-glass windows of the Byzantine church down the block.

Dad devoured it. He said the *ragù* smothered fresh, al dente pasta that snapped like a rubber band between each bite. As he ate it, the most peculiar things were the tiny drumsticks he kept pulling from his mouth. The meat of them slid right off the bone, not much bigger than a toothpick, though he might have exaggerated. He pulled a bone from his mouth, holding it between his fingers and studying it. He looked to Frank for the answer. Grandpa Sciara saw him and laughed. "*Mangia, mangia,*" he said, motioning with his hands from the plate to his mouth, eat, eat. Dad did, nibbling anything left on the fragile bone. He asked Frank, "But what is it?"

Frank, shy about it, shrugged.

"Spar. Spar," Grandpa Sciara said. Grandpa Sciara saw that Dad didn't understand, so he stood up, flapping his arms. "Spar, Spar. Tweet. Tweet."

Dad asked Frank, "Sparrow?"

"Yeah," Frank said, "dumbass."

Grandma Sciara hit Frank's arm. She knew a few bad words in English.

After dinner, Frank and Dad went to the attic, which was triangular with a small window at one end and a vent at the other. The window was open but the attic still smelled of old papers and moth balls. There were mouse droppings everywhere. Bird seed and shit dotted the ledge of the window. "Grandpa breaks their necks," Frank said, then defensively added, "It's not a lot of meat but it's good."

"Yeah, they're great," Dad agreed. "One hundred percent." He thought for a minute and said, "I hadn't thought of eating these birds before."

"Now you have. You can eat almost any bird," Frank said, scratching the back of his neck. "Grandpa says so." Dad smiled at Frank, thinking.

A few sparrows flew down, resting at the sill. They watched the boys with one eye, then turned and watched with the other. When no sudden movements were made by either party, the sparrows punched their heads forward, snatching seeds in their pointed beaks.

Then swift as if he was in the boxing ring, Dad jabbed, catching one of the sparrows in his fist. With a quick twist, he snapped its neck. The bird went limp in his hand. Frank turned to him, silent, his mouth falling open.

"For Busia," Dad said, pleased with himself.

If you ask me, I think Dad sometimes enjoyed killing things. He loved this story. He loved how he killed the fish and the birds.

CHAPTER 14.
NESTING

SITTING AND WRITING SOMETIMES LOOKED A LOT like sitting and doing nothing.

From inside the cabin, Anna yelled, "There's too much laundry." Our guests had left and that's what happened after the weekend. There was a lot of laundry and a lot of cleaning to do. I finished my chores and when I was through, I sat outside on the porch and read. I got a bit of writing and journaling done. Beyond the porch the birds were loud and that was nice. The wind blew the leaves, I listened. That's when Anna yelled. It was the leaves blowing, birds chirping, then her yelling. She often got stressed and her reaction to stress was to yell about the thing she was stressed about. My reaction to stress was often to stuff it down, pondering it all night while silently freaking out.

I sat on a cooler on the porch where I often sat next to our screen door. After it got dark, I would read by the light of two lanterns. It was nine in the evening and that time of the summer where it was getting dark a little earlier though it wasn't completely dark yet. It stayed light out here later than lots of places. It was a wonderful thing that also sort of messed with you. We were on the westernmost edge of the eastern time zone, which meant it stayed light longer. On the day of the summer solstice the sky didn't become completely black until midnight.

I didn't want to stop what I was doing but I knew I needed to help her. I looked at the horizon where the sun was about to set, casting a few last rays through the tree line. I wondered how old those trees might be. I thought about the trees and the loggers, how they once used pulley systems and draft horses to move the logs to the river where they'd run on the current to the sawmills. There were lots of rivers in the Upper Peninsula. They might have cut the lowlands back then but it didn't seem they did that much now with their machines, which couldn't navigate the steep hills as well. This region's economy was built on logging, iron ore, and copper. It had a different group of peoples than the Rust Belt. Of course, there were the Indigenous peoples who were here first, then Scandinavian and Dutch loggers, Cornish, Irish, German, and French Canadian miners. It seemed it hadn't changed much. For a while there was a prosperous period in the Upper Peninsula, but the Great Depression ended it. Lots of the natural resources up here went fast. Today much of the reason you moved here was because, in a sense, you wanted to live off the land. We did that, we homesteaded, but we did have perks like solar power, propane, a pretty good well, and a washing machine.

Most of the time we hung up the laundry to line dry. It was really a wonderful smell the sun baked into the sheets. I'm not sure there was anything else like it. There were lots of miraculous things the sun did out here. On the small table next to me was a bottle of farmhouse ale from a brewery called Barrel and Beam. The beer was pleasant, one of my favorites. The dim light coming through the amber-colored bottle showed it was half full. I bought several of these bottles each week and saved them for the day the guests left. It was my reward to myself, having a nice bottle of beer, relaxing while I read, wrote, and thought about what I was thinking. I took another sip of beer and dog-eared the book I was reading. It was too bad I had to go inside because I was enjoying the sunset and listening to the birds.

It had taken a while for my "prayer" to be answered. When the birds arrived this time, they stayed. I assumed this was because the logging wasn't as close as it had been before. Not long ago a hummingbird flew onto the porch, looking for flowers, and had flown into a window and died. I had been sitting in front of the fireplace with my feet stretched before the glass door. Early that morning I had gone outside without shoes and my socks got wet. I was exhausted. I was drinking coffee while reading the news, drying my socks, when there was a bang against the window. I jumped and turned, seeing nothing. I figured it had been a branch carried over the porch railing on a swell of air.

A few hours later, I went out for a cigarette and I looked at the window, seeing nothing, but then on the porch floor, below the window, I saw the most iridescent hummingbird lying there stiff. Her wings were a shiny emerald color with streaks of black and her belly was full of ruby feathers, so small they were like miniature jewels. For the next couple of months in the late morning while I read on the porch, brushing mosquitoes from my arms and ankles, I'd hear an almost mechanical noise, and if my eyes were quick enough, I'd see another hummingbird. I imagined he was looking for the one that died. I said to him, "Careful, there's a window there," and I pointed with my thumb behind my shoulder.

Anna hollered for me again and that's when I tucked away my notebook, pencil, and book. I took another sip of the beer and went inside. She was in the room we called the Deer Room. She had decorated it with mounted antlers that the owners before us had left. We also had some throw pillows with antlered fauna printed on them. The sheets on the bed were a plaid flannel of gray, red, white, and black. Over the sheets was a black wool blanket with cream-colored geometric designs. There was a faux fur throw at the foot of the bed. It was a very pretty room, if somewhat masculine. On the nightstand furthest from the door was a framed photo of Bunny. She and I looked quite a bit alike. Sometimes people asked me if it was a photograph of me from when I was younger. The photograph was from when she had first become a respiratory therapist. She was probably somewhere between the ages of twenty and twenty-two. The photo might have been for an ID card, but it looked a lot like a school portrait. That photo would have been more than forty years ago. Nature did a good job mixing our parents' DNA.

Bunny was beautiful, more so than any of the rest of us. Myself especially. I didn't feel so good-looking, not anymore. Maybe that's how things went once you passed the age of forty. I was filling out. A few nights before I had taken a pot edible and stood before the mirror. I didn't really notice I was stoned until looking in the mirror. Just don't stand in front of a mirror when you are stoned. *I've come of age.* This past year or two must have aged me more than I would have otherwise. I think many people have a similar feeling. Or maybe how I felt was just what happens when you're past forty? Your pores get bigger. Your lips turn down at the ends in an unintentional frown. Your jowls start to sag and creases form from east to west and north to south over your fore-head and neck. Maybe I was just filling out in the way that women do. Men fill out later in life too; they literally balloon into their skin. Body dysmorphia, which I'd never thought I had, was telling me I needed to look different. But maybe the truth was that I was just becoming myself. I thought the extra skin under my chin was from my slowed metabolism, *but was that just how it worked now?* I wondered how the hell that was ever going to go back the way it was, and while looking in the mirror I pulled the skin taut under my neck and chin, pushing my eyes and lips back a little with my palms, seeing myself at thirty-five. I was now many more pounds than I had ever been. Anna called it our pandemic weight. I positioned the mirrors so I could see my profile and became extremely disappointed. *It's okay, you are stoned,* I reminded myself, *it might not be that bad. Try again in the morning.* Anna, from our bedroom, called out, "What?" I told myself to shut up and when I left the bathroom, feeling older than I had been going into it, I said, "Nothing."

She was stubborn. "You were talking to someone."

"No I wasn't," I said.

Bunny was so beautiful, though. I miss her. I bet she'd be stunning at sixty, which is around what her age would be now. She got married three times before she died at thirty-nine. Traumatized by her death, I rarely pictured my own life after thirty-nine, but I'm past that now. I guess it made sense she was married three times. She was easy to love. She was an Aries. People with an Aries sun sign are usually pretty people and always funny. I have never met an Aries that didn't make me laugh.

I've been married three times too, and all three times before I was thirty-nine. My marriages weren't the same, though. The first time was so that my partner at the time who was Israeli could get her citizenship. While I was in college, I found two men, an American Serbian and a Serbian, who were in a similar situation and with gay marriage not being federally recognized at the time, we swapped partners. Of course, none of us are together anymore but my ex-Israeli girlfriend is now an American citizen and Darko, well, he ended up moving back to Serbia anyway. While we were married, Darko and I had a good time celebrating the Slavic foods from our childhoods, comparing what our families did differently or the same. He moved back to Serbia I think because his family was well off; it wasn't easy to be gay there, but he would have a better financial life than he did in the U.S., where he worked in restaurants as a server. For a long time, though, he wanted to have the freedom of love rather than wealth. Then, I don't know, I guess he got older. I drew up our divorce papers and we ended the marriage at the courthouse.

Then I got married again because I fell in love with

someone, but the marriage didn't last. I think that's some-times how things work. Not everything can be forever.

Now I'm married to Anna and it's good; she's smart, beautiful, and funny. I love her very much. Working together is hard, as it is for many couples that work together. Most of the time we are happy working together, though sometimes there's this hollering about laundry.

⌒⤙

Birds are monogamous—they pick a partner and stay together. I've read this and in real life I've seen them work together as partners. It's a very lovely thing.

It was one of our early springs out here when in May I watched a warbler mom build a home for her soon-to-be babies. She built the nest where the logs intersected to support the bellied roof of the porch. She crafted it carefully, making it her own. In June she fortified and occupied it. Every day she sat in her nest. When she saw me, she'd fly away from it. But when she saw the dogs, she looked at them with one eye, deciding to stay seated while they passed. To her, I was much more of a threat, being taller than the dogs. I'm sure she imagined I could reach up and slap away the nest or steal her eggs. Her instinct was real. I could see Dad using her babies for a meal, but I would not.

She spent a lot of time in her nest, fat and feathery, her bill tucked under her lovely wings. She left the nest in the mornings, hunting for insects, berries, and grubs. It was the time for wild strawberries. I watched her in the yard. She'd come back, landing on the nest's ledge. I couldn't see what was happening inside, but I imagined the baby birds with their shiny heads, jaws hinged wide open and their large, searching eyes on their mother as she dropped the minuscule ruby berries and squiggly worms between their mandibles.

That was the same summer of biting flies. Everyone around us in the UP had said the flies would be coming. They didn't lie. The flies were especially terrible where the forest had been logged and still more terrible after a rain.

One day the sky got light gray in color. There was a quiet drizzle and I went for a bike ride. I bounced over the bumpy path where the roots from one tree to the next on either side were exposed. I was on a Specialized Fatboy bike and I skidded out when a twig became jammed between the back spokes and chain. I fell and wanted to cry in the same way I would have as a child, wanting sympathy from Mom but not really being hurt. No one had seen me so I sucked it up and began fixing it. The biting flies landed on my arms and shoulders in clumps, so close together their wings layered like the shingles of a roof. Their bite was sharp. It hurt and little bumps formed over my arms and shoulders where they removed chunks of skin with their sharp fangs or whatever it was they had.

Eventually the whole warbler family was gone one day, along with all the other birds. The sound of the logging was loud while trees felled, chainsaws whined, trucks lumbered in and out. After a while I got the courage to look inside the nest. Vacant. The black flies were gone too. I left her nest where she built it, with no intention of moving it either. It's still here.

After the birds and flies left the snakes showed up, which made sense since there were no red-tailed hawks to carry them off. Before, I would stop and watch the hawks fly over the path with snakes wriggling in their talons. The owls hadn't left, though. I saw one swoop down and nab a fuzzy vole. And I heard them having a lot to say at night.

The bats hadn't left. They were still nesting. At dusk we saw how the bats flew out of our chimney, like a cloud of gunpowder blasting apart as they flew off in every direction. They found their way in and out of our chimney as they awoke from hibernation. Wood shavings had fallen from where the sides of the ceiling met the wall, littering our carpet beneath. I looked at the wood shavings and at first thought it was many mischievous mice. Turned out it had been the bats back in early May that had been scratching and crawling their way between our roof and the wood beams of our ceiling. I learned what guano looked like and worried we'd get "bat-shit crazy."

The birds may have been gone, but the bats took down more winged insects at night than the warblers, or any of the other birds for that matter. The bats consumed many of the biting flies still holding out. We saw bats dip in and out of the floodlights posted high up on the sides of the cabin.

Anna hated the bats. Each time they sounded off, she pulled her head into her shoulders like a tortoise, as if one might swoop down to grab her with its tiny mouth and nimble toes and carry her away by her hair. Echolocation was how they saw, I told her. They needed to make those squeaking sounds so they could find their way. The squeaking ricocheted off whatever obscure flying insect they were about to engulf, or alerted them to their course so they could fly above or below a branch, pole, wire, or two-legged monster who stood below them emitting the circle of light cutting their path. That would be me; I liked to watch them in the yard with my flashlight.

Once a bat got lost in the cabin. Her sonar must have been not quite tuned or something, or she might have been ill—instead of up and out the chimney, she came down and in, attracted to the dim light from our computer as Anna streamed the news late at night. Our bedroom door was cracked, and the bat must have sailed in soundlessly with her wings extended. She must have realized she was in the wrong place when the low voices from the computer's output were unfamiliar; the sound of our dogs' heavy breathing was something she didn't like, and the millions of tiny insects and dander in the dogs' coats probably wasn't too appealing either. She sounded off, finding our locations and sizes, and then her wings started beating frantically, and with everything in the closed-up room echoing back at her, she realized she didn't have anywhere to go. Anna woke me up, yelling that there was a bat in the room, and we scrambled into another room, taking the dogs with us.

But that next morning after the night the bat was in our bedroom, I told Anna not to worry, I was determined to find the bat and release her safely. I put on a pair of yellow-dyed leather gloves and a pair of clear aviator goggles made for chopping wood or things like that in daylight. I walked up our stairs stealthily. I went to our room, searching for her along the ceiling, behind the dresser, under the bed, where our bath towels and robes hung on the back of the door, inside my bookbag hanging from the wall, through the closet, and even in our dresser drawers. I couldn't find her. I threw everything that hung on something out the window, hoping if she was in there, she would find her way out. If I just tossed her out the window that way, I thought, *would she just turn to a cloud of dust when the daylight hit her body?* Vampires and viruses have really messed up our ideas of bats. Eventually I built a house for the bats over on the ridge, luring them away from the cabin, and this worked. I fixed the area around the chimney where I thought they had entered, and we haven't heard any scrambling since. Now at night they come up from the trees on the ridge near where their new home is.

The underbelly, hind legs, and bony toes of a bat make it look like a cross between a mouse and a bird. They fly and the tips of their wings graze the tops of flowers as they swoop down on insects that thrive off nectar, collecting pollen all the while, ensuring reproduction. Fabulous pollinators, bats. Flowers have growing patterns nestled in their DNA that evolved for this very purpose, and their dusty orange, white, and yellow pollen is designed to cling to a bat's hindquarters and the undersides of their wings as they go up and down, decimating insects in flight. They descend and the pollen trails them—like a crop-dusting plane, in essence. The pollen falls on neighboring flowers in a fine, shimmering layer. It settles on the flowers and is drawn in, fertilizing the ovule, generating a new seed. This is not unlike, in a sense, how humans complete this process, the same way you might have learned about the birds and the bees.

The day after the bat incident, Anna said she thought the wilderness was closing in on us: a bat in the bedroom, snakes in the yard, toadlets in between every blade of grass, birds nesting on our porch, bears and otters in the river, owls snatching mice from between berry brambles and carrying them overhead,

coyotes hollering, wolf packs trotting and howling, dried this-
tles, dead nettles, buttercup, devil flowers, the wild marigolds,
and other weeds—edible and not—outlining the cabin. The
truth was the wilderness hadn't closed in on us any more than
we and other humans had closed in on the wilderness, where
the animals had been pushed out from their trees, caves, dens,
trails, and bushes, and maybe ended up here. Their homes had
been grabbed with claws like the ones in the game where you
put in a quarter and try to pull out a toy. Their homes and
trees were flung onto the truck beds of semis, and hauled out.
The animals had entered our yard on their way to somewhere
else, somewhere safer, a part of the forest where I wanted to
believe the growth was older or untouched, somewhere on the
other side of the river maybe, home to new nests, estuaries,
and sandbars full of eggs, where the tortoises stood on guard,
where they all could be safe again. While the birds and other
overstory dwellers went on their way first, the wolves, foxes,
coyotes, bears, and one lone mountain lion followed. I saw
all at one time or another, crossing the land during the time
between when the logging began and after the warbler family
had left the nest.

Not long before the warblers were gone, I conducted an
experiment. I came up to the porch from the yard on my
hands and knees, curious to learn how much the mom knew
about me. It was early in the morning. I was at my strangest
in the mornings, so I felt fine about it. I knew Anna was
sleeping and hoped she wouldn't wake up to find me crawling along our porch, but it didn't really matter anymore. At
that point I was deep into dabbling in various life experi-
ments—forest ones and substance ones like weed, psilocybin,

alcohol—and I'd even decided to go back to school. Like any good college kid, I was ready to experiment.

I knew the warbler was in her nest, and after having let the dogs out, I crawled up the deck with them, doing my best imitation, allowing my behind to swagger from one point to the other with the forward pace of my arms and thighs, left right, left right. On all fours, I was their size, but it turned out the mom was smarter than me. She flew away, and the male warbler, her partner, appeared on our post, looking down at me and I thought, snickered.

CHAPTER 15.
EPHEMERAL SEXUAL ORGAN

DAD WAS THE BOLETUS. MOM WAS THE CHANTERELLE. Dad was the forest. Mom was the kitchen. Dad was the forager. Mom was the chef. Dad was outside. Mom was inside. Dad was nature. Mom was nurture. Dad caused problems. Mom solved problems. Dad was violent. Mom was safe. Dad was anxious. Mom was depressed. I fruited from them, and I was all those things too. I was also the sheep's head—wily, twisting—and the honey mushroom—stretching, symbiotic.

Mushrooms are sexy. Some are multigendered. Others are male and some are female. Some reproduce together and some are asexual, able to reproduce on their own. Mushrooms are more like animals than plants, but I don't know exactly how. I'm not a mycologist. I'm not a botanist or an anthropologist. I'm just a person who prefers mushrooms to people and trees to tall buildings, a person who spends many hours alone, thinking too much about what I'm thinking.

I do study some of what I write about. I have tried to understand how mushrooms reproduce and the best explanation I've heard was told to me by my friend Rebecca, who *is* a mycologist. "The fruiting body is the ephemeral sexual organ of the mushroom. The rest of the organism resides underground as mycelium. The part that we see just fruits to fulfill a reproductive function." She told me this and I wondered if this was why mushrooms tasted so good.

In any case, mushrooms are fascinating. People hunt them, dream about them, fall in love with them. Some people even have festivals to celebrate the different seasons and species of them. And out of the many wildly beautiful organisms in the forest, mushrooms will more often than not stop you in your tracks for a closer look.

On August 17, 1979, sometime in the late morning, I fruited. I was swaddled against Mom's chest by the time Dad got to the hospital. He was dusty from Grandpa's farm. He'd been out on the tractor in Grandpa's field, sculpting a new patch of land for next season's corn when he got the call that Mom was in labor.

He had two sheep's head mushrooms bundled in paper napkins. He stood in the hospital room's doorway, the mushrooms swaddled against his chest. He stepped into the room and with his free arm he reached out for me. Mom turned, shielding me from his reach. She told him to wash himself off first. He set down the mushrooms on the tray table at her bedside. After he washed up, he held me for a couple of minutes. Passing me back to Mom, he said, "Found two sheep's head," and nodded to where he had set them. "Come real early this year. Been some good rain, though," he said, scratching his cheek. "I never found 'em this early before."

Mom didn't respond right away. She was exhausted but awake enough to tell him to move the mushrooms from her tray table.

The sun rose over the window. A distant church bell confirmed it was noon. The window was open, and a fan churned where it was propped against the screen. A couple of bees, pulled by the fan, bumped against the screen. The air of room 3E was warm and thick and smelled of fresh baby and starched hospital sheets. Dad sat in a chair beside the bed. In Mom's arms, I was seven pounds and a few ounces against her breast. My sisters would arrive soon but were late as well. Dad asked what was taking them so long. Mom didn't answer, figuring whatever it was, they were up to no good. Dad pressed the shiny pads of his calloused palms together and hung his hands down between his knees like he was praying to the floor.

⌁

Mushrooms have eleven chromosomes. And some strains can have up to twenty-some thousand variations of gender. There are three stages of sexual reproduction in mushrooms. Early on, in the meiosis stage, the "daughter" cells separate, and the DNA gets all shuffled together, which can lead to many combinations of the parent strains. The way I understand it, this happened with me and my sisters, splitting into four. Mothers at the time of their own birth have close to a million eggs inside of them. They have far fewer by the time they're able to reproduce, but there are still hundreds of thousands of potential siblings sharing her insides with you: the blood, the DNA, all the things she's tasted. If you look at pictures of me and my sisters from when we were all around the same age, we look like we could've been quadruplets. With mushrooms this all happens beneath the surface. It does for humans too, I believe.

Dad recently told me that his dad, before he was an owner of Jennie's Café, had owned a gas station. "Sinclair it was called, I think. Yeah, Sinclair." We were inside his sunroom, sitting at the table where he often sat to watch the birds.

I said, "Isn't that the one with the dinosaur?"

He said, "I'll be damned, it is."

He scratched his chin. "He used to run a gambling business through there. Poker, bingo, blackjack, name it."

"He was laundering money, then?"

"Well, ah, ah, I guess so. He was a bad gambler. My mom made him stop and that's when he bought into the restaurant."

"Still sort of gambling then," I said.

The day I was born, the tractor pulled a stretch of blades that turned up Grandpa's soil. The metal blades sliced through the grass and weeds, sending crickets and grasshoppers flying. The tractor blades cut neat lines through the haphazard patterns of the knapweed, curly dock, and goldenrods. The weeds were severed, and their seeds were folded back into the earth from the blades, replanting themselves. Along with the soil, the weeds, and the grass came the mycelium, the sex organs of which—somewhere far beyond where he plowed—would fruit into the mushrooms Dad and I would dream about hunting and devouring. At the time, Dad didn't think about that. He saw weeds to conquer and rows to plow for the coming season. Corn was coming in at two dollars and sixty-nine cents a bushel, and could be going up next year. The people who had this land before Grandpa had taken out many of the oaks, maples, cottonwoods, elms, and birch in large plots for gardens. If you looked at it from above, the long square blocks offset from the road were carved out like a chessboard—rows in one block went horizontal and in the next, perpendicular. Working the John Deere was Dad's form of artistic expression. He squinted his eyes against the sun. The big wheels on each side of his seat kicked up the land. He could smell it: "Nothing like fresh soil."

Acres away, Grandpa stood in the driveway and waved his arms to get Dad's attention. From that far out, backlit by the sun, Grandpa looked like an animated stick figure. His arms went back and forth mixing with the imaginary rows of corn. Dad was gunning for *amber waves of grain*. Dad loved being on the tractor. The silt, sand, dust, and pollen settled into his forearms where the hair was the thickest. He gripped the rusty wheel. On the tractor it was as if everything that was manly coursed through him. He felt powerful. But when he saw his dad waving like that, he killed the engine. It was quicker to run back to see what the matter was than to drive the tractor back in. He didn't want to cut into land he had just so carefully manicured.

Dad got the news Mom's water had broken, that she was at the hospital. He took off, abandoning the tractor for the Oldsmobile. He pushed the seat back as far as it would go, giving himself room what with his hernia and all. The station wagon's tires fishtailed as he spun it out of the sandy driveway and sped north on Route 421. He wanted to be there for my birth. He was certain Mom was finally going to have his son. He flew over the rocky pavement, nearly passing the intersection, and flung himself west. The station wagon sided up, wanting to glide on two wheels, but its wide bottom kept it on the pavement.

The sun was behind Dad, glaring in the rearview mirror. The soft flutter of what seemed to be a hundred butterflies flew up from several clusters in the road and slammed into the Oldsmobile's grill. He cussed his favorite phrase, "Goddamned son of a bitch and dirty bastard," when suddenly lights flashed red and blue behind him. He skidded to the side of the road. He leaned over to tuck his cowboy gun from the glove compartment under the seat. He liked to have it on him. I'd be the next one to use it, but not for some years. After he explained to the Jasper County Sheriff that his wife was having a baby, he was let go with a warning.

Dad patted the wily structures of the young and spongy sheep's head mushrooms he'd hunted that morning, and which sat there in the passenger seat. He thought this was surely a sign of all the mushrooms he and his boy would find together. He'd *never found them this early before.* The mushrooms were so clean. But nothing came from the forest without something else attached to it. Several acorn caps, decayed birch leaves, and three beechnut shells were imbedded in one of the mushrooms' bottoms. Sheep's head grew around whatever lay in its path. And while on the passenger seat, the mushrooms released several small beetles, hundreds of microscopic arachnids, three slender rust-colored bugs with what seemed like hundreds of legs, and two stink bugs. Dad flinched, brushing them off the seat where they hitched a ride from Medaryville to Merrillville.

Dad made it to the hospital, but late. I was already there. He couldn't think of what to talk about, so he talked about the mushrooms.

Mom eventually said that all sounded really nice about his find and while her eyes were closed, she continued, "That's nice. Cook them later." But she imagined if he did, she'd have to clean up after him. "Or don't cook them, wait for me to do it," she added.

As Dad sat there, with his hands hung between his thighs, praying to the ground, an awkwardness filled him. He didn't know what else to say to his wife, the mother of his fourth daughter, who looked like the rest. He probably thought a little about what a boy would've looked like. A boy would've been longer and weighed more. He imagined he'd surely have a big baby boy. He didn't say anything like that out loud. He didn't bring up how they had been wrong in thinking about the gender of the baby. He had told Mom about the mushrooms. *Now what?* It'd probably be stupid to ask her how she was feeling; he understood it probably wasn't too good.

He said to her about the mushrooms, he said, "Shouldn't be out till Labor Day," while ever so acutely aware of the several bees banging against the screen, caught in the fan's vortex; he slapped his arm, thinking one had landed there.

Being post-labor Mom didn't have much else to say. Her pelvis ached. Her tailbone throbbed. Her vagina and the tubes inside of her were sore. She wanted him to know that she felt less than medium. And for a quick few minutes she thought maybe they could try, together, to get above it. Like start over or something, but she didn't have the energy to explain what she meant if she were to say it. Anyhow, she figured it was the drugs making her sentimental or something.

Unfortunately, Dad never asked her how she felt. Instead, he looked at her like he was in pain—his hernia. She wormed her way, each joint wiggling and taking courage from the next, and created space for him in the narrow bed.

Dad got in and settled next to her. He said to her, "In a little bit?" His eyebrows cusped like a curious child's. "Soon. We should make a playmate for Iliana." They had already decided on the name, pronounced *ill lane uh*, after an ancestor from a long time ago.

"You're out of your god-damned mind," Mom whispered. Behind her closed eyelids, she rolled her eyes. She didn't want to talk too loudly because if I woke, I'd start squawking again. She felt too old for this, if younger than I am now. But with three teenagers and a new baby, it wasn't fathomable to think of a fifth. They weren't *that* Catholic, hardly at all. *Absolutely not.* She felt like she had already lived a couple lifetimes. "No way, we ain't having another kid. Four is enough. We can barely afford the ones we have."

He wanted a son. She knew he wanted a son and said, "This one will do," and because she knew, she added, "this one can be your little boy."

So, I became his little boy. I came about it naturally. I didn't have a penis but the things that went on inside my brain were probably the same as if I did have one. I always thought I was a boy, even before Dad ever said I was. I didn't see any difference between me and my boy cousins, but I felt very different from my girl cousin, even though when we took baths together, she and I looked much more alike than me and the boys.

Dad said I was a boy because he knew that made me happy. It made him happy too. He would do anything to make me happy. When I was very small he'd drive me around in the car for hours if I was unsettled because the rhythm of tires on the road put me to sleep. He went out late to get me the specific brand of pacifier I suckled, called a doo-doo. He scoured every store, sometimes until the wee hours of the morning, making sure he got it right. He bought me the He-Man action figures I wanted. He took me hunting. He showed me about guns. I was his sidekick. He was a good dad even if some of the stories I've told make it seem otherwise.

And maybe it was with all his wanting a boy that I wanted the same. I'd go on to ask god to help. Every night I'd ask god, "Can you turn me into a boy tomorrow?" But no matter how much I prayed that god would turn me into a boy, it didn't happen. I'd check my pajama bottoms in the morning to see if I had a similar apparatus as my boy cousins and it wasn't there.

When we took baths together, all about the age of five, Mom made sure to clean behind our ears. She used Q-tips to clean out what dirt had accumulated in them during the day that the swimming pool didn't wash out. We got grimy a lot because we built forts and played football. Sometimes we just got down in the mud because we could. Mom scrubbed our elbows, knees, and privates.

But when we took the baths, the three of us together in the baby blue enamel tub, while our chests looked somewhat the same, beneath the water things were different. They had little pale-colored nubs that floated up between their thighs. I didn't have that. My privates were less than theirs, just a crease between my legs. Mom had us stand up one at a time, to scrub our privates and butts. Our butts were all the same, round moons with a shadow sliced between them. Mom held us by our upper arms, working the lather over our bodies. And once we were done, one by one, she sat us back down in the tub. I saw her watching me look at them and she knew I was disappointed by the difference.

Genetic variation occurs within generations of mushrooms. Like many organisms the variations help the mushrooms adapt to changing environments.

To taste the beginning of time, to taste the earth as far away as you can imagine, consume the honey mushroom. Named *Armillaria mellea*, they are also called honey caps, pipinky, pinky, gypsy mushrooms, and *opieńka* in Polish. Dad grew up calling them *popinki*—what Busia called them, which was maybe a nickname. When he brought them to her from the forest, her eyes got big, and she knew exactly what to do with them. Honey mushrooms can be slimy. To love these mushrooms you have to love the texture of slipperiness. They are good pickled with vinegar, fermented with salt, in a stew, or roasted with butter, salt, and pepper. Honey mushrooms are asexual.

When all else failed, Dad and I collected the honey caps come fall. It's not that we didn't want them, we did, but we wanted the sheep's head more. The texture of the sheep's head was choice in comparison. Dad fermented the honey caps like he did sauerkraut. He put them in a crock with allspice, star anise, caraway, and bay leaf. He salted them between the caps, removing the stems. He layered the last remaining herbs from the garden between them. He used a weight inside the crock and covered it with plastic and every other day or two he removed the plastic to burp the gas that had built up inside the crock. The fermented honey caps were sour and fragrant. He used the juice from the ferment to season his pickled pigs' feet and other concoctions.

Many of his homesteading projects Dad reserved for his friends or my boy cousins to help him. He differentiated between what were the boy things and what were the girl things. I got to participate in the girl things, so I could do the fermenting and pickling. The boy things like butchering and harder stuff I had to watch, making mental notes. And sure, it might have been that he was worried I'd get hurt. But in a way, worried or assuming I'd get hurt and couldn't take it, but that the boys or men could, meant a lack of respect for girls and women. That might be picking it apart too much, but I think I'm right.

✦

I learned early on, even before 1984, that it seemed like the world was fairer to boys than to girls. That's a thing when you're young, trying to decide what is fair and what is not. So much seems unfair. Dad treated boys differently than girls, but I wouldn't say better.

Aside from Wonder Woman, it was mostly boys who got to be superheroes. They got to play sports on television, get messy with impunity, learn karate, play games where they could get hurt. Men and boys yelled, and it seemed okay. Dad yelled and it was just how it was. My sisters cowered when he yelled, but sometimes they laughed after his back was turned. And sometimes if he yelled, they ran because they worried they might get hurt. They didn't feel that way about Mom. When Mom yelled, they yelled back and sometimes called her a bitch. The physical threat wasn't the same.

Boys got a pass; they were allowed to do more things. Girls got held to standards. I didn't want to be standardized. I wanted to do what I wanted.

In grade school, the boys and I had crushes on the same girls. As I got older I had a hard time reconciling it unless I pretended to be a boy. At home I retreated into my imagination and pretended to be a boy and in that world it was fine for me to have crushes on girls. A couple times—actually many times—the crushes slipped from pretend into real life. I thought I could deliver love letters to certain girls and that it would work out, but it did not, and I got ridiculed by the other kids. The kids said that because I wasn't a boy I couldn't do such things. But girls had crushes on me too. I noticed it once we got older, when they knew the difference and knew they shouldn't. I figured it happened that way because I seemed more like a boy than a girl even if I didn't look it anymore.

I've told you Mom pierced my ears before I was old enough to protest because as a baby, people thought I was a boy. People thought I was a boy even when Mom dressed me in pink. I had a boy's aura. I was androgynous without meaning to be.

Eventually, going to Catholic school was different than home. I was forced to be like a girl. I had to wear a skirt or jumper. I hated it. We were required to wear shorts underneath the skirts too. That was another thing about boys—we had to wear shorts because the boys wanted to look up the skirts. Looking up skirts didn't interest me. I knew what was there. I didn't want to see the girls' underwear.

Later, at Catholic high school you had to wear uniforms too, but when October 1 arrived, girls got to wear pants because it was colder outside, and you were allowed to be more covered up. I liked that part. The pants had to be navy, and it was hard to find a fit you'd like. I didn't feel cute in the navy slacks, but I felt more like myself in those than in the skirts and jumpers. And in high school you got to wear navy shorts in the warm months, so I didn't have to wear a skirt at all, and the jumpers were long gone. I wore navy shorts cut from the slacks I got too tall for but the nuns made us roll up the hems if the shorts were frayed. We couldn't be messy about it. No, no. And because you couldn't have the frayed part showing, that was how I wanted to wear them. I got in trouble more than once for that. The nuns would make me roll the shorts up in front of them, then later I'd roll them down again. Also, you couldn't have your shorts or your skirt any more than two inches above your knee and if you did, you'd have to change into an extra skirt or shorts from the nurse's office that was never the fit right. I didn't really care for having my shorts too short. But you had to abide by these rules on length because the girls had to be regulated so we didn't tempt the boys by showing too much of our thighs. So, in a sense, the boys got a pass for that too.

It seemed to me that boys didn't have to learn much about self-control or how to be in the world, because everything revolved around making sure they were okay. Girls had to mind all their manners, dress certain ways, and live with the threat of physical violence or rape. Boys had to worry about feeling uncomfortable, tempted, or ridiculed. Physical violence and rape could happen to them too, but they had more ability to defend themselves being somewhat stronger. Of course, there's more to it all, but that's how it seemed to me then. There was very little balance. I knew that much was true. I knew that before I even had words for it. Boys had the power.

It's hard for us as a species to understand anything if it's not in relation to us. We've completely altered the world to our liking. And even within that we've divided ourselves into so many categories, which when you consider things, are constricting. Things shouldn't have to be so certain. By dividing ourselves we create the boxes we work so hard over the course of our lives to escape.

There are some things about our species that are quite beautiful, and I could go on and on, but instead what I want to tell you about is the mushroom, which is a beautiful and, in a sense, genderless organism. The spores come from the fruiting body, the ephemeral sex organ, which can be likened to a sperm or egg. But it's probably more accurate to call it an egg. And the oxygen, trees, rivers, sun, and rain—everything is the world—is the path the egg travels, the way human eggs travel through mothers' fallopian tubes. The spores are carried by the wind, on animals, the feathers of birds, the cuffs of our pants, and in the hairs of our arms, and when they fall, it's as though the soil, the environment overall, becomes like the uterine lining. Here is where they then begin, in a way, to become embryos.

Now it feels strange to say men could be dangerous and violent, because I know so many who are good. But this was how I learned about it in my heteronormative upbringing: men have guns and brass knuckles. Men play hard games and roll around with one another. Men work outside and hurt themselves. Men have certain bonds. They shoot stuff, blow things up, skin the animals, and gut the fish. Men are bigger than women and, in many cases, stronger. Women do laundry in waders, can vegetables, ferment, cook, save seeds, feed and clean the children. Women have the children. Women do the softer things. They have certain bonds too. Women are mothers. Even though my parents stretched gender boundaries, there were still boundaries.

Back then I wanted to be a boy. I wanted the power of a boy. I wanted to be a man to have that power, but the truth was I just didn't want to feel so afraid. Sometimes I think I would still like to be a man because I don't feel like a woman. But I don't feel like a man either. I feel more akin to a mushroom.

In the forest, hunting mushrooms with Dad, carrying our mesh sacks so that the spores would drop, ensuring reproduction, I felt like I was doing something worthwhile. I could exist in between. I didn't have to have to be one or the other. I was a catalyst. I didn't have to be the boletus or chanterelle or have a penis or vagina. I didn't have to be a certain thing to be in the forest. I just needed to love it and I did.

CHAPTER 16.
SHEEP'S HEAD

I KNOW WE'VE BEEN KISSING THE WALLS AND TRAVEL-
ing through time, but I must take you again to a late summer
day in 1984. By then I'd seen a bunch and knew a bit about
some things. I knew how to aim and shoot Dad's cowboy
gun. I wished I'd had it with me that day, to point it at Uncle
Georgie. Not to kill him, but to make him afraid like he had
made me afraid. To tell him to stop being a bad guy.

He'd already come over and shot up the farmhouse in one
of his rages. Mom laid over me on the floor when we all had
to get down as a couple bullets hit the siding and stuck in the
support beams. One bullet had also come through the window. Mom was heavy on me. I felt like Play-Doh like when
you flatten your palm over it. Her breath was warm on the top
of my head when she asked if I was okay. "Yeah, I'm okay," I
said. Her breath smelled like zucchini. Mom was mad at Dad
like he was the one who had done it, and I guess if you thought

about it enough, he had done it because he hadn't stopped his brother from doing it. Soon as Uncle Georgie showed up, swerving his Buick up the driveway, Mom told Dad not to let him get out. "Don't you let him get out of that car." And Dad, being the guy he was, not wanting to have any sort of confrontation with his brother, thought he could talk him down from whatever ledge he was on. Dad knew his brother was on a ledge because he was always on a ledge. We all knew that. I knew that and I was small. Some people are just like that, you know, on the ledge. Dad looked at Mom as he hurried out of the house to meet his brother in the driveway. Dad's face said he wasn't going to stop him. He just couldn't do it.

~

Near the forest's edge at Grandpa Regan's farm in Medaryville was that old Dodge pickup truck from the 1940s. Dad said at one time they hauled pigs in it. Dad said before that, he and his Jaja, his dad's dad, would load it with grapes from the Sunday market in Gary and take them back to Jaja's house to make wine. Jaja lived in a shotgun house up a hill from one of the main arteries in town. Jaja had two acres. He had lots of oaks where his yard met some forest preserve out back. "It was a good house. Jaja done real good," Dad said.

Dad's family liked to hang on to everything. Nostalgia made good stories. Some of it was nice stuff too, but no one kept it nice or fixed it once it wasn't nice anymore. When the thing was done or broke it was a goner. If it fell apart then it was in pieces. Time passed faster than you thought and suddenly things that were once new became relics.

Now, these truck windows were shattered from gunshots.

Webbed fragments and shards hung on from the windshield's frame. Uncle Georgie and one of my cousins thought it would be fun to shoot stuff, so they did. At some point the truck's doors were flung open and stayed that way. Rust had frozen the hinges and there was no closing them. From the truck's bench seat, moss and saplings grew. The contrast of the dark, worn leather seats and moss was quite pretty. The seeds of thistle flowers were carried in from late summer through the opened doors and enough water and sunshine came in through the busted-up windshield to give them life in the floorboards. Weeds and wildflowers gone to seed were arranged in the hundreds, freckling the truck's cab. A few large oaks squeezed through cracks in the truck's bed where the pigs were once stuffed in, grunting. The pigs used to lick the sides and floors of the truck bed, tasting the sun-dried grape juice from years prior. They would have loved the acorns from these oaks. Seasons of acorns had fallen over the truck.

A few yards away, there was a camper. The door was broken off and rested against its side. The walls were ripped out, whether by a person or time, it was hard to say. The bones of it were exposed like in an X-ray film. The floor was swollen and rotted where Queen Anne's lace, thistle, and milkweed stood up. Where the kitchen sink might have been, maple saplings sprouted along the counters.

Depending on how you saw it, this farmyard was a treasure or a horror. In the pole barn, hammered together with square-cut box nails through repurposed pine and corrugated iron walls, were old drum sets, baseball cards, stacks on top of stacks of magazines and newspapers, coffee cans full of nuts and bolts, antiquated farm equipment, tools, stalls for horses, other stalls full of towels, old clothes, and a mattress. That barn was as big as our barn at home, which had similar contents like a smoker, commercial-sized icebox, cast-iron sausage stuffer, cedar and iron wine press, and wine barrels. It was all there, even small things like the red vinyl bar stools and booths from Jennie's Café, and its soda fountain with the tubes behind it like an octopus with crystallized soda clogging in the tentacles. I imagined Dad as a young boy, like George Bailey in *It's a Wonderful Life*, passing the soda fountain and making a wish: *I'm gonna be Jacques Cousteau. I'm gonna be Tom Joad.*

Wind blasted through where the iron walls were no longer attached. It rippled along them, making a sound like a xylophone. I sat behind one of the old drum sets, tapping my five-year-old fingers as hard as I could against it. "Where's the sticks?" I asked Dad. He didn't know, said I should find them. "Could sell that drum set if we fixed it a bit," he said, and added there were Mickey Mantle baseball cards around here somewhere. He told me once he had a Babe Ruth card too, worth a couple million—probably both their rookie cards, his and Mantle's. He said he'd never gotten rid of them, that I'd be able to find them in a brown paper bag, rolled down like a lunch sack.

I creeped off again. Finding anything like that was impossible. First you looked one way, then the other, and then you realized everywhere you looked there was a brown lunch sack. I searched one after the other. Nuts. Bolts. Screws. Nails. And in the bigger bags, rolled down the same way, were just magazines or newspapers. There was a headline from an ancient *Time* magazine that questioned whether Nixon would be a good president. I figured this was how all families were— they just hung on to everything. One of the best things I came across was Busia's burger press. "Well, I ain't seen that in years," Dad said. By the time either of us would talk about that burger press again, we'd both have forgotten it would still be here, and I'd steal it but you already know this.

In this barn, families of mice filled the corner holes. Bats hung from the rafters. Cats stretched and pawed at the ground, meowing. An occasional owl came in and swept the place for dinner. Dust collected. Paw prints upon paw prints dotted everything. Even the slow drag from the underside of a tortoise's shell cut trails in the layers of dust and farm dirt. A squiggly path announced a garter snake had passed through.

Dad's mom was the hoarder, not his dad, at least that's what it sounded like in retrospect whenever anyone talked about it all. It was probably easier for everyone to blame her. She wasn't a favorite. She had to keep it, they said, even if it didn't mean anything at all. Grandpa Regan wasn't orga- nized anyways, so it didn't bother him much. In the end, people figured Grandpa thought that's what pole barns were good for: housing things you couldn't get rid of, things that became part of who you were. He probably wasn't wrong. And no one bothered him about it. He never had enough animals to fill it, so it got filled with future relics that in 1984 looked a bit like junk. Dad was the same way. The garage and the pole barn at our farmhouse were just like this one. You couldn't make a move in it without banging a shin or slicing the tender flesh on your ankle. Mom hated it, but that's how it was. Dad still used the big smoker, warming boxes, and upright refrigerator from Jennie's Café so that was in his favor. If you used the thing then it wasn't really hoarding it, at least that's how I think he saw it. In 1984 Dad worked that smoker hard—a real diesel truck pumping out plumes of blue smoke. Filling the barn with smoke, Dad said, "It'll find her way out." The guy who was always worried we were going to die in the obscenest of ways was the one most likely to take us out. Asphyxiation was one of many possibilities.

Dad stood at the edge of Grandpa's barn doors, rifle strapped over his shoulder and pocketknife tucked in his boot while I pretended I was a pirate, searching for treasures. I looked for anything resembling drumsticks and, in each paper bag, hunted for the collectible baseball cards. I figured if I found those, I could trade them in for at least a hundred bucks at the Buy, Sell, and Trade store in downtown Hobart. All they had in that shop were baseball cards—old ones, and new ones; the kind wrapped in plastic with a hard stick of gum.

If you peeled the façade from that barn it would light up like a dollhouse. On one side there was open space the length of four pine-paneled Oldsmobile station wagons and the width of two. This was where I searched among the bags, furniture, tables, stools, old cars, rusted plows, and seeders. Dad said a draft horse used to pull one of those plows before Grandpa got his tractor. Off to the side was an area sectioned into six horse stalls, though only two of the stalls had horses in them. The horses, in sync, bowed their heads and nudged their muzzles into the hay. One broke rhythm by raising his head, lifting his tail as if on a switch, and letting out four coal-shaped turds. Relieved, he turned his head back down and pushed his long face back into the hay. There was a skinny walkway of compact earth between the stalls, lit by two circles from exposed bulbs dangling from wires. The walkway led through a particle board wall that separated the stalls from the rest of the barn. Through that walkway, a lean-to housed three pigs and opened to a small paddock. Outside, the plump sows bathed in the muck. Dad, always worried about the pigs, reminded me to be careful. He never wanted me near them. But when they had babies, I was allowed to put my hand through their pens and let them smell me before I fed them apples. He'd take the babies out and I'd hold them like they were puppies. I'd pet and kiss their soft heads between their ears.

And alongside the paddock, when no one was looking, deer stole up from the forest. They crept through the black walnut, poplar, and oak trees, barely crunching the dried leaves as if floating, and stuck their heads through the barbed wire. Over time those wires got bent from them stealing their dinners out of the pig trough slopped up with acorns, corn, smashed apples, and whatever food scraps that came from the house. There was a cow too, a pretty one. The lone heifer stood at the other side, away from the pigs and barn. She was mostly black with a few white spots along her flank and tenderloin, and one large white spot on the right side of her face making one side of her face white, and the other black. Depending which way she stood, it was like looking at two different cows. In the yard she tried out different postures, but you rarely saw her move. You'd see her standing there like a statue, and after the few seconds it took you to blink or check over your shoulder, when you saw her again, she was facing the other direction. She seemed sad. I walked into the paddock and held out my hand to her. She came near and pushed her nose onto it. I scratched her snout between the nostrils. She was familiar with people. She and Grandpa had a good relationship. Several times Dad offered to kill and butcher her, but thankfully Grandpa wouldn't let him do it. I was like Grandpa in that way, knowing I'd never be able to kill any of my own livestock.

Several barn cats lingered on the sidelines, watching us. One was on top of a post, another in a tree, a third on the ledge of the lean-to, and a fourth was between the roof and rafter. Once I counted at least ten different cats here but that wasn't even half as many as in our barn, so we had that going for us. The cat on the post was calico and the one in the rafters, hovering over the pigs, was black and fluffy with pumpkin-colored eyes. I looked at her looking at me. I called to her, "Here, kitty kitty kitty." She knew I was talking to her, so she ran away.

Dad called my name as I called for the cat. In the paddock, I had begun sinking in the mud. The heifer was at arm's length. The pigs, while unmoving, looked at me with all six of their black eyeballs. Dad, still standing in the open barn doors, called into the dim and dust. "Lanie, let's go," he said again. Suddenly, I heard him gasp when he must have seen I was sinking in the mud. I barely noticed it myself. He squelched his way towards me. One boot got stuck and he came up barefoot. He left the boot behind, coming at me with panic on his face as if I was in grave danger. He plucked me out of the mud and said I should never leave his sight again unless he told me it was okay. But *he* had told me to look for the cards and he sort of always let me out of his sight. I chose to not say anything. Then he said something else about quicksand and that got me scared, especially after he was hounding me under his breath about suffocation and how he once knew a guy who no one knew anymore because he had gotten swallowed up by the earth, which could happen to me, to anyone for Christ's sake. He was certain that somehow, whether eaten by pig or earth, trampled by horse or cow, I was a goner.

On that Sunday morning, not long after we found chanterelles on the day of a sand tornado, we were getting ready to hunt for mushrooms again. I sat on the living room floor of my grandparents' farmhouse with my legs crossed and a bowl of ramen noodles between my twiggy thighs. I was watching *The Lone Ranger* and dressed to match in a button-down shirt with embroidered breast pockets and pearl buttons, straight-leg Levi's, and hefty belt buckle. My cowboy boots sat beside me. I was eating the packaged kind of ramen noodles, Maruchan. Grandma Regan was not a good cook like Mom, not even as good as Dad for that matter. She couldn't even make the packaged stuff taste good. I couldn't figure out why. Dad could make it pretty good, better than it was supposed to be. He used all sorts of extra toppings, though I did get sick that one time. His ramen was satisfying. Grandma gave me soggy noodles. The ratio of dry seasoning to water was off. Just well water would have probably been tastier. I knew how to do the ramen better myself. This was one of many reasons I liked our farmhouse more than theirs, though I did love to forage for mushrooms with Dad and Grandpa. I loved this forest. And with all that wonderful stuff there was bad stuff too. Like lunch, the television options, and of course there was always the possibility of Uncle Georgie being around. But I went anyways, excited to be between the trees.

The Lone Ranger ended when he got the bad guy. I liked looking like a cowboy, but I didn't love cowboy television. There wasn't anything else on. They only had three channels.

After lunch, I took my empty bowl, spoon, and fork to the sink and washed it myself because that's what Mom told me I was supposed to do at other people's houses. Even at my grandparents' house I was to clean up everything I touched. And I ate everything too because she said that was how I should do it. "If you don't like it, you better do it," she said. Dad was out in the garden with Grandpa, so after I set my dish in the strainer, I went to look for baseball cards in the basement, thinking maybe Dad misremembered where they were.

The farmhouse Grandpa had built was a bi-level home. Everyone seemed to have a house like that. I liked ours better because the layout was unique. Dad did a lot of our home himself. I heard when Grandpa got the land here, there wasn't much more than the well house and outhouse on these one hundred acres. The acreage was studded with wooded areas and tiny abandoned log homes no bigger than a single room. Some of the land was flattened into big square spaces large as city blocks, made for planting corn and beans. Dad always said he wished he knew "more about them mineral rights 'cause there was probably a lot of oil under that farm we were missing out on." The upstairs of Grandpa's house had lots of light coming in from the windows on the south, east, and west sides. The north side of the house was shadowed by old oaks and walnuts. The kitchen was on that side of the house and always darker, not to mention grimier.

The basement was dark and dingy. Indirect light came in, casting shadows over the many boxes and boxes of things. In the southwest corner, sectioned off by a few walls was Uncle Georgie's bedroom, and I stayed far away from that side of the basement. The basement, like the barn, was full of treasures, never to be used again but stored for safekeeping just in case, like the porcelain statue of a cherubic-faced woman. She had a sash around her shoulder and her breast was exposed where the nipple was gone. She held a basket of mulberries. When I asked Mom one day about the statues—there were more than just the cherub—she couldn't explain it other than to say, "That's something lots of Polish people like to have for decorations." The truth was she didn't like Grandma Regan's taste.

"Hello," I said to the statue, squaring up to her, giving her cold, hard lips an innocent kiss. She was my height after all, it only seemed natural. A chunk was missing from her cheek and the rest of her was glued together from hundreds of small pieces as if it had been shattered before. Somehow without knowing for certain I understood it was Dad who had done it.

An old dining room table with ornately carved ladder-back chairs took up a large portion of the room. Other furniture, like worn end tables and old lamps, was stacked on top of it. Surrounding the table were the boxes, some filled with papers that may or may not have been important, some with other things. And in here too, were more brown paper sacks, both lunch and grocery-sized, that held other miscellaneous items: small tchotchkes, trinkets, whatchamacallits.

Spider webs lengthened in the corners. Some connected

all the way from one end of the room to the other. I ducked beneath them, fought with the ones I hadn't seen that caught my sleeves, and pulled other ones out of my fine hair. Field mice left evidence everywhere. I never thought this was a nuisance—just part of what it meant to have a farmhouse. A house, even if it's not vacant, can fall apart quickly. You just brushed away the mouse shit and spiders, moving on. As I peeked in one bag I thought could contain cards but was only cards for playing, like poker or War, a few fluffy brown mice skittered from one side of the dining table to the other.

The mice were so very cute, which increased my desire to hold them. Mom told me not to because they carried diseases. I couldn't help it, I must. When Mom yelled to keep the doors shut tight at night because of the rodents, I made sure to put the stopper on the screen doors just short of closing so they could come in from the cold. I wanted them to find their way to my room. I left crumbs as a sign that I was a comrade, but they never came to me. I feel bad about that now. Obviously, it took years before I had my own place and realized I didn't want them.

On the east side of the room was a flimsy door fashioned with a brass knob. I feared what was behind it but was sucked in. I knew beyond the door, the garage held even more treasures. I was afraid because I hadn't seen Uncle Georgie or heard him that day but that didn't mean he wasn't there. It meant he could be anywhere. He knew how to materialize from nothing like the worst kind of supervillain. I went into the garage anyway.

To my left, was a traditional garage door. The kind you grasped from the bottom and threw upwards, and it chuckled along the aluminum tracks. But you couldn't get to that door from where I was. There were too many boxes, bags, fabrics, nests, and webs. The mice had also made their mark. I brushed the poop aside, inspecting the contents of bags. I quietly sang to myself the theme song of *Inspector Gadget*. In the middle of the garage was Dad's old two-toned 1958 Chevy, his first car. If I extended my arm just enough, I could touch it.

I had been in that vintage car plenty but never when it was working. It was royal blue at the bottom, light blue at the top with white on the hood and front fenders. The backside flared out with fins on each side, with cherry brake lights. I wished I could have ridden in it when it had worked, at least once. Dad told me stories about it, how he drove to Great-Grandma Hubbs's house in Lake Station to pick up Mom for their first date. He drove it to fish, taking the entire Sciara family with him, fishing poles strapped to the roof and the trunk full of ice. With the Sciara family in it plus himself, the shocks cried as he drove as close to the water as they could get, the Gary Harbor. He had saved up every little bit he could for a long time to get that car.

I had sat in all its seats knowing those stories. I imagined I had a fisheye view of each story, hitching a ride on the roof, seeing through the eye of the fishing line's shiner. I was even the dead crappie, bluegill, perch, smelt, bass, and catfish they had caught, gawking up at the trunk's ceiling, my lips stuck in the shape of a small circle. Sometimes I sat behind the driver's seat and pulled on the wheel like I was steering a rig. Other times I slunk down in the seat, pressing on the gas pedal saying, "vroom." I'd yank the wheel left then right, tilting the opposite way as I fishtailed. I pressed my palms against the worn leather seats. I let my hand glide over the dashboard, dusting it, but also feeling its energy. I had imaginary dates in there, too. Sometimes we just parked. My date, a pretty girl with a heart-shaped face and dimples, sat next to me. I scooted over into the middle of the bench seat, between the driver's seat and my date. I placed my legs on each side of the column. She placed her hand on the knobby part of my knee as our thighs touched. I leaned over, kissing her. My hands went around the hollow frame of her face, holding it close to mine while our lips moved clumsily. I felt her breath on my face.

I knew that car well. Under the driver's seat was a rusted jack. Under the passenger's seat was a tire iron. The backseat held various odds and ends. The trunk hung open because it didn't latch anymore. Inside the trunk were waxed boxes with handles. Inside the boxes were receipts and papers with scribbles on them, meant to be some sort of bank ledger but I could never make it out quite right. All the receipts were squished into files, year after year until the boxes looked pregnant. I searched through the files looking for paper money, thinking maybe someone had forgotten it in there. If I found some, I planned to buy all the toys I circled in the Sears catalogue that came every winter before Christmas. I figured with all this mess around, someone was bound to have misplaced some money. I imagined Grandpa with those papers in his hand, looking under a desk light at the scratches, then adding them up on a calculator with the tape spooling out the other side.

I knew those worn leather seats. I had memorized the crevices the way a palm reader traces a life line with their finger. I had played with the radio dials a million times. Once, when I was littler, I turned the keys left in the ignition and the car turned on, static played for a split second before the car died out. Now the keys were long gone. Of course, there was a coffee can full of keys on a workbench. I had tried each one, but none worked.

I was about to open the car's door and stopped when I was utterly spooked. I jumped back like I had been electrocuted. I saw the outline of a man behind the dirty windshield, sitting in the driver's seat. I couldn't calculate how long I had already been in the garage, so I didn't know how long he had been spying on me. That was a terrifying feeling—realizing you were being watched—and I began to shake. I was always afraid of that sort of thing. Sometimes my sisters spied on me when I was playing pretend, talking to myself, or kissing a wall, and it hurt my feelings because I would hear them laugh but it never scared me the way this did. I felt dogged. I hoped he hadn't seen me kiss the statue in the other room. I didn't want him to know that I knew what kissing was.

I knew that car, but I didn't know it with him in it. Unrecognizable now, with his hands on the wheels. Through the windshield his eyes were blackened, deep within their sockets. Still, I knew he was glaring at me. I imagined how his eyes must have been following me all this while, as I'd been humming my song. I got upset at myself for being in there and not seeing him in the first place. I should have seen him, but it was hard to see. The car was dusty. It was a hard thing to know.

I backed up against the workbench until I couldn't move back any further. The basement door was several feet away. I worried if I ran, and he knew I was scared, the thrill of the chase would only increase his desire to grab me. I was mad at myself. I had always been so conscious of where he was, but for some reason I hadn't thought to look in the car. I'd been too eager to rummage. I imagined if I had the cowboy gun things would be different. I'd be in charge. My eyes flicked left to right, scanning for anything I could grab to protect myself, or murder him if it came to that.

The Chevy's door creaked open. A stuffed Incredible Hulk doll with a soft, green chest and white shorts peeked out from around the door. The doll was in Uncle Georgie's hands. I didn't move any closer. The hair on the doll's head looked fluffy. It was so cute; I wanted to have it and he knew how much I did.

"You like the Hulk, don't you," he asked.

Just run, I thought. This was the kind of thing Mom talked about and how McGruff, the Crime Dog, said to stay away from the strange guy who offers you candy or a ride. I kept my distance, wanting the doll, but it wasn't worth it. He knew it. I knew it. He said that if I got in the car, the Hulk was mine. "Here, I'll scoot over," he said with an innocent look on his face. He slid to the passenger side and patted the driver's seat. I was supposed to consider this a friendly invitation. I knew the seat would be warm from his heavy thighs. I hesitated, looking at the door again, thinking I should run and just how to do it.

"Come on in, and you can have the doll," he said. "I won't bother ya." There was a bottle in the seat next to him. I knew because he unscrewed the cap and took a drink. He tilted his head back, suckling the bottle like the baby pigs did with their mother only not as cute.

"I have to ask my dad," I said, stalling, fighting down

the knot in my throat. I was afraid the smallest movement toward the door would sic him on me. I was shaking while also finagling my way, half inch by half inch.

"You don't have to ask your dad. He *said* I could give it to you." I knew he was lying.

This was it. No one was coming. I didn't have much more time. I had to get away or this *thing* was going to happen. A thing that was scarier than the grim reaper in the mirror, or the sharpness of a knife's blade at your throat. I wasn't exactly sure what the thing was, but I knew it was something I would live through, which made it all the worse.

Suddenly, I ran. I grabbed the door handle and passed through the threshold, slamming the door shut. I held it closed with the weight of my body, back and palms pressed against it. I found the lock and turned it. I exhaled. I heard him breathing on the other side. The door handle jiggled. Dad called to me from somewhere inside the basement, "Lanie," he said, "Lanie." Never was I so happy to respond to him. "Here," I hollered back, loud enough for Uncle Georgie to understand Dad was nearby. He knew Dad would mess him up. Dad had already put Uncle Georgie in the hospital once. That time ended with his jaw wired shut for saying something grotesque to my sisters. I knew these stories though I was too young to know them.

I gulped air and unlocked the door. I was afraid if I kept him locked in there, the payback later would be worse. He would want revenge and things might not happen as slowly next time. He stayed behind the door. He wouldn't come out, not with Dad around. He knew if Dad saw him come out of the garage behind me that Dad would know something was wrong. Georgie knew if Dad knew, Uncle Georgie would be a dead man. Somehow me and my enemy were on the same page. I wanted him gone, yes, but I didn't want it to be because of Dad. I made a few strides toward Dad's voice and found him standing near the statue of the lady. For a moment I wondered if he, too, had ever kissed her.

"Come on, get your boots on," he said, which meant he'd put them on me. He held my boots in his hands. They weren't much larger than his palms. He kicked out a chair and sat on it, lifting me into his lap. One foot at a time, he pushed them in. The boots were white with scuffs at the toes and worn down on the outsides of the heels from the funny way I walked with my legs sort of bowed.

"Let's get going," he said. "We've got to get sheep's head." I followed him out the basement's back door into the grove of walnuts and oaks. We walked over the sandy soil where my boots sunk down with each step. We trudged down the path and my heart thumped, still rattled. I looked down, thinking I might see the pounding through my shirt. Dad wasn't concerned; I don't think he noticed I was shaken. He didn't ask why I was in the garage. It was just how it was. You could easily disappear around here.

"To find sheep's heads," Dad said, "look at the base of all the old and dead oak trees. That's where you'll see a sheep's head, there on the ground." He pointed at the ground then bent over with a grunt, picking up a leaf. "See here." He traced the leaf with his fingertip.

"I see."

"This one here is oak, so when you see these leaves on the tree or the ground with acorns near the tree, then you know to look. But make sure it's a big tree. No little ones. Or if it's dead, that's good too." We kept walking.

This day was Grandpa's birthday. Grandpa was movie star handsome. His dark, thick brown hair was speckled with white. It was wavy like the bark of the oaks. He wasn't ever going to bald—even when the white took over, it all stayed. He wore it short around his ears, which made them stick out. It was coiffed at the top, though he didn't style it at all. He woke up like that; he was a beautiful man.

We took the sandy path that led into the forest. Grandpa came running, catching up to us. He was dusted in all sorts of things from the corn harvest. Earlier when we got there we'd looked out at him amid the big clouds of it all rising from the tractor's wheels. We heard the bearings and gaskets clobber one another, the sounds of grease spattering up into the engine around coils and other mechanisms. The exhaust pipes released brown smoke. Grandpa cut some of his corn in early September for feed; the rest he'd let dry longer, and that'd be for the bushels. Sometimes he had sweet corn and we ate that in August. He didn't end up selling bushels for long though. He was retired; he could only do so much. Dad dreamed he'd take over for him someday. Dad told him, "Don't worry, Pa," he said, "I'll see to her." But he wouldn't. He couldn't work his job, work his own property, and work his dad's.

Grandpa caught up to us and wiped his hands on his chest. He wore a white T-shirt and dungarees and a straw hat over his pretty hair. He was a real Tom Joad. He was everything Dad wanted to be. I saw it in Dad's eyes. My eyes shined that way too when I looked at him. Together, we all passed the clapboard lean-to and the paddock where the heifer stood looking at us with the white side of her face. Dad loved to say how he built the barn, paddock, and lean-to. He stuck out his chest and adjusted his posture. He said, "I built those," just about every time we walked past them. We passed the thorny blackberry brambles. I picked the last ones of the season, collecting as many as I could, until my hands were painted with the purple juice.

Because I was small, Dad said, as he usually did, that I had an advantage finding the mushrooms. Because I was closer to the ground, they'd be easier to spot. After a while I thought he just said this because he knew he wasn't good at finding them himself anymore. He never spotted the mushrooms first; it was me or Grandpa who did. Dad would see something and point at it thinking it was a mushroom and it wasn't. I knew he could hunt them good; I just hadn't seen it. It was the same with hunting and fishing. He told me stories about all the fishes he'd caught over the years, yet I rarely saw him get a bite. He talked a lot about the deer he'd shot and the wild turkeys he'd bagged, but nope—hadn't really seen it. Supposedly he'd done all those things, and well too, but it was mostly before I was born. Then there were the sheep's head he'd found the day I was born. He always told that story. It was a good one. Because of that, we'd always look around my birthday, but that was the first and last time he found them so early. Earliest I ever found them was August 23.

But on this day, Grandpa's birthday, we often found them, and I did. I found the sheep's head. Grandpa gave me his pocketknife and explained, "Now, cut it at its base." I already knew this part, but I pretended like he was telling me for the first time, something I'd learn to do with men for a long time.

I held the tender mushroom in my hands. A few potato bugs scattered from burrows along the underside. I flicked them off. I closed the knife on my thigh and stuck it in my boot like I'd seen Dad do a hundred different times. I never cut or stabbed myself like he sometimes did, but he still told me not to do it that way because I would. I didn't listen to him. And I didn't cut myself. I gently shook the mushroom to release any more critters, pinching away the leaves and twigs.

The sheep's head was beautiful. It was the size of a softball and the shape of a brain. I held the sheep's head the way I held baby bunnies when I found them. I lowered it carefully into the mesh sack I had over my shoulder so the spores would sift out through the holes. We got to be pollinators in a way, and that was a pretty thought.

I found several more and Grandpa found one and exclaimed, "Always on my birthday!" Afterward, we sat them along the picnic table beneath the only willow on the farm. Next to the willow was the well where Dad and Grandpa washed their boots. I did the same. Grandpa told me to pick my favorite specimens first. I picked the youngest ones, the ones that were as cute as real-life baby sheep heads. I was having a nice time, but I didn't want to stick around to cook them. I wanted to go home. I kept looking at the garage door, hoping Uncle Georgie wouldn't reappear. Every time Dad moved around the table to get a better look at what we had found, I kept magnetized to his hip. I hooked my finger in his pocket. Touching him made me feel safe but I wanted to go home. I wanted to be with Mom. I missed her already.

Dad might have known the spots to get the mushrooms, but Mom knew how to cook them. We got home and laid them out on the kitchen table. Mom broke the clusters by their petals. She tossed them in corn starch and shook off the excess. Next, she dipped them into a pale-yellow pool of egg yolks mixed with buttermilk—about two or three yolks to about half a cup of buttermilk. The buttermilk came from the butter she churned. She always saved the buttermilk for things like that and for pancakes. She left the butter that made the buttermilk out on the counter, so it'd stay easy to spread over bread or whatever we wanted to put it on. She cooked the mushrooms in that butter, and it was like nothing else. Dad said it tasted like veal raised in the forest and I agreed.

The mushrooms floated in the egg yolks and buttermilk, and we pushed them down with our hands to really soak them until everything was gluey from the starch and proteins. From there, we put them in a large bowl and coated them in flour with lots of pepper, salt, garlic powder, onion powder, and paprika. Mom told me to wash my hands before my next job which was to take them out from the bowl of flour and spices and neatly line them on a tray next to the cast iron where she melted the butter until it foamed. She added the mushrooms, four to six petals each, depending on size, to the twelve-inch skillet. They sizzled, scenting the kitchen with the decay of summer, toasted black peppercorn, brown butter and flour, black walnuts, and acorns. The whole kitchen was aromatized in the best possible way with the funky mushrooms and the oil split from the butter. The butter solids became dark and crusted to the outsides of the mushrooms. Once they were very golden and glistening on one side, Mom carefully flipped them with a fork so the other side would get looking the same, crunchy too. That was it. It was perfect.

When the mushrooms were done, we put them on a tray with a paper towel beneath them to catch the excess oil. We piled them onto a plate and stood near the kitchen island where Mom kept on cooking. We didn't wait to sit down or make a big fuss of it. The sheep's head were best eaten right away. They were crispy, salty, and spiced. I ate them and tasted the forest. And for that, even with all the scary things I knew, I would keep going back.

Chapter 17.
MILKWEED

On the summer solstice, it was nearly midnight before the stars appeared. I had been an hour deep into the forest in the Polaris, just after the sun was setting, when I decided to make my way back to the cabin, slowly stopping to gather things here and there. In a sense, it was silent, but when I closed my eyes, my eardrums wanted to blow. The entire forest throbbed.

I stopped to collect firewood at what I called Apocalypse Zone Number One. It was a part of the forest where I first saw the annihilation from the logging. It looked just like the end of the world there. It was a stretch nearly five acres long going from south to north and thirty acres from the path to the west. The loggers might have cleared this rectangle a couple years before, I wasn't certain. Piles of logs, dried and washed from the sun and rain, waited for the loggers to pick them up. I understood what the loggers had to do, but the leaving piles of logs behind I could never understand. In the spring and fall you could see the stack of the dried logs very clearly but in the summer the brush grew up around them, and I always knew where the leftover piles were, so I always saw them even when I couldn't.

But why these logs were left behind, I didn't know. They seemed they might have made lovely pieces of furniture. Sometimes I stopped to collect them for firewood. I picked out nice long ones, logs that were dryer and thus less heavy. Little grubs along with worms, potato bugs, ants, spiders, and other things I couldn't possibly begin to see scattered when I picked them up. This time of year the cicadas were at their loudest. I stood in the Apocalypse Zone for a bit, allowing the sun to blanket my skin. And at 10 PM out here, it was like how it felt at 7 PM back in Indiana at the farmhouse. Sometimes when I was little, I stood in the yard, facing the west, thinking about how big the world was and feeling really tiny, like a red ant, the kind I had used a magnifying glass to set on fire. Moments like that made me realize setting fire to ants was not a nice thing to do. Here in Michigan, though, the sun's heat released the terpenes from the pines surrounding me and the whole place was one big Yankee Candle.

I carried the logs, two times the length of me, up to the path, where I used the chainsaw to cut them to sizes that would fit in the bed of the Polaris. As I walked through the tall wild grasses, I startled grasshoppers that shot out and banged me in the chest, arms, and head. The goldenrod, not yet bloomed, and snapweed were about waist high. They were preparing to attract the pollinators, hard at work trying to put things back the way they had been before. Something that would take, maybe, forever.

It was a time when I might've for once been in the Now. I might've, for once, been able to fall asleep right then and there. If I could stretch out under this sun, then I thought maybe I could sleep forever.

—⊷

When I got back to the cabin, I split the firewood into sizes that would fit in our stove in case it got chilly. Even around the solstice we sometimes had to have a fire at night. I also cut pieces that would fit inside the fire pit where I did a lot of cooking for our guests. Many of the dishes I prepared were cooked over the open fire, which gave an exceptional flavor to the food. The first time our neighbor that lived closest to us came to visit he brought us a welcome gift of Lake Superior lake trout—a big one, maybe eight pounds or so. The fish was right from the lake that day. I gutted it immediately, coating it in brown sugar and salt and started up a fire out back. I hung the trout with a hook in her jaw from a tripod over the fire. She hung there for many hours. I occasionally moved her around to where the smoke was, adding more brown sugar into her mouth from where it hinged open. The brown sugar melted from the heat, coating her insides. Later that evening when I took her down, I removed the skin and bones and pulled apart the muscle tissue, placing the flakes over fresh sourdough smothered in butter. After I tasted it, I knew this was exactly what I was going to do every weekend for our guests. It was one of the best barbecued fish I ever tasted.

I sawed the logs to size, then I split any logs larger than

six or eight inches in diameter with a heavy wedge. Some people used axes, but for me the axe didn't seem strong enough to split them right. I'd hurt myself before using an axe. I'd been chopping wood for some guests who were staying in the Airstream, which had a small fire pit in front for the guests to use at night. I wasn't wearing protective eyewear and a piece of wood ricocheted into my eye. I dropped the axe, screaming. It hurt and I was scared. I put both hands over my eye where I had been hit. Anna came running out of the cabin. I was afraid to move my hands from my face as I curled up on the grass. I thought if I moved my hands my eyeball would fall out and hang down my cheek. Anna pulled my hands from my face and said, "It's okay. You're okay."

"Is my eye in the socket?" I asked, crying from the hurt of it all. It wasn't often that I wanted to run into Mom's arms like I did when I was little (that's a lie—I want that all the time) but that's what I wanted.

"Yes, your eye is in the socket, but there's a little cut and your eye is going to end up black."

"I can't see though!" I said, feeling my cheek and my hurt eye. Then I realized my contact lens was there, stuck on my cheekbone. "Oh, my contact is out," I said.

"Okay, that's good. Go rinse your eye with soap and water."

I went into the cabin. Inside, Anna reminded me I needed to wear goggles. She was right. After that I never used the axe to chop wood again.

⌒✕

Having a good fire was important. Especially when we had

guests. Trout is still the thing I like best to cook over the fire. Our neighbor sometimes brought us one or two trout a week. He was obsessed with fishing. He never got tired of trout, I don't think, and he must've eaten a lot of it.

As afraid as I was of some people, our neighbor made me feel safe. He was originally from Ohio, and I can't say that I've always loved people from Ohio, but Brian became the big brother I never had. He was the same age as my sisters. He lived and worked close by, in one of the larger towns. For him, coming out to camp was almost a two-hour drive, depending on whether the path was shitty or not. He helped us with all sorts of stuff, like fixing the gate after George broke it, and putting the chain back on a small four-wheeler I had for a while, things like that. I gave that four-wheeler to some other neighbors who had a camp out here too. There was a pond behind their camp, a large pond to be exact, where there were maybe bass or catfish. Those neighbors were nice too and said we could use the pond. Anna and I thought it might be nice to go out there when no one was around and swim. They told us if we did to "watch out for leeches." We decided we probably didn't want to go swimming there after all and stuck to the river, even though we couldn't really swim in it due to the current.

Brian showed me how to use my chainsaw correctly and change the blade and chain. He showed me how to make sure there was enough oil in it, and all those sorts of things. When I first got up here I thought I knew what I was doing, but he knew before me that I really *didn't* know what I was doing. This was a lot more than camping. It was truly living in the wilderness, even though we had a lot of comforts. His cabin was about four city blocks from ours, a half-mile or so. If he was out there working, I could hear him, that's how quiet it usually was. He was a tall guy, probably six-two or six-three. He had a Russian last name. I thought Dad would like him a lot but he hadn't met him yet. But someday, I knew we'd all fish together on his boat. Sometimes Brian went to countries in Central Asia, like Kazakhstan, Pakistan, and Georgia to hunt and eat with the locals. He had recently been in Patagonia. He would send me pictures of meal spreads that looked unlike and better than anything I'd seen in magazines or elsewhere. I didn't know if that sort of hunting was right. But he wasn't a big-game hunter as far as I knew; if he were, I didn't think he'd advertise it, at least not to me and Anna. I think he knew we were tree huggers. Didn't matter what we believed, he was a good guy and I came to love him.

I don't mind regular hunting, not when anyone does it, though some people really dislike it. It's a very silly thing to dislike hunting unless you've got strict vegan or vegetarian principles. But anyone who eats meat from a store or elsewhere and then says they don't like the idea of hunting—well, there is zero sense in that. If I'm going to eat meat, I'd much rather it be an animal that was hunted in the forest rather than living in a factory farm or even a small farm for that matter.

The wild game Brian brought to us tasted like how Wayne told Mom it tasted—like what those animals ate themselves: berries, grubs, shrubs, mushrooms, cedar, acorns, walnuts, so on. Brian once gave me a tenderloin of mule deer. I salted it and rubbed it with a touch of a homemade white bean and wild rose miso. I hung it over the fire for a while to give it some smoke, then kissed it against the open flame after it was done hanging. That was the best piece of protein I ever had in my entire life.

Brian had a nice boat docked on Lake Superior. He did what was called troll fishing, where the lines were set and then pulled behind the moving boat. In the cabin area where you steered the boat there was a small computer screen in front of the wheel where you could see the depths of the water and a sonar beeped, revealing schools of fish below. I had a hard time believing it would work. Dad had one of those in his fishing boat too, which wasn't as fancy, and it didn't work too well. But when we were on Brian's boat, we caught two big trout exactly where the sonar showed there were fish. He knew when there was one on the line. That was when he slowed down the boat and grabbed the rod from where it was stationed, handing it to me. "Reel it in," he said. I did. I could tell he was very excited. The line and rod arched. He told me to hold it up, so I did, and to "reel that way," which meant a little to the right. I reeled it in, to the right. He got his net out and when the trout came up and fought with me near the lake's surface, he waited, ready to reach out with the net soon as the trout was close enough.

Once the fish was in the net it was all over. Brian brought her in and set her on the floor of the boat. This was the first one we caught that day. He reeled in the second one and I used the net and he pretended like I was helping but he mostly did it. The one I had reeled in was smaller. The second one he could tell was larger so he did it because he knew I wouldn't have been able to do it. It was okay. I might have lost it or got taken overboard.

Lake Superior was beautiful. As the eagle flies Lake

Superior was about twenty miles north of us but to get to it from our cabins took about two hours. When I was out there with him, I felt as if we were on the Atlantic, fishing somewhere off the coast of Maine or Newfoundland or some magical place like that. The sky was gray and the large cliffs along the shore were a perfect burnt orange and green, covered in pines, and from far away you saw the water hit them, spraying up into the sky, creating a pleasant spectrum of bluish-gray, orange, ochre, brown, and green. We went at the end of August one year and it was a chilly day. The pandemic was in full swing so we wore our face masks, but when he took a picture of me holding the fish, I took down my mask so you could see how happy I was holding the fish. And I was. I was really happy.

By the time I got back to the cabin that day the trout were cadavers. I had asked him if I had to knock them out like I knew Dad did. He looked at me strange and said, "No, they'll die soon enough."

The larger of the two trout had been too long for the cooler, so even after I took her out she stayed bent in the way Brian bent her to get her inside it. I gutted the small one first, cutting it from the small hole where excrement was released to just under the head where the jaw opened up. First, I snipped the entrails from the one end where I knew they were connected to the butthole (for lack of better anatomy) and just under where the tongue met the esophagus on the other end.

I can't really say how I knew to do this or how I learned. No one showed me. But teaching myself new things, somehow I knew Busia was doing it for me, from the inside.

I removed the entrails all at once. They spilled over my

hands onto the cutting board. I scooped them up and placed them into a sterilized Ball jar beside my workspace. I wiped the cutting board with a towel and took the trout to the sink and ran a little cold water over her, enough to remove the blood, then patted her dry with paper towel and wrapped her in plastic wrap and placed her into a fresh cooler full of ice packs. I don't like to place a fresh fish directly into ice or water. Then I went on to the larger one. I ran my knife against the honing wand, then went at this one the same way, carefully. "Holy smokes," I said to myself as the blood and guts spilled onto my hands, spreading like oil paints over the maple cutting board where I worked.

The kitchen light hung over me and I felt the warmth of it on the cowlick at the back of my head. Around that time, I had cut off all my hair, which was what I did sometimes when I was angsty, or fearful that I was losing my hair from stress. I'd cut it to make sure it was still all there. That might not make sense, but it did to me. The warm light on my head felt good.

The trout spread open. I cleaned out the guts and the khaki-colored intestines. Then the grand finale—roe, thousands of them, in a skein the color of orange pith, hung limp in my hands. I held up the roe sac excitedly to show Anna. "Wow," she said but with a tone that meant she didn't want to really look. I used small scissors to cut the sac along the seam, careful not to pierce the tiny marbles. I ran my fingers over it, squeezing the roe like toothpaste from a tube into a bowl of salt water. *So many babies.* The blood was maroon. The other entrails I could identify were the stomach and the lungs, which were like greenish-yellow sponges; the kidneys like small beans, named similarly; and the heart, red. I pushed my finger into it going, *bum-BUMP, bum-BUMP.* Anna told me to cut it out.

That trout made a lot of meals. We didn't have guests that summer because of the pandemic, but I prepared it several ways. I seared it in ham fat, or like Nick Adams did in "The Last Good Country," in salted pork fat and bacon grease. I cooked it spiced with vadouvan. I used the trout in a stew, smoked over the fire, as cakes, and in pasta. I imagined Busia and Dad did the same with the catfish and crappie and smelt and bluegill he caught, using it for a meal every night. The roe we used as a topping for latkes, salad, homemade bagels, and bread.

When I make trout for our guests, still to this day, I cure it in brown sugar and salt like that first time Brian brought it to me. I smoke it gently over the open fire, where I use the wood I collected from the Apocalypse Zone and serve it with a gribiche made of wild sheep sorrel folded in with scallions I've marinated in homemade wild strawberry vinegar and wild onion oil. It is an astonishing thing.

⟋⟍

At times in the Apocalypse Zone, shallow pools formed in the ruts from where the dinosaur-sized logging machines had settled for the nights when they weren't in use. Now that they were gone, evolution was doing its thing again. From one week to the next it was incredible how quickly things changed. Already tadpoles were racing across the surface of puddles. Tadpoles were extremely precious.

I stopped here often. Enough to know how life shifted. After I collected the wood, sawed it, and stacked it neatly in the bed of the Polaris, I hopped over that shallow pool, looking around a bit. I left the machine running. Jefferson Airplane was being played on the local radio station, where every so often the manly announcer would say they were "rocking our faces off in Escanaba." My favorite song played, "Volunteers." I figured if the bears were out this evening, they'd stay away from the tunes and the rumble of the Polaris's motor.

In this logged field I found joy, distilled. I went out to gather one thing and always ended up discovering more. A veil of blackberry brambles lined the devastated field. I collected them too, filling an empty cardboard pint container I'd saved from the farmers market. Wild blackberries were heirlooms, the ancestors of all other blackberries. I couldn't fight my compulsion to count them while I picked. Turned out I could fit as many as forty-five wild blackberries into one pint, depending on their size.

I took a deep, pine-drenched breath and I knew this was maybe the closest I would ever get to the farmhouse. Collecting blackberries here felt like collecting them at Grandpa Regan's farm. Plucking them from the brambles felt like home, especially when the thorns scraped against my arms. For a moment, even with the ideas of bears, wolves, or the Leshy watching me, I felt safe, even with as scared as I usually was. Perhaps because in moments like this, at the edge of the forest, the logged field, the late sunlight when it should be dark, it was all wonderful *and* scary—and that was what safety felt like to me. That, too, was a scary thought.

With the blackberries in hand, I got a deep feeling that I had done all this before. The feeling made a well in my stomach. Like I was looking in two mirrors, one before me and one behind me, multiplying myself. A feeling like I was in a memory of a memory of a memory. As I stood there, I felt my soul had left my body and I was two things, a husk of myself and my soul, which stood beside it. I saw my life from beginning to Now, all at once. I saw it like the rings of a tree—a circle of me from young to old, all the versions of myself, holding hands. Somehow, I was in the middle of them, of myself. I didn't know which version was memory or which was real. I didn't know which version was me. They all felt the same and I wondered even if this was *my* memory, or Busia's, or Dad's. Or maybe it was my future child's. We were real-life nesting dolls, fitting inside one another.

And I had collected berries this exact way at Grandpa's farmhouse, where tall rows of corn and soybeans squared off before the forest. Life flared out like old oaks. It was everything, all at once—an epiphany or maybe a real, spiritual experience.

I know this seems out there, and it truly was, because I don't think I could ever tell you *exactly* how the forest makes me feel. But it was something like that.

I plucked as many blackberries as I could before a slice of what would be the Sturgeon Moon came up over the trees in the east. I left plenty of blackberries behind for the bears and birds. I wondered without really thinking about it if after I left, the cubs would use their clumsy paws to rake through the berries. I knew I'd leave before they all arrived.

Before I got in the Polaris, I looked carefully at the milkweed mixed among the blackberries. Looking closer I followed the path of a wood ant. She was like three dots of ink dropped on the sage-colored leaf. Her legs were like eyelashes crawling along the leaf. This was what she did in the summer, after the monarchs drank nectar from the pink, rubbery flowers, after they had their love fests in bear, wolf, and fox scat piled in the middle of the path, after they laid their eggs and the pupae emerged, eating holes in the leaves, after they slunk down the bright green stalk and cloaked themselves for metamorphosis; she—the ant—walked along the milkweed leaves, wrangling aphids, and collecting honey dew.

The milkweed flowers had already begun to seed, splitting at the seam on the curved side of its body, releasing hundreds of seeds attached to white fibers like cotton candy. When the pods holding the seeds first grew, they were tender enough that you could eat them. It was beautiful because first all those flowers that were so fragrant turned into the seed pods. The pods when they were young and small, less than three inches, were the best things I ever ate. They had to be collected at just the right time; if they became mature, the seeds and silk were too fibrous to eat. And I loved them so much, but when I took them, I only took a few, and left the rest for the monarchs. And none would ever be wasted. And those few I took, I liked to soak in buttermilk left over from the butter I churned just like Mom did. Then I'd dredge them in a mixture of flour, salt, pepper, paprika, and garlic and onion powders and fry them. They tasted like a cross between fried okra and a jalapeño popper without the spice. The silk of the seeds on the inside sort of melted and they had a little funk to them, kind of like a ripe cheese.

As for the ant, you could touch her if you wanted. If you positioned your arm against the milkweed, she'd crawl onto it, walking up and down. Her fine legs tickled. You could also pick the ant from your arm and, turning her upside down, watch her legs wriggle against the sky. You could also try to squish her between your fingers, but I didn't. But if you did, her exoskeleton would crunch, and a milky white substance would gush out, just the same as when you snapped the milkweed pods from the plant. I know this about squishing the ants because I had heard that was what would happen. Or maybe I remember that's how it was because when I was little, I might have done that sort of thing to ants. I can't say for certain.

I used a foldable, pocket-size magnifying glass to watch the ant until the headlights from the Polaris became brighter than the natural light. She held a globe of honey dew in her mandibles. She pulled it to her mouth and the sticky juice ran down her nonexistent chin. She followed the aphids over and under the winding curves of the milkweed's leaves. She was full of sugar, buzzed, stumble-swaying like a drunk person. Watching her, the Jurassic machines that took down the trees came to mind. She moved like those machines: lifting, carrying, crushing. I shouldn't ever fool myself into thinking ants or critters like them didn't have feelings. Ants have brains and nervous systems. They respect their dead and elders, especially the queen; they never allow another to take over until the first one was gone for good.

Now, the ant with her abdomen full and her body sticky, she climbed headfirst down the milkweed stalk with another globe of honey dew. She sent out pheromones, letting her sisters know she had dinner covered. They would take the honey dew back to the queen.

Eventually the sun was completely gone, and I could no longer watch. I picked up the container of berries where I'd sat them on the ground. I hopped over the puddle of tad-poles. The baritone of the bullfrogs became a choir. Far in the distance was the falsetto of coyotes. And with millions of stars in the sky, I felt millions of eyes on me. At night, the animals reigned. They knew my eyes didn't adjust like theirs. My hearing was not as refined. Compared to a bear's, my sense of smell was pretty much nonexistent.

I cleared the pond. My boots clobbered the ground; a mushroom cloud of sand puffed up around me. At the edge of the path, illuminated by the machine's headlights, peeping at me through the grass, was one perfect, bright red, misshapen mushroom. Finally, a lobster mushroom. I parted the blades of wild grasses and found several more. I looked up the hill, and where mossy mounds grew over what looked like stumps from hundreds of years ago, a few more grew from the sides. I knew these were likely the last of the season and I felt very happy I'd found them. I knew right away that I would sauté them with the fava beans or dragon's tongue from our garden with a bit of fresh churned butter, salt, and pepper. I'd add a bit of crushed garlic and lots of fresh thyme, also from the garden. I'd serve all the green and bright red-orangish colors of it in a perfect pale-blue bowl in a light broth of dried mushrooms and I pictured it and I thought that would be really nice. Finding the lobsters, I felt the hole I had inside me close up a little.

I sliced the lobsters at their base with the curved blade of my mushroom knife. I used the brush on its other end to loosen the sand and dirt. I smiled to myself, thinking about this pretty dish, and that now I knew where lobsters would grow. And how each year I was looking one way when all the while they might have been right behind me.

CHAPTER 18.
THE KID

SOMETIMES WHEN YOU WANTED SOMETHING BAD enough, it showed up—but it wasn't always a real thing. The same was true of things you didn't really want, like fears, or behaviors.

It was sometime in August, one of these summers, a few months since we had last inseminated me. We had done the insemination on our own. Anna inseminated me, at home. We knew this was the least likely way to achieve a viable conception. I was no flower, but sometimes these things were easy. But more often than not they weren't.

Like mushrooms, some flowers are asexual, reproducing on their own. Others need help. There are bees, ants, wasps, bats, hummingbirds—creatures that can really get in there, carrying the pollen for the flowers. After that there are the wolves, squirrels, foxes, chipmunks, coyotes, and occasional mountain lions that pass through, and the obvious bear plopping down, cloaked in everything from the forest, right in that spot. The wind is good at carrying pollen and spores too, like how sometimes little mushrooms sprout from the soil of the plants in our windowsills. Anna inseminating me was like that—like the chances of the wind. If everything was timed just right—we even had the Walgreens-brand ovulation kit and tenth-of-a-degree thermometer—then there was a slight chance. Honestly, it was going to take a lot of luck.

Yeah. That was the likelihood, though we had high hopes for our little Nora or Norman Wayne. We had decided Wayne was going to be the middle name whether it was a boy or girl. Wayne was Anna's dad's middle name as well my grandfather's first name. Norman was Dad's middle name. We also figured we could wait for the baby to tell us if they were a boy or girl and then change the name from there, if need be, I guess to whatever they would want. The first time I got pregnant, it all happened so fast. We were certain I was fertile and thought maybe we might be lucky enough again, but that was several years ago now. A lot happens to a middle-aged woman in that amount of time.

⸺

The specimen had arrived in a container delivered to our front door. It was a hollow tank full of tags with stickers of all the locations through which it had traveled: New Mexico, Texas, Missouri, Illinois, North Carolina, Michigan, Colorado. It was secured with a lock and a combination that the sperm bank had sent us in an email to open it. Inside was a liquid nitrogen canister, called a dewar, which held a tiny tube of semen. We had instructions indicating that we should wait to open it until the ceremony was to begin. They didn't call it a ceremony, but doing it at home, rather than in the doctor's office, there was a ceremonial aspect to it. We didn't get spiritual about it, though I suppose we could have if we wanted.

Anna was nervous and had Nina, the nurse in our family, use a syringe to retrieve the semen. I lay in bed with our dogs flanking my hams. Anna came into our bedroom where I reclined with my hips up on two layers of pillows. My knees were bent and a towel was over the bottom, naked half of me. Anna held up the syringe as if she knew what she was doing, flicked out any bubbles, and we laughed, now fully in our roles.

"Here's daddy," I said. "Is conception this way more or less romantic?"

"Are you ready?"

"Yes," I said. I helped her guide the syringe. Here's the thing: at this point only so many eggs were left. Plus statistics say only about half of the sperm are viable after semen is frozen. And getting pregnant at my age was considered "geriatric." I'd have better odds with a twenty-dollar scratchy. I guess in a sense, we did sort of have a ceremony planned. I had picked a song, and then she'd leave the room, and maybe I'd masturbate. We had read chances were better if you had an orgasm because that made the cervix open and vacuum the sperm into the uterus. It made complete sense but maybe was an old wives' tale. I can't remember the exact reason why we chose not to have sex instead. The pandemic had really thrown a wrench in things mentally, physically, emotionally, and sexually, so that was probably why. I don't think we were the only ones feeling disconnected. Being intimate now was a harder thing to do when both people were experiencing a slow-burn trauma layered with depression, anxiety, and whatever other ailments you could add to that. Truly the list went on and on.

The song I chose was "White Rabbit," by Jefferson Airplane. Anna put it on Spotify and set my phone on the dresser. She left the room, and I eventually gave myself an orgasm thinking about the before times. I held my hips up like the internet had instructed, forming an L-shape by pushing the soles of my feet toward the ceiling. I stayed that way for about ten minutes, relaxed, then fell asleep. The next morning when I went pee, I smelled like how my straight girlfriends described themselves after sex. And I sort of knew that smell myself, but it was easy to forget things that you didn't want to remember.

It was a late night in August and on the cabin's porch, it was loud. Down the way the wolves howled, and coyotes cackled, owls hooted. While I stood at the northeast corner of the porch, the area where it opened to the sky, I looked at the stars and our Old English Sheepdog, Bunny, curled at my feet and farted. Squirrels, chipmunks, and rabbits scurried through the leaves down below and something else was out there, further away. I heard the rustling in the leaves. One red squirrel without a tail and a large rabbit of sorts had been hanging out a lot lately, sniffing around the fire pit where I cooked the trout and they were undoubtedly lured by the aromas. The only thing that was silent was the sky. The Perseid meteor shower had just ended.

I closed my eyes and inhaled deeply. I had a vision that

someday I'd be able to show a kid this place, and someday in the future, in a moment like this, it would become a strong memory for them, of us standing on the porch, out here, in the middle of the wilderness, counting fireflies in the yard or at the edge of the forest, something dreamy like that but I wanted to share it so badly and at the same time was drastically afraid of what the world might be like for such a kid twenty or thirty years in the future.

I exhaled. While I probably wouldn't be on my deathbed in thirty years, I probably wouldn't be able to protect them while they grew up in the way Mom and Dad had protected me. I wouldn't be able to remind them every day to take the gun. *Or maybe I would.* I wondered about that for a moment and instead of dwelling on it, I imagined the kid and me in the yard making rings out of fireflies and dandelion stems, playing make believe. I'd tell them not to kill too many fireflies in the production of it all, that it wasn't a good idea to kill more bugs than necessary. I imagined how nice it would be for them to have this chance to see how otherworldly it was out here. I imagined what it would be like for them to practice kissing the log walls of this cabin, how everything would taste, and what it would be like when they traveled time. Despite all the danger and sadness that surrounded us sometimes, they'd know something this beautiful meant that this whole planet we inhabited was uniquely beautiful. If I homeschooled them, our religion class would be a walk through the forest.

I imagined hard, with my eyes shut tight, and I saw the kid's face materialize behind the screen door. "Mom, watcha doin'?" they asked. I waved my hand, inviting them to join me. I walked to the door and opened it. The kid came out and stood alongside me. I put my hand on their shoulder. We walked to the end of the porch where it met the yard. The sky was black and the constellations were sharp. "We should count the stars," I said. Now, with this small person at my side, I took their hand. "Let's go further," I said. I liked the feeling of having my kid's hand in mine.

With no wind the forest was deafening, more silent yet louder than it had ever been. The kid asked, "Why so quiet?" *How do you explain?* I stopped and listened. The wind started up as it often did. "Shhh," I said. "You have to listen to what you're not hearing," which was everything.

I said, "It's very loud."

"How?" the kid asked. "How is it loud?"

"Because things don't always have to sound like how we think they should sound. Loud things don't have to make you jump."

Into the dark night, the kid and I began to walk the path. The stars were fluorescent blue and yellow dots. Occasionally, one star darted from this point to the next, right out the corner of my eye, and by the time I pointed, it was gone. *Look there! Look here!* The leaves of the beech trees whistled. Mosquitoes buzzed and maybe a fly or two hung around and we got bit.

The Joe Pye weed's heavy purple flowers swayed side to side. Joe Pye weed was named after a Native American doctor who taught the colonizers how to use it, but over time those remedies were lost. However, I've read it might have helped me from wetting the bed. I'd have to use it on this little one. I'd use it, getting them dry before bedtime to avoid messes in the night.

"We are so small, don't you think?"

"Yeah," they said.

"The universe is very big," I said to them.

We walked down the steepest part of the path near the logged field that had not long ago been so dense, that ten feet in turned black, miles and miles away from any humans, and I felt something watching us. A pain gripped my shoulder, like sharpened canines meeting the bone; like my body was Busia's and the Leshy was upon me. Fears were catching up to me. I snapped out of it when the kid said, "Look, there," and pointed to another star cutting through the sky.

Eyes were watching us through slits, marbles, diamonds, octagons, circles, and ovals. A lady spider with her eight eyes spied on us while she was upside down. Most spiders are female, you know. Well, I don't know that for certain, but most bees and ants are, I told the kid. I knew how to say truths and untruths at the same time from having listened to Dad all these years. And if I said it matter-of-fact enough, and I believed it, and I got everyone else to believe it, then it sort of became true.

I hugged the kid into my side. They were the height of my thigh. "It's good to be out in the middle of nowhere," I said, "don't you think?" They nodded in agreement. Where the men had logged, 95 percent of the trees were gone. A true massacre. A few spindly maples, pine, and young oaks, ten to fifteen years old, remained. Where some trees had been felled, the ones they didn't haul out would remain. Eventually I'd collect them for firewood.

We got farther into the wild but stayed where it still felt safe enough for the two of us. I spread out a blanket. We sat with our legs folded and our boots were at the blanket's edges, holding it down. I asked the kid if they were worried about bugs, spiders, or animals coming for us. They shook their head, no. "Ten shooting stars since we sat down," the little face told me. I smiled. They were counting, and I turned to look at the sliced bole nearest us, sensing eyes on me where hundreds of little creatures I couldn't see watched us. I got a wet, sticky feeling along my legs when I remembered how the slugs slithered along the dahlia's leaves at night. Quickly my eyes flashed left to right over our blanket, looking for land mollusks, expecting them already to be encompassing our toes but there were none. I thought that by coming out here, we could show the trees and the Leshy that not all of us were bad. *We hadn't caused the destruction, but we hadn't stopped it either.*

Because of the logging, entire underground mycorrhizal networks had gone static. Some sparked while they fizzled to gray, struggling to remain on. And in this pine bole to the left of us, next year would grow maple, birch, and beech saplings, each from a slice between the bark and cambium layer. Just enough rainwater would have gotten in and enough nutrients would pass through the layers to force themselves back into the empty field. This was how they protested. No matter what, the trees kept coming back, they kept trying.

Forty-five minutes went by and I knew because "See, there," I pointed, "the International Space Station. It's passing right through Ursa Minor."

"Where?" they asked as if they could follow my directions.

"Just below Polaris," I said, looking into their dilated eyes. They didn't see it. "All right, I'll show you again next time, but you might be sleeping by then," I said softly, noticing their eyelids growing heavy. They fought back the tiredness, staring into the sky. I remembered a time when I was that age and I fell asleep in the back of the Bronco after one of Mom and Dad's Trivial Pursuit nights with friends, where I was encouraged to engage with other children, and when I finally did, tired myself so much that I zonked out across the backseat. Mom or Dad carried me into the house that night. If I woke up, and they knew I was awake, they would have had me get in the bath before bed. I played possum. I knew just enough to stay that way, pretending I was dreaming. I was warm in their arms. This kid would do the same with me. I knew I would have to carry them back to the cabin.

The moon was over us; the silver-blue glow felt better on our skin than the orange-yellow heat of noon. The pines pitched toward the moon and bats rushed to it; geese flew past it. The kid's eyes popped open when the geese honked. The geese came cursing like rush hour, and always late at night. They were very rude about their timing. But the geese weren't going anywhere, even when the loggers were at their worst. They were smarter than the turkeys and had heard what had happened on the high ground, several hundred feet above sea level and four to five acres south of where they called home. The loggers couldn't get their Caterpillars so easily down the steep hillsides. It wasn't worth their time and energy to log that far down. The geese were smarter than everyone else realized. They flew across the sky after midnight. They followed the wind, from the north to the west, honking their heads off so that everyone knew just what they knew, which was a lot. They knew where to go.

A bit further away at the edge of the opened field, a lone wolf walked, her snout in the air. Because I saw her outline against the trees, I could tell she was young. I wondered if she was the one who called out, the one I cried for and with so many nights. She pretended like she didn't know we were here. She went along as silently as the pads of her paws allowed, sinking into the sod. In my mind's eye, her paws were calloused and swollen with the forest. Microscopic mushroom spores crowded between the creases in the leather of each toe's pad. I imagined pollen dangling from the lactate of her swollen nipples. I watched her move from west to east across the tree line. A tree line against the logged field that not so long ago, didn't exist. But had it not existed I'd have never seen her.

In the far distance, the howling of her pack sounded. She sprinted away. I elbowed the kid and said, "We should probably go. You're falling asleep." They woke up. We both knew that not only one wolf but many wolves were not too far off. And as exciting as that was, it meant we should go home.

I pushed my hand onto the ground and got up. When I stood up I felt the flow of warm blood seep through my underwear onto my thighs and the insides of my jeans. There was nothing I could do. I rolled then tucked our blanket under one arm. As I suspected the kid said, "I'm tired, Mama, carry me." I hoisted them onto my hip. They wrapped their arms around my neck, like I used to do to Mom and Dad, and laid their head onto my shoulder. When we got back to the cabin, I left the kid at the doorway where they had first appeared. I took off my jeans on the porch and just threw them away. They were no good anymore. I went inside, got cleaned up, and that night I was so tired, so drained, that I fell dead asleep right away.

$\mathcal{S}$OURCES AND $\mathcal{R}$EFERENCES

I AM NOT A MYCOLOGIST, BOTANIST, ECOLOGIST, OR anthropologist. Much of the way I write about the world and nature in particular is how I have imagined it to function. While I have studied some of these subjects over the years, I have not been formally schooled on them. Below is a partial list of books and other resources I have made use of in studying the topics and phenomena I write about here.

Constantine, Albert, Jr., *Know Your Woods*. Simon & Schuster, 1987.

Dean, Evelyn, and Steve Brill. *Identifying and Harvesting Edible and Medicinal Plants*. HarperCollins, 1994.

Perry, Brian A. "Are Mushrooms Genetic Individuals or Genetic Mosaics?" *MykoWeb*, December 2007.

Schwab, Alexander. *Mushrooming Without Fear*. Skyhorse, 2007.

Smith, Alexander H. *The Mushroom Hunter's Field Guide*. University of

Michigan Press, 1969.

Tekiela, Stan. *Start Mushrooming*. AdventureKEEN, 1993.

Thayer, Samuel. *Nature's Garden: A Guide to Identifying, Harvesting, and Preparing Edible Wild Plants*. Forager's Harvest, 2010.

Thayer, Samuel. *The Forager's Harvest: A Guide to Identifying, Harvesting, and Preparing Edible Wild Plants*. Forager's Harvest, 2006.

Walker, Glenn. "The Sexual Nature of Mushrooms." *Mycopia*, November 21, 2017.

Zim, Herbert, and Alexander Martin. *Trees, a Guide to Familiar American Trees*. Random House Children's Books, 1989.

ACKNOWLEDGMENTS

Books take a lot of time to write, at least for me they do. I go through many drafts and many edits. I'm often absent mentally and physically from my friends and family through the process. With that, I think it's important to thank my wife, who supports me while I'm working on these books. I should thank our dogs, too.

This book requires the acknowledgment of my entire family, from the roots of the tree to the top, and especially my mom and dad. My sisters Kelley and Nina, who provide the stories of all the wild things they did, and what Bunny did, and their memories of how it happened. If I could write a tenth of what they've lived, it'd be astounding—there are so many more stories to tell. Of special note are those who have passed: Busia, Wayne, Bunny, and Grandpa Regan. Without them I wouldn't have these stories to tell or have ended up where I am, with these bones, blood, and skin.

I wouldn't be able to write or tell my stories without Doug Seibold, and his belief in my ability to do it. He is part book publisher, part editor, and part psychologist and mentor. I am proud to be working with such a fine company as Agate. There are many people on his team that are very invested in my writing and for that I'm extremely grateful.

The School of the Art Institute of Chicago, Master of Fine Arts in Writing program has given me a lot to think about. My appreciation goes to James McManus, writer, teacher, and poker historian, who mentored me through much of this book's crafting and has become a true friend. Ruth Margraff, a talented professor who reminds me of what people might want to feel, smell, touch, and taste. By proxy of my writing, she's fallen in love with my family. I'm glad my work had that effect on her and by proxy I've fallen in love with her. Jesse Ball, novelist and poet, who allows me to pick his brain when I'm wondering where I should go next and simply, how to do what we do as writers. He is one of my writing heroes and in a way has become a brother. Mary Cross and Rosellen Brown for their time and dedication to my work while completing my MFAW. Jourdain Barton, MFAW colleague, who took time to review and discuss my manuscript in detail. Every em dash is dedicated to her. Finally, Elise Paschen, who mentored me while I tried my hand at poetry and helped me bounce back and forth between prose and poetry.

The Native Tribes of the Upper Peninsula, while I live here and write, this land truly belongs to them.

The forests I grew up in and all the flora and fauna. The Hiawatha Forest in which we now live.

Lastly, I think it's important to acknowledge our guests at the Milkweed Inn. The people who have become my audience and readers. I love that I get to share my life and thoughts with them. In real life I often whisper, but through writing I get to shout about all that I experience.